ORBÁN

PAUL LENDVAI

Orbán

Europe's New Strongman

HURST & COMPANY, LONDON

First published in the United Kingdom in 2017 by
C. Hurst & Co. (Publishers) Ltd.,
41 Great Russell Street, London, WC1B 3PL
© Paul Lendvai, 2017
All rights reserved.

The right of Paul Lendvai to be identified as the author of
this publication is asserted by him in accordance with the
Copyright, Designs and Patents Act, 1988.

A Cataloguing-in-Publication data record for this book
is available from the British Library.

ISBN: 9781849048699

This book is printed using paper from registered sustainable
and managed sources.

www.hurstpublishers.com

Printed and bound in Great Britain by Bell and Bain Ltd, Glasgow

CONTENTS

PREFACE

This book deals with the history of Hungary since the collapse of the Communist system and above all with developments since the conquest of power in 2010 by Viktor Orbán and his Fidesz party. My main intention in this work, which was first published in German in 2016, was to provide a truthful and dispassionate account of Viktor Orbán's stunning career, even of politics and actions which I deplore.

Still in his early fifties, Orbán, the ablest and most controversial politician in modern Hungarian history, has not only shaped events in Hungary, but has also played a major role in European politics. He was the youngest prime minister in Europe in 1998–2002, and since his two overwhelming electoral victories in 2010 and 2014 he has ruled Hungary as the undisputed Number One.

I was born and brought up in Budapest, and as a child and a young man I was both directly and indirectly affected by the demons of nationalism and ethnic hatred. After my flight to Vienna following the crushing of the 1956 October Revolution, I worked as a foreign correspondent (with twenty-two years on the *Financial Times*) and as a political writer and television commentator. My books on Austria, the Balkans, Hungary and Eastern Europe have tried to present a balanced picture, avoiding partisanship toward any particular nation or cause.

PREFACE

As a Hungarian-born Austrian author with Jewish parents and a Hungarian wife, now living in Vienna but travelling and lecturing frequently around the world, I have always tried to avoid sweeping generalisations. I have neither assets nor interests in my native homeland and my undivided loyalty is to Austria, which since 1957 has given me—like hundreds of thousands of other refugees from many countries—the chance to start a new life in freedom.

In view of numerous important events, I have added a comprehensive new final chapter to the translation of the German text. Following my frequent trips to Hungary both before and after 2010, the insights offered here into the often turbulent history of a country of extraordinary contradictions have been formulated neither with cynical indifference nor with partiality toward any particular group. The book is based on documents, as well as on personal impressions and conversations with politicians, scholars and many friends in Hungary and abroad.

I must thank above all my wife, Zsóka, who, despite her engagement with Nischen Verlag publishing German translations of contemporary Hungarian literature, has done her best to provide ideal working conditions for my writing this book.

Vienna, June 2017

THE PERSONAL TOUCH

How important are people and personalities in politics? In the democratic states, the political and economic crises that have afflicted the world since the banking collapse of 2008, the consequences of international terrorism and cross-border migration, are reflected both in a great critical unease about parliamentary debate and in opinion polls expressing a passionate longing for a 'strongman'. The human factor remains difficult to comprehend, even incalculable, yet without it all historic events are incomplete. All too often not only in global history, but also in the contemporary history of Central and Eastern Europe, conflicts between progressive and reactionary forces, between openness and isolation, have been bound up with almost dramatic changes in the personalities of political leaders.

The maxim that 'men make history' originates with the notions of hero worship expressed by the once very popular Scottish historian Thomas Carlyle: 'The history of the world is but a biography of great men.' According to the German philosopher Georg Friedrich Wilhelm Hegel, however, the spirit of the world and of the age is much more decisive than either people or personalities. Karl Marx and Friedrich Engels believed that politics is dependent on the material conditions of production. The question of which forces have moved a leading politician and which forces he himself has set into motion—that is, the combination of external factors and personal action—still constitutes the central problem in describing and evaluating political personalities today.

If chroniclers of contemporary history wish to consider the important role of the personal element in political decision-making, which should never be underestimated, then they need only recall the words of the Swiss historian Herbert Lüthy: 'Contemporary history is not anonymous. It is known to us as something that really occurs only to the extent to which we wrest anonymity from the actors as well as we individualise and identify them ... Dates and facts mean absolutely nothing when we are unable to create for ourselves any image whatsoever of the consciousness of the acting players.'[1] In the age of the global communications revolution and the dissemination of social media, such reflections have become even more pertinent.

The turbulent history of the Central and East European states, and the perplexing changes in the positions of the men and women at the head of their governments and states, confirm time and again the warnings of Isaiah Berlin, the great British thinker born in Riga, who in 1988—that is, before the great political upheavals of the following year—cautioned that history should not be seen as an 'autobahn from which major deviations cannot occur ... I believe in pluralism and do not believe in historical determinism. At crucial moments, at turning points ... chance, individuals and their decisions and acts, themselves not necessarily predictable—indeed, seldom so—can determine the course of history ... We haven't much choice. Let us say one per cent. But that one per cent can make all the difference.'

In discussion with the Iranian philosopher Ramin Jahanbegloo, Berlin explored some historical counterfactuals, taking Churchill in 1940 and Lenin in April 1917 as examples. What would have happened if Churchill had not become prime minister or if Lenin had died earlier?[2] This train of thought, of course, could easily be continued. What would have happened if, on 10 March 1985, not Mikhail Gorbachev but another of his less progressive rivals had been elected General Secretary of the Communist Party of the Soviet Union? Or if, in 1947–8, Josip Broz Tito, with all his experience and authority, had not stood at the helm of communist Yugoslavia and openly refused to take orders from Stalin? Even the metamorphosis of János Kádár, from being despised throughout the world as the pitiless 'Gauleiter of Moscow' following the bloody crushing of the autumn 1956 Hungarian uprising to his becoming the symbol of 'goulash communism with petty freedoms', illustrates the importance of the personality.

In his 1989 essay 'The Heroes of the Withdrawal', the German writer Hans Magnus Enzensberger ironically described the achievements of Kádár and Gorbachev, as well as the Polish head of state General Wojziech Jaruzelski, as those of 'demolition contractors' in the dismantling of their own systems. But an equally valid assessment of these and many other personalities is Hegel's verdict that, when the historical moment is past, when the heroes have completed the task they had to fulfil, then history throws them away 'like empty shells'. This ultimately is what happened to such contrasting figures as Chancellor Konrad Adenauer, the founding father of the Federal Republic of Germany, or Willy Brandt, the architect of the German Ostpolitik, and, on the other side of the Iron Curtain, the geriatric Hungarian party boss Kádár, who in declining health and after a series of mishaps was toppled with the agreement of Gorbachev. The careers of some leading politicians reflect what Jakob Burckhardt called 'relative greatness' in his famous *Reflections on History*; they also confirm that talk of a political personality's indispensability can very quickly turn out to be hollow.

Sometimes, however, history not only drives seemingly indispensable leaders from office but also throws onto the rubbish heap the governing parties they head. In Hungary, the land of the greatest popular uprising in post-war Europe, that was the fate of the three political groupings most important first in setting the course of the 1989 annus mirabilis' great political changes, and then, with the exception of four years of Fidesz government (1998–2002), in decisively moulding the nation's post-1989 politics and economy. In contrast to the other countries of the Soviet bloc, the system change in Hungary was not associated with either a political upheaval or a dramatic revolution. Among the Hungarian people at that time, unlike during the few days when the 1956 uprising appeared successful, there was no feeling of moral renewal or any intense desire to settle scores with the dignitaries of the old regime. Not one leading communist functionary or head of the various secret services was ever convicted of a single crime.[3]

In contrast to the violent clashes and mass protests elsewhere in the Soviet empire, the relationship in Hungary between those in power and the opposition was marked on both sides by self-restraint and a willingness to engage in a dialogue. Given the indelible memory of the hopes and tragedy of the 1956 revolution crushed by the Soviet tanks, the state party's monopoly on power was never questioned. All sides strove, right until the end, for a gradual reform, and then later for an orderly change of power. The right-wing radicals of today, but also the left-wing critics of the smooth transition to parliamentary democracy, easily forget that in 1989 there were still approximately 70,000 Soviet soldiers, 1,000 tanks, 1,500 armoured military vehicles, 622 artillery pieces and 196 missile battery sites provisionally (until the dissolution of the Warsaw Pact in 1991) stationed in Hungary, and that the party controlled not only the intact and immense apparatus of the secret services but also the units of the so-called armed workers' militias.

When considering the long and tortuous path of János Kádár (1912–89) from executioner and jailer to the 'father of the nation' and the 'good king' during the thirty-two years of the regime inseparably linked with his name, we must in retrospect emphasise the immense political significance of his personality; and this in full knowledge of his evil role (behind the scenes, but long since fully documented) in the execution of his former comrades in arms, László Rajk (1949) and Imre Nagy (1958). The typewriter mechanic and lifelong full-time functionary always differed in his public appearances from the other leading communist politicians. This was something I was able to experience at first hand in an extended interview with Kádár in 1981.

On account of his almost puritanical lifestyle, his personal modesty and sense of humour, Kádár, despite the bloody settling of scores with the freedom fighters and the inner- and intra-party opposition, had by the 1970s and 1980s managed to achieve a benevolent toleration of the regime by the broad mass of the population. The esteemed national poet Gyula Illyés said in a TV interview with me in the spring of 1982 that Kádár had succeeded in gaining the trust of the people through 'objectivity, modesty and accomplishments'. In contrast to all the other leaders in the Eastern Bloc, Kádár did not tolerate a personality cult built around himself. No pictures of him were to be found hanging in official offices and buildings, and even at ceremonial parades none were carried. He was 'a dictator without personal dictatorial tendencies', as a Hungarian political scientist aptly noted.

Despite the historical responsibility that weighs heavily upon Kádár, all opinion polls taken since 1989 have revealed that the betrayer and murderer of Imre Nagy, the prime minister of the revolution who morphed from a Muscovite communist into a national statesman, is remembered as the jovial father of the nation and as the 'hallmark of a golden era'. At the end of the 1990s, 42 per cent of those questioned considered Kádár the 'most congenial Hungarian politician of the twentieth century'.

This glorification of the Kádár regime may of course in part be explained as a consequence of his shrewd tactical policy of carrot and stick, which bore considerable fruit relatively quickly. It is statistically incontrovertible that incomes tripled in real terms between 1956 and 1989. And it may also have been in part a reaction to the huge new problems that arose after 1989.

As a foreign correspondent and later as editor-in-chief of the East European desk of the Austrian broadcaster, ORF, my double role as a reporter and, thanks to my local and linguistic knowledge as a native Hungarian, as an insider, allowed me to observe the process of half-hearted change in Hungary. Until he was stripped of power in May 1988, Kádár was thought to be indispensable for a peaceful change and, at the same time, the embodiment of the staying power of a 'strongman' put in place by the Kremlin. Kádár was, indeed, a strong man. Over three decades, as he tacked between the pressures from Moscow and the deeply rooted fears of his people, he neutralised potential rivals with subtlety, cynicism and, if necessary, with brutality, but always with inimitable tactical skill. The ambivalence of the judgements passed on this communist regime in the service of an alien dictatorship—and also on the authoritarian Horthy regime, the last ally of the Third Reich and responsible for the deaths of 560,000 Hungarian Jews—provides the key for an understanding of the tendency, so marked in Hungary, of seeking refuge in the past.

The reckoning with the three basic taboos (the one-party system, foreign rule and the stigmatisation of the 1956 uprising as a counter-revolution) took place at a monumental funeral service in front of 250,000 people at Heroes' Square in Budapest on 16 June 1989. This was before the formal resignation of the ruling party and before the withdrawal of the Soviet occupying troops. Purely for its location at the entrance to the City Park and at the end of Andrássy Avenue (at almost 3 kilometres, the longest street in Budapest), this square of the collective national memory works magnificently. At its heart stands the 36-metre-high column that was erected in 1896 to mark the thousandth-year anniversary of the Magyar conquest of the territory of Hungary. Atop the column is a 5-metre-high figure of the arch-angel Gabriel, who holds in one hand the Hungarian crown and in the other the apostolic double cross. The monument to Hungarian heroes, and the semicircular colonnades and statues dedicated to the memory of the fourteen kings and heroes of Hungary, dominate the scene. Two buildings dating from the years before the turn of the century and designed in the neo-classical style of the late nineteenth century, the Palace of Arts to the right and the Museum of Fine Arts to the left, complete the architectural unity of Heroes' Square.

The black velvet catafalque towered over the six Corinthian columns draped with black flags. Above, on the steps, lay the five coffins containing the remains of the martyrs who had been sen-tenced to death in a secret trial and then immediately executed thirty-one years previously: Prime Minister Imre Nagy and his four companions of fate. The sixth coffin had been left empty, to symbolise the 300 executed freedom fighters of the uprising in October and November 1956. Over the unforgettable scene hung an air of mourning. But there was also a menacing determination never to give up the freedoms now being gained. The entire demonstration was broadcast live on Hungarian TV, as was the subsequent interment of Imre Nagy and his comrades in plot 301 of the same cemetery where they had previously been buried in unmarked mass graves. As a compromise, the guard of honour for the coffins was formed not only by family and friends of the martyrs and members of the democratic opposition, but also by those functionaries of the ruling party who had adapted them-selves in a timely fashion to the new political situation. Austrian TV, like many others, transmitted the moving pictures. I did not report live from Budapest but commented off-camera in the studios in Vienna. My voice at times almost failed, faltering with emotion and excitement, and tears rolled down my cheeks during the funeral oration given by my friend Miklós Vásárhelyi, who as Imre Nagy's chief press officer had been responsible in 1953 for obtaining my release from an internment camp.

Six people, victims and opponents of the communist dictatorship, spoke at Heroes' Square. The political sensation of the day, however, for the media and for me too, was the speech of a completely unknown young man with a beard. His name was Viktor Orbán and he was just twenty-six years old. On behalf of the younger generation he delivered the final speech, one that was both concise and clear; in view of the conditions still prevailing, it was also in its demands for democracy and independence an extraordinarily sharp oration:

> If we trust our own strength, then we will be able to put an end to the communist dictatorship. If we are determined enough, then we can compel the ruling party to face free elections. If we have not lost sight of the ideas of 1956, we will vote for a government which will at once enter into negotiations on the immediate beginning of the withdrawal of Russian troops. If we are courageous enough, then, but only then, we can fulfil the will of our revolution.

Even in retrospect, and regardless of his subsequent political actions and more recent cosying up to the Russian head of state Vladimir Putin, the trailblazing character of Orbán's courageous and politically rebellious words, which went beyond the limits of protocol, has to be recognised. After this appearance, which lasted a mere six-and-a-half minutes, the young man became, from one moment to the next, famous both in Hungary and abroad. In the words of József Debreczeni, his biographer and today his harshest critic, this was the 'meeting of an extraordinary luck with an extraordinary talent'.

2

THE LONG CLIMB FROM BOTTOM TO TOP

In 1989, as Kádár's Hungary was being laid to rest, who would have thought that just nine years later the bearded young revolutionary would (in the words of his biographer Debreczeni) shoot like a 'meteor in the sky of the Hungarian people'? Minus the beard and now aged thirty-five, in 1998 Viktor Orbán was the youngest freely elected prime minister in the history of Hungary, following the sensational victory under his leadership of the erstwhile youth party Fidesz. Even fewer observers could have imagined that, after two consecutive electoral defeats in 2002 and 2006, the young politician, driven by an unbridled lust for power and blessed with exceptional personal talent and tactical skills, would go on to score two epochal electoral triumphs in 2010 and 2014, twice winning a two-third parliamentary majority. Orbán then proceeded to fill all positions of state power with his own supporters, without any regard for the principles of the rule of law or the EU's set of values. Since his spring 2010 victory, he has aggressively assumed the leadership role, unwilling to delegate decision-making. In his profound analysis of the methods and practices of the Orbán regime, the distinguished independent legal expert, Tamás Sárközy, speaks of a 'new land grab' (a clear allusion to the Magyar conquest of territory in the Danube region in 896 AD) by a Freikorps of plebeians, who are enriching themselves in the interests of their mission and want to create a new order, with a new elite and the new middle class.[1]

Sárközy points out a phenomenon unique to Hungary, one that has been completely overlooked in the Western media: nowhere in the world (apart from the family clans or dictatorships in Africa and Latin America) is there a democratic country in which a small group of ten to twenty former students, who have known each other for about thirty years, occupies to such a degree so many key positions of power. The offices of the highest dignitaries (the state president, the prime minister and the speaker of the National Assembly) are held by three old friends, János Áder, Viktor Orbán and László Kövér. The core of power in the Hungarian state is formed by a band of friends, now in their mid-fifties, who have been together since university, college or their time in the military, or who have forged friendships through their wives. It is due to their unreserved personal loyalty to Viktor Orbán, and not because of any particular personal talents, that they have risen to key positions in government, the administration and the economy.

A good starting point for any description of the exercise of power and leadership within the authoritarian regime established by Viktor Orbán in 2010–16 is Max Weber's well-known definition: 'power is the opportunity, within a social relationship, to have your own will prevail even against resistance'; 'ruling should mean the opportunity for an order of a particular content to be obeyed by the assigned person'.[2] Orbán's system of government does not depend on naked oppression as do the regimes of Vladimir Putin in Russia, Alexander Lukashenko in Belarus or Nursultan Nazarbayev in Kazakhstan. Through the distribution of offices with sinecures the ruler of Hungary has assembled around himself a great army of devotees, one that extends far beyond the administration, police, secret services and military. Over the decades, long before winning his two-thirds majority, Viktor Orbán created for himself enormous personal room for manoeuvre. From the very beginning, his opponents in the party were incapable of resistance. They either lacked the will or acted too late and failed. Even when taking into account the particular context and historical circumstances of the last three decades, the personalised rule of Orbán can be explained primarily through his life history.

The fact is that most of the politically or financially powerful men around Orbán come from the poorest layers of society, from difficult backgrounds; overwhelmingly, they are not from Budapest, but from socially marginalised environments in the provinces. This has led some Hungarian authors to make bold comparisons between leading Fidesz politicians and the heroes of novels by Balzac (Lucien de Rubempré) and Stendhal (Julien Sorel). But these allusions, in spite of parallels in the behaviour and lifestyles of some of Orbán's new friends (such as the flamboyant Árpád Habony),[3] are false. The circumstances of the social rise of both Orbán himself and the most influential Fidesz members of his circle correspond in no way to the milieux described by these French masters.

In 2003 and in 2009, the Hungarian political scientist and journalist József Debreczeni published two separate biographies of Orbán. Together they total 1,020 pages and are very different in tone. It is not Balzac's encyclopaedic moral portrayal of France but these books, written six years apart and before the decisive election victory in 2010, alongside interviews and TV recordings from the early days, that provide the key to understanding those particular circumstances in the long and contradictory Kádár era that shaped the lives of Orbán's family and friends.[4]

Viktor Mihály Orbán was born on 31 May 1963. Most of what we know about his family life and childhood in the tiny, wretched village of Alcsútdoboz, about 50 kilometres west of Budapest, comes from Orbán himself. Initially, the whole family, including Viktor's brother (two years his junior), lived squeezed together in the cramped house of his paternal grandparents. The central figure in the family was his legendary grandfather. A physically very strong man, a dock worker, he joined up in the Second World War, served on the Eastern Front and, after the collapse of the Second Hungarian Army, eventually returned home from captivity in Austria, unscathed but not without some adventures to tell. With his wife, a former cleaning woman, he settled in the tiny backwater of Alcsútdoboz. Orbán's grandfather was, for a time, employed as a sort of surgeon (doctor's assistant) alongside the local vet. The young Viktor admired this strong personality who took his school leaving certificate at the age of forty-eight, just to make his mark in life. And it was from this extraordinary man that the five- or six-year-old Viktor got his passion for football. Together, grandfather and grandson regularly listened to radio broadcasts of football matches and read the sports pages.

When Viktor was ten, as a consequence of arguments between his mother and grandmother, the family moved to the somewhat larger neighbouring village of Felcsút. In a dilapidated house at the end of the main street they had to begin all over again. The circumstances in which he grew up were certainly orderly, but without doubt very poor. It was only later, looking back on these years during interviews, that Orbán recalled how unbelievably hard he and his siblings had had to work in the fields as young children, at times having to help neighbours, and always in the school holidays: pulling beets, sorting potatoes, collecting corn-cobs, feeding the pigs and chickens.

There was no running water. Hot water was a luxury that had to be heated in a tin pot on the gas stove before washing yourself in the sink. It is easy to imagine what all this must have meant for a bright boy growing up in such conditions. At the age of thirty, the successful young politician, by then the president of Fidesz, described what an 'unforgettable experience' it had been for him as a fifteen-year-old to use a bathroom for the first time, and to have warm water simply by turning on a tap. That there was another world, one of prosperity, was something he had yet to encounter personally at Felcsút.

Orbán has never made any secret of the fact that his parents' social rise was closely associated with the political and economic consolidation of the Kádár regime. In the 1970s and 1980s, there emerged in Hungary a new figure, that of the successful petty bourgeois, whom the political scientist László Lengyel has characterised as 'Homo Kádáricus', as opposed to the 'Homo Sovieticus'. In Lengyel's analysis, the Homo Kádáricus in the towns and countryside made a living from various side jobs. In the heyday of 'mature Kádárism', public and private life was divided under the guiding principle of 'We up here play politics—and you down there live.' This tacit agreement, under which the ruling party and the people both knew the boundaries of what and what was not possible, permitted a Hungarian variety of communism.

Orbán's father, Gyözö, born in 1940 and a party member from 1966, was without any question one such Homo Kádáricus. In the local farm collective in Felcsút, he belonged to the party leadership and was head of the machinery department. Hard work combined with ceaseless learning were the keys to the family escaping its poverty. Orbán's father was thirty years old when he resumed his previously interrupted studies by means of a correspondence course, and he completed university as a mechanical engineer. His mother became a teacher for children with special needs after attending teacher training college as a mature student.

Viktor was good at school, but even at an early stage his tendency to indiscipline, which in later years would arise again and again, was recognisable. As the second smallest in the class, he was not going to be a leader, but in scraps he always fought fearlessly. He admits himself that he was an 'unbelievably bad child. Badly misbehaved, cheeky, violent. Not at all likeable. Repeatedly I was thrown out of all schools ... The adults couldn't stand me and I couldn't stand them ... At home I had constant problems with discipline; my father beat me once or twice a year.' From school to his military service and then studies at the law faculty, his maxim remained unaltered: 'If I'm hit once, then I hit back twice.' In an unguarded moment, the young politician let slip that even as a seventeen-year-old he had been thrashed by his father for his loutish behaviour.

The social rise of the family coincided with Viktor's acceptance to one of the most distinguished grammar schools in Hungary and the household moving away from the tiny village of Felcsút to the town of Székesfehérvár, the country's medieval capital. Here, in the two-room flat of 54 square metres, the fifteen-year-old not only experienced the small miracle of that first bathroom but also passed the social test of encountering urbane surroundings and his new classmates (thirty-one girls and only six boys), many of whose parents were better off than his own. In an interview, Orbán later mentioned that it took him half a year to successfully overcome his rural accent and behaviour. In this he was aided by his mother, but also by his own self-confidence. At the grammar school the young firebrand got into arguments and fights and was even thrown out of the boarding home. Luckily, by that time his father had already found a job and the family had moved to Székesfehérvár.

In his first two years at this school, the eager young schoolboy, as secretary of the Young Communist League (KISZ), helped organise various social and sporting events. Orbán has never attempted to retrospectively present himself as a young fighter against the regime. On the contrary, politics was a subject he never discussed either with his much-loved grandfather or his parents. It was simply not a topic within the family. Nobody read newspapers, nobody listened to political news. They accommodated themselves to the Kádár regime, which, in comparison to those elsewhere in the Eastern Bloc, was milder and more bearable. In Orbán's own words:

> It is remarkable but there is not a single factor or reason in the history of my family which would have explained why I became an anti-communist. My father was a party member. The family did not want to involve itself in politics. A typical reaction to the post-1956 mood. I was told to learn hard, work and to take care of your own business. Don't think about social questions or the outside world. We can't influence them anyway.

In this manner, the Orbáns, like most Hungarians, adjusted to the communist regime. His father was promoted to a higher position in a quarry and in 1982 got a job as an engineer in Libya. This was initially for a year but was prolonged; in the second year he was able to have his wife and youngest son (fourteen years Viktor's junior) join him; Viktor also visited his father in Libya as a student.

Meanwhile, football had become the greatest passion in the schoolboy's life. He played in the youth team of a top club in the Hungarian first league. He trained four times a week and spent 90 per cent of his free time on the football pitch. These were his best years yet, even if he had 'no particular talent as a player' and had to work extremely hard to get a place on the youth team.

Though he was fully aware of his ultimately limited skills on the pitch and did not overestimate his abilities as a centre forward, Orbán has always cultivated an intense, uninhibited and, it goes without saying, media-effective relationship with football. At the grammar school he grasped that in the world of football it is possible to reach the top even if you start at the bottom. Football also offered a chance to shift his social boundaries, an opportunity to be tested and to measure personal strengths as an equal among equals:

> In the grammar school we led a far too dull a life. That was different in the football team; in it could be found all kinds of people: rich, poor, dull, clever. At the same time it formed a very good community of friends. The game brought together people from different backgrounds and classes. Every time I changed team, I also changed cultures.

By far the most important person amongst Viktor's friends at school was Lajos Simicska, who was three years older. This was somebody who had started out right at the bottom. Hardly any other pupil had plunged the depths he had. According to Simicska, his family was so poor that he had to steal coal to keep them from freezing. His father, a metalworker, had been morally and physically destroyed by his role as the secretary of a workers' council during the 1956 uprising. The openly anti-communist Simicska had been thrown out of one class and had to repeat the year because of his rebellious demeanour, so that he was now only two classes ahead of Viktor and his contemporaries. They all admired Simicska as a battering ram. According to Orbán, Simicska had a 'fantastic brain. He was the cleverest of us all.' He only joined the Communist Youth in order to be accepted to university. Simicska ended up starting and completing his studies at the law faculty at the same time as Orbán and his other friends.

They were all soldiers together. Young men accepted for university had first to complete their military service of almost one year. Military service was a particularly hard time for the future students because they were considered 'privileged' by the other recruits and, above all, by the officers and non-commissioned officers, who did not hesitate to bully them. For Viktor Orbán these months were a real trial. They coincided with the World Cup and, because of all the limitations placed upon his free time as a conscript, he ran the danger of missing important games. On several occasions he was sentenced to three days' imprisonment for going AWOL or failing to appear for duty because he was watching football matches. Once, the headstrong Orbán had to spend ten days behind bars because he had struck a non-commissioned officer during a personal altercation.

Although he was still politically unengaged, this period marked emotionally a turning point in Orbán's life. In the army, for the first time and at first hand, he was confronted with both the brutality of the military machine and with the sheer crudity of the indoctrination justifying the system. These experiences prepared the ground for his subsequent political activity and for his turning into a conscious opponent of party dictatorship. It was also at this time that the omnipresent secret services, which were particularly active in the army, tried to win him over as an informant. He turned down the offer, but said nothing about it to his friends. Only after a press report referring to this emerged in June 2005 did Orbán publish a document from the archives of the state secret services, according to which the 'attempt was unsuccessful'.

His friend Simicska was also considered something of a black sheep during his military service because of his critical attitude towards the Soviet attempts to suppress the trade union opposition in Poland. A whole array of future Fidesz politicians, including Orbán's closest friends from his student days such as Gábor Fodor and László Kövér, had similar experiences in the army. Kövér, who comes from a Social Democratic workers' family and is almost four years older than Orbán, often tends towards hyperbole: he once described his time as a soldier as a 'mini-Auschwitz'.

This group of friends grew closer through their political activities in the law faculty students' union. But it was above all their time at the Bibó István Special College for law students, founded in Budapest in 1983,[5] that forged their close links and the network of personal and political friendships which, directly and indirectly, have shaped not only these individuals' careers but also, through their subsequent rise, the whole political landscape of post-communist Hungary. The fact that Orbán shared a small college room at 12 Ménesi Street in Buda, first with Simicska and then for almost two years with Gábor Fodor, means that these key political figures have an intimate knowledge of one another, which has determined time and again their personal reactions in the interplay of cooperation, rivalry and animosities over the following decades. Even today sixty students, each paying about 12,000 forints (approximately €40) a month for the privilege, live in twos or threes in the only 12-square-metre rooms at the college.

That this island of autonomy and self-determination could exist, indeed flourish, in the 1980s, was due primarily to three factors. First, there were the general reforms and concessions of the late Kádár regime. Second was the fact that the director of the college, István Stumpf (only five years older than Orbán), was himself a reformer and, as the son-in-law of the powerful and long-time Minister of the Interior István Horváth, enjoyed a degree of personal latitude. Last but not least, a great deal was owed to the active support of the Hungarian-born multimillionaire George Soros, who from 1986 onwards promoted the college and generously subsidised its politically active students, as well as their journal *Századvég*, through language courses, bursaries, foreign trips, printing costs and so on.

Through lectures and personal contacts, Orbán, Fodor, Kövér and their like-minded friends forged close links with the intellectuals and politicians of the left-liberal opposition. These connections, intensified through playing football together and family ties, ensured that the former grammar school pupils, army conscripts, Bibó roommates and neighbours remained a tightly knit group even after graduation. It was no coincidence that in 1984, shortly after the founding of the college, the twenty-one-year-old Orbán was elected chairman of the executive committee of its sixty students.

'In politics, power is first, second and third.' This observation of the German-American political scientist Ernst Fraenkel is, according to the sociologist Rainer Paris, as true today as it ever was. 'And for that reason, the only person who can lead is the one with the will to lead. That is the person who, even if forced into it, decides fundamentally on it and from a particular moment onwards accepts and aggressively assumes the leadership role.'[6]

The absolute will to power has moulded the character of Viktor Orbán ever since his time as a student leader and throughout his entire political career, even though he has succeeded, not least thanks to a compliant media, in conveying the image of a goal-oriented politician, one with character, modesty and clean hands. He has long understood the value of being able, if necessary, to distance himself from officials in his own party who were maladroit or had become unacceptable, and not to let himself be held 'responsible' for any mishaps or slipups.

Gábor Fodor, the close friend with whom he shared a room at the Bibó College, and who later became a rival, observes that 'Even as a young man in the 1980s Viktor Orbán was already possessed of those domineering, intolerant ways of thinking and behaving that are all too evident in him today. There was also an expediency about him, one without any principles. But not only that. He was, in addition to all of this, sincere and likeable.'

The character of Orbán as a man admired by his supporters but feared by his opponents, with both widely recognised leadership skills and a deeply rooted cynicism underlying his political practice, has remained ambivalent throughout his life.

3

THE RISE AND FALL OF A SHOOTING STAR

To understand the astonishing developments since the collapse of communism in 1989 in general, and the singular rise of the Fidesz Party from 1998 (and especially since 2010) in particular, it is necessary first to recall the personal and political infighting within its small core group, differences which were ultimately to prove irreconcilable. On 30 March 1988 in the approximately 30–35-square-metre great hall of the Bibó College, Viktor Orbán and thirty-six other students founded the Alliance of Young Democrats (Fiatal Demokraták Szövetsége, or Fidesz) as an independent youth organisation. This daring challenge to the crumbling ruling Communist Party at first only interested the secret police, who immediately tried, albeit without any success, to put pressure on its founding fathers. None of the three dozen law and economics students, all in their mid-twenties, could have thought then that they were establishing what has evolved into perhaps the most successful political party in Hungarian history.

Fidesz's founding document declared that its goal was the creation of a new, independent youth organisation, intended to gather together the politically active, radical and reformist youth.

There were two prerequisites for membership: the age limit was fixed between sixteen and thirty-five, and membership of the Hungarian Young Communist League was prohibited. Within four weeks Fidesz had 1,000 members. The wider public, however, only learned of the new grouping's existence after Orbán's sensational speech at Heroes' Square on 16 June 1989.

That year the course was set for the transition from dictatorship to democracy. After Mikhail Gorbachev bluntly informed Hungarian Prime Minister Miklós Németh in March 1989 that the Kremlin would not oppose either a multi-party system or the introduction of private property, a desperate power struggle broke out within the Communist Party. Hungary went down the same path as Poland, setting up a round table to commence negotiations between the opposition and the ruling party. Viktor Orbán and László Kövér from Fidesz took an active part in these meetings.

New political parties and groups mushroomed. By the end of 1988 there were twenty-one, and a year later sixty different groupings. The strongest party by far, and the best organised nationally, was the middle-class Hungarian Democratic Party (Magyar Demokrata Fórum or MDF), led by József Antall, who later became prime minister (1990–3). The Alliance of Free Democrats (Szabad Demokraták Szövetsége or SzDSz), formed in November 1989 with the philosopher János Kis as its intellectual mastermind, maintained in this new situation the tradition of the democratic opposition, which had been extremely active in the underground. Together with Fidesz, the Free Democrats represented the spearhead of the anti-communist opposition. Among the groups established at this time, only two pre-war parties, the Smallholders and the Christian Democrats, survived as politically significant organisations. The newly founded Social Democratic Party sank into oblivion after just two months. The Socialist Party (Magyar Szocialista Párt or

MSzP), forged by the reform communists, tried in vain to assume its role.

In October 1989 the second Fidesz congress decided to transform the youth organisation into a political party in order to participate in the first free elections scheduled for the following spring. Orbán had been working part-time since April 1988 for George Soros' Open Society Foundation, and, with a grant from the Foundation, had moved at the end of September 1989 to Pembroke College, Oxford to complete a nine-month research project on the idea of civil society in European political philosophy. He travelled to Budapest to take part in the congress but was not elected to the leadership. The rapid political developments in Hungary, however, created a completely new situation in his life. The planned nine months in Oxford did not even become four: in January 1990 Orbán returned to Budapest with his wife and their four-month-old daughter, both of whom had in the meantime moved to London. This was his fateful and irrevocable decision to become a career politician. In his absence, his former roommate at the Bibó College, the popular, sociable and very handsome Gábor Fodor, had become head of the party.

After his return, Orbán threw himself into the election campaign with unbelievable energy. He was already displaying such leadership qualities that in the vote on the order of the party list of candidates he was placed first and Fodor second. If we look at this 1990 list today, even the praise of a social psychologist as critical as Ferenc Pataki becomes understandable. In his book on the 'Fidesz phenomenon',[1] he writes of the 'fairytale' achievement, 'unique in modern history', of a handful of students who, in spite of splits and changes, have remained at the helm of their party for thirty years, able to protect their group identity and to seize total power over a whole country. In order, the first five candidates were Viktor Orbán, Gábor Fodor, János Áder, József Szájer and László Kövér. Apart from Fodor, a special case dealt with below, the other four still hold the leading positions in both state and party today: Orbán as prime minister and head of the Fidesz Party, Áder as president of Hungary, Szájer as a vice-president of the European People's Party in the European Parliament and principal author of the new constitution and, finally, Kövér as speaker of the Hungarian parliament.

At the first free elections in April 1990, Fidesz won twenty-two of the 386 seats, a result that Orbán later justifiably declared as a great success for a 'party of youth'. But after the massive electoral victory of the middle-class MDF as a 'calming force' proclaiming conservative, national and Christian values, it was that party's chairman, József Antall, who played the leading political role. Until his premature death in December 1993, he governed the country as an internationally respected prime minister at the head of a bourgeois coalition with an absolute majority, during the transition to a market economy and independence. The Free Democrats formed the main opposition with ninety-four seats, whilst the post-communist MSzP garnered less than 10 per cent of the vote and a mere thirty-three MPs. However, voter turnout was disappointing: 65 per cent in the first round and only 45.5 per cent in the second.

Shortly after the election, the inexorable decline of the first democratic government began. The announcement (after previous denials) of an overnight 65 per cent hike in petrol prices sparked off street blockades by taxi drivers. At the height of the tension it became known that Antall was fighting cancer and was in hospital after a major operation. The tense situation was only relaxed by reducing the price increase and by a TV interview that the prime minister had to give from hospital in his pyjamas.

Presumably no government could have coped with the system transition without shattering the artificially high levels of employment and inflated wages and salaries, both sustained only by an enormous foreign debt. The people, however, had expected a rapid economic upturn and nothing but benefits from the changes of 1989. Hungarian society was totally unprepared for the unexpected and tremendous stresses and strains of the transition. Just a few examples: GDP shrank by 20 per cent between 1988 and 1993; real wages fell by 4 per cent in 1998 and 8 per cent in 1991; inflation was 35 per cent in 1991, 23 per cent in 1992 and only fell under 20 per cent in 1993. The previously unknown phenomenon of unemployment briefly reached 12 per cent. Thousands of enterprises were liquidated and half a million jobs disappeared.

Under pressure from both the vociferous left-wing and liberal opposition, and the extreme-right, nationalist and anti-Semitic wing of his own party, which sustained his majority, the terminally ill Antall could not carry out the policies of compromise that his own personal and political convictions favoured. His approval ratings fell sharply. Nevertheless, after his death almost a quarter of a million people paid their last respects to the prime minister, laid out in state in parliament. Heads of state and government from all over the world attended his funeral. In contrast to most leading Hungarian politicians since 1989, József Antall was above reproach, honest and in every respect personally incorruptible.

In the years of the Antall government, the twenty-two Fidesz MPs remained true to their youthful image. Their beards and long hair, their jeans and open-neck shirts in parliament, their verbal fireworks and casual repartee endeared them not only to other MPs but also to the public at large. They advocated liberal positions in their economic, educational and social policies, and were quick and uninhibited in their judgements on the nationalist and anti-Semitic undertones skulking around in the governing parties. And, on occasion, they had no hesitation in voicing their biting criticisms of the close relationship between the coalition and the Catholic Church.

As the parliamentary leader of his party, Viktor Orbán maintained this liberal line of 'no ifs or buts' in his speeches and interviews. After his report, in 1992 the party congress endorsed an application for membership of the Liberal International. Orbán became vice-president and was a proud host of the Liberal International congress held in Budapest in the autumn of 1993. Due to TV broadcasts of parliamentary sessions, at the beginning of 1991 he was already the third most popular politician in the country, whilst Fodor—still the party leader—was fourth. In April 1993 Orbán was voted the first president of Fidesz, unopposed and with an overwhelming majority, confirming his undisputed leadership position at the age of thirty.

Quotations from Orbán's interviews and speeches at this time (often used against him by today's opposition), in which he laid out his programmes, leave no doubt as to his position on basic political questions of the day:

> The leaderships of the governing parties, and particularly of the MDF, are very much inclined to reject criticism of government policy by suggesting the opposition or media are undermining the standing of Hungary, are attacking the Hungarian nation itself. Such statements do not augur well for the future of democracy. Such an attitude indicates that the leaders of the ruling parties tend to conflate their parties and their voters with the nation, with the country. Sometimes, in moments of enthusiasm, they have the feeling that their power is not the consequence of a one-off decision of a certain number of Hungarian citizens but that they express, in some mystical manner, the eternal interests of the entire Hungarian people.[2]

Or this, from a speech given on 7 February 1992:

> We have always refused to see our struggle in terms of there being on the one side the good, and on the other the evil, on the one side there are patriots and on the other traitors ... The nationalistic idea, populist politics, is in sharp contrast with liberalism. Liberals demand freedom for the people so that they can run businesses and vote. The populists,

on the other hand, want to elevate the people ... It is evident that in the churches the MDF is seeking political allies against society. The churches can only then have their due position in a modern society if they protect and win back their autonomy. If, however, they see the actors in political life in terms of some being enemies and others allies, then they will become themselves political actors ... Fidesz should in the next legislative period become a completely open, liberal People's Party without any age limits.

In this post-1989 period there were growing tensions in Hungarian society, triggered by the economic crisis and the demonstrative shift to the right, reflected in anti-Semitic tendencies and measures to control the public service media. Nevertheless, the popularity of Fidesz, as a youth party unsullied by the sins of the past, rose from month to month. In 1992 polls showed that the party had gained the approval of 30 per cent of the electorate, and amongst voters who were certain to take part in the election in May 1994 this figure rose to 45 per cent. It is no wonder that the reports about the rapid growth in the popularity of Viktor Orbán and his closest friends went to their heads. According to Gábor Fodor, the inner circle was already beginning to speculate on the composition of the future government, naturally under the leadership of Fidesz.

Behind the glittering facade of all the political successes, from 1992 a political differentiation, which would later become a deep rift, began to emerge between Orbán's absolute claim to leadership and the still extremely popular Fodor. The moody and culture-focused Fodor demonstrated neither political clout nor resolve in the power struggle, or indeed in his subsequent career. There were also fundamental differences concerning Fidesz's policy of alliance. From the very beginning, there was a tense relationship with the Free Democrats (SzDSz), a group founded by urban, left-wing intellectuals and with four times as many members of parliament as Fidesz. Whilst Fodor maintained a personal friendship with the then leader of the Free Democrats, János Kis, Orbán and his closest political crony, the impulsive László Kövér, who, according to all sources, was hostile to Fodor on personal grounds, emphasised the full independence of Fidesz. 'We don't want to be the youth organisation of the SzDSz,' Orbán stressed on more than one occasion, and his line was clearly supported by the majority of the party leadership.

In any analysis of the estrangement and open conflict between Fidesz and the older liberals, the differences in personalities and social status have to be taken into account. The leading Free Democrat politicians were overwhelmingly left-wing intellectuals—philosophers, sociologists, economists, who had broken with Marxism and often came from ex-communist, bourgeois, sometimes Jewish families. They were well read, open to the world and fluent in foreign languages, in contrast to the first generation of Fidesz intellectuals, who were mostly from a rural or small town background. The leading Fidesz politicians were, moreover, predominantly lawyers with practical knowledge. Furthermore, the differences in lifestyle and family traditions between the two groups were often conspicuous. Reflecting on his time at grammar school in a much cited video interview from spring 1988, Orbán said:

> In our circle of friends there were boys who came from another social background. The milieu from which I sprang had no specific cultural traditions whatsoever. Such a white collar class ... my father had no connection with the peasantry; it's true we kept animals so we did this type of work, but in our village there had been for a long time no peasant culture, no workers' culture ... Not to speak of any bourgeois culture ... I came from such an uncultured, from such an eclectic something, but there were boys whose fathers were priests and came from a Protestant tradition and there were also one or two lads who came from a conventional middle-class tradition ... Only one of them was older, Lajos Simicska; he was the smartest amongst us.

Orbán and his closest friends were moulded by these deeply rooted differences in their childhoods, upbringing, lifestyles and standards. These roots marked, first subconsciously but later openly, their attitudes towards liberal politicians, who were often overweening, even arrogant in their behaviour. Their initial admiration for the brilliance of some liberal and left-wing intellectuals evolved over the years into an aversion fed by inferiority complexes, later into almost open feelings of hatred. A famous episode was immortalised in some verses by the poet István Kemény. At a reception for newly elected parliamentarians in 1994, the well-known Free Democrat MP, Miklós Haraszti,[3] went up to Orbán, who like the other Fidesz representatives was appropriately attired, and adjusted his tie with an insolent gesture of the hand. Orbán blushed and was visibly incensed. Kemény celebrated this symbolic and never forgotten moment in a poem, as a key experience in the life of the 'last prime minister of the drowning country of Hungary'. This personal background of perceived inferiority has to be understood, as it lies behind the outbursts of animosity against the renegade MPs around Gábor Fodor who 'betrayed' Fidesz in 1993 and 'sold' themselves to the post-communists; it is also reflected in the disdain for cosmopolitan Europhiles repeatedly and vociferously manifested by Orbán's friends, especially by the speaker of parliament, László Kövér. The turning away from liberal positions and the espousal of grassroots nationalist values, in contrast to the 'alien' left-liberal governments, has run like a thread through subsequent debates, peaking with Orbán's open avowal of 'illiberal democracy' in the summer of 2014.

Untroubled by any sense of scruple, Viktor Orbán, not yet thirty, single-mindedly and quite openly pursued his goal of seizing total control over Fidesz. With the help of his loyal comrade Kövér, he cannily outplayed his former friend and subsequent rival in every trial of strength—for the last time in 1992–3, when

Fodor sought the post of chair of the enlarged executive. At that time, Fodor was by far the most popular Fidesz politician and the second most popular political figure in the country. Finally, in protest against the underhand pressure and intrigues, Fodor and two other MPs quit the party in November 1993 and resigned their parliamentary seats. Some months later, two further well-known MPs left Fidesz for political reasons. In all, according to Fodor, the party lost between 400 and 500 active members.

Even before the final break, the media were commenting upon Fidesz's internal differences in general and Orbán's absolutist claim to leadership in particular. In this period he gave a key interview to the critical journalist Zsófia Mihancsik.[4] She pointed to charges that Fidesz was prepared at any moment to give up its principles in favour of seizing power and added that Orbán's attitude as party leader was dedicated to engendering fears amongst ordinary people. For his part Orbán dismissed the allegations about settling personal scores by pointing to democratic, majority-based decisions, as well as the claims that people were supposed to be frightened of him. Amongst other things he was quoted as saying:

> My personality has a number of defects (I'm not going to say what they are, that is for my opponents to find out) and offers a ready target for such personal attacks. I am considered to be a resolute person; I like rational arguments and also that style of politics in which resolve is an important element. My mentality also offers a target in the sense that by origin I am not a sensitive intellectual of the twentieth generation and this throws up some questions of style; there is in me perhaps a roughness brought up from below. That is no disadvantage as we know that the majority of people come from below. But this struggle also gives an opportunity for such attacks. In my opinion, in certain conflicts, confrontation and not compromise has to be pursued because only in this way can subsequent, even greater conflicts be avoided.

At the 1994 parlimentary elections, Fidesz paid a high price for the dispute with Fodor and his followers. When they left the party Fidesz stood at 20 per cent in the opinion polls and its Free Democrat rivals at 8 per cent. Yet when the elections were held a mere six months later, in May 1994, the Free Democrats won more than 19 per cent of the vote, and Fidesz only 7 per cent. Instead of the 100 (or at the very least sixty) seats anticipated by Orbán, Fidesz had only twenty representatives in parliament, two fewer than in 1990. The party dropped to last place, even behind the Christian Democrats, who now had twenty-two MPs.

This was a bitter disappointment for Fidesz, which had been so certain of victory. An additional, painful slap in the face was the entry into parliament of the three rebel MPs, on the Free Democrat ticket. After a brilliant rise and a completely unexpected fall, Viktor Orbán, and Fidesz with him, stood before the greatest test of his life.

4

THE ROAD TO THE FIRST VICTORY

The election of May 1994 marked the nadir of Viktor Orbán's political career. The post-communist Socialists quintupled their vote and formed a coalition with the Free Democrats for political appearances' sake even though they had a clear majority; together the two parties held over 72 per cent of the seats. In contrast Fidesz had become the weakest party in parliament. Yet, only four years later, in May 1998, it won the election and Orbán became prime minister, the youngest head of a government in the history of Hungary and, at that time, the youngest in Europe. How was this possible? What reasons lay behind this truly sensational change?

Before discussing the errors of the Socialist–Free Democrat government, we must first return to the role of the personality, to Orbán himself. I first met him on 22 September 1993, before his electoral defeat. The occasion was a speech he gave at the Institute for Human Sciences (IWM) in Vienna, in what was then a still far from polished English. Afterwards I spoke with him at an intimate dinner given by the Institute's director, Krzysztof Michalski. Orbán struck me with his frankness when discussing, for example, his rivalry for the party leadership with Fodor, as he did with his solid liberal attitudes in opposition to the conservative policies of the then Antall government. At the time he impressed us all—his audience, his host and myself included—as a progressive politician of the young generation, a man with a promising future. This first encounter was followed by others; these, however, were in the period after Orbán had turned his back on liberalism in favour of nationalist, right-wing politics.

After the election defeat it soon turned out that the liberalism of Orbán and his closest friends had been little more than a thin veneer. They quickly grasped the necessity of making a smooth accommodation with the new circumstances. The Free Democrats, in the past radically opposed to the communist regime, were now prepared to form a coalition with Prime Minister Gyula Horn, a former communist, and his victorious Socialist Party. Gábor Fodor, once the symbol of Fidesz, even accepted the post of education and cultural minister in the coalition government. These dramatic and surprising developments seemed to justify in retrospect the hard and distrustful line taken by Orbán and Kövér towards their stronger, centre-left rivals. After the formal resignation of the entire party leadership and a clever mixing of self-criticism and condemnation of any cooperation with the Socialists, Orbán, Kövér and their friends were confirmed in their functions at an extraordinary party congress in July 1994. Though in his speech on that occasion Orbán excluded any shift to either right or left, this was just a ruse.

In the summer of 1994, after the Fidesz debacle, Orbán's former adviser and subsequent biographer József Debreczeni taped a long interview with him while collecting material for a book on the recently deceased prime minister, József Antall. Only nine years later did Debreczeni make these off-the-record comments available to the public in his first book on Orbán. In the wake of Fidesz's worst electoral defeat in its history, Orbán reproached

THE ROAD TO THE FIRST VICTORY

Antall with extraordinary acerbity for his failure to create or leave a legacy of either a communications framework or an economic basis for any future conservative government:

> Antall bears the personal responsibility. Not because we are in opposition but because we are standing buck naked with our bottoms bare in opposition ... There isn't a single newspaper. Some of the newspapers were stolen, and he allowed the others to be robbed under his nose and the rest he left in state ownership ... there is no radio, no TV channel. There's nothing. And for this there is no excuse.

Orbán saw as the late prime minister's other great mistake

> his having neglected to cultivate personal contacts with the eight to ten big capitalists ... What should have been done with them? Make it clear in front of the bankers that these eight to ten people are our people. And then let big business arrange everything else according to its own logic. These people could perhaps have been helped in the investment funds, in the calls for tenders ... After an international negotiation he [Antall] was asked in a small group of people why he had not proposed some possible joint economic ventures. Antall replied that he had not gone to do business but to improve the position of his country. In his view, business had no part in politics although it is the very substance of politics ... He had no feeling for anything like this. Absolutely no feeling.[1]

For many readers of Debreczeni's book, these attacks were puzzling, because Fidesz propagandists were already busily spreading stories that shortly before his death in December 1993 Antall had personally bestowed his political testament on Orbán.

Nevertheless, these remarks reveal even at this relatively early stage the relationship of the young politician to the acquisition and exercise of power, as well as his understanding of political communication and media management. Drawing on the instructive experiences of his predecessor Fodor's alleged shortcomings, Orbán, whilst still opposition leader, put Lajos Simicska, perhaps his oldest friend from his grammar school and army days and a 'genius' at financial transactions, in charge of fundraising for Fidesz.

At the seventh party congress in April 1995, only nine months after his categorical rejection of any swing to left or right, Orbán committed himself without reservation to a political shift to the right.

In my view, the formation of blocs, the emergence of a socialist centre-left and a moderate centre-right dominated by the middle classes is in the interest of the country ... In the centre we have, if we stand alone, no chance against either left or right. To my mind there is no possibility of cooperating with the left. My answer is that Fidesz must seek cooperation with the forces politically right of the centre.

In keeping with the new line the party now called itself Fidesz—Hungarian Civic Party (Magyar Polgári Párt).

The volte-face, a great surprise for many, was soon reflected in the language and personal style of the Fidesz leadership. Increasingly the erstwhile rebels, who had once been bearded and casually clothed, were dressing 'conservatively' and had their hair neatly styled. In the speeches of Fidesz MPs, and particularly in Orbán's own rhetoric, current political and economic questions were increasingly interwoven with professions of faith in the nation, in Magyar tradition, in the homeland, in national interests, in respectability, in middle-class values, in the family, in love of the mother country. It was a smooth transition, one gathering speed all the time, as the politicians who had previously scorned and caricatured conservative values now began to stand shoulder to shoulder with the Catholic and Protestant churches and, above all, to deliberately play the card of the Hungarian nation founding myths against their left-wing and liberal rivals.

Fierce critics from the left maintained that the Fidesz leaders were chameleons, without a shred of principle and always ready to bend with the wind. Such emotional accusations missed the point because they overlooked the deeper motivations of the all too conscious and superbly executed turn to the right. After splitting off the weak and, it must be said, skilfully isolated left wing, Orbán exploited his only realistic chance for future success against the left: the right-wing conservative, nationalist, populist option. In the first freely elected parliament, Fidesz had inevitably been the left-wing opposition to a right-wing government. Now that the government was overwhelmingly socialist and left-liberal, everything was naturally reversed. Thus in parliament on 27 September 1994 Orbán was able to taunt the Socialist–Free Democrat coalition (much to the delight of the Smallholders' Party and the Christian Democrats) with Willy Brandt's famous quip on German reunification: 'What belongs together is growing together.'

In any explanation of why the Fidesz leadership lurched to the right, the long concealed but highly explosive force of the national question, above all the Trianon trauma, must never be forgotten. What Nietzsche called 'cowardice in the face of reality' applies equally well to the forty-year-long silence of the communist regime about the national tragedy and, after 1989, to the suppression of any discussion by the post-communist left of this subject, one exploited and exaggerated by right-wing nationalists. The treaty that was signed on 4 June 1920 in the summer palace of Trianon at Versailles distributed two thirds of the territory of historical Hungary and 40 per cent of its peoples among the three neighbouring successor states of Romania, Czechoslovakia and Yugoslavia. 3.2 million Hungarians now lived under foreign suzerainty. That Hungary won back 40 per cent of the lost territories in the Vienna Awards of 1938–40 as a consequence of its alliance with Hitler's Germany was a taboo subject for the Kádár regime. (After 1945, the pre-war borders were reimposed.) Despite this, in the 1980s, 70 per cent of those polled stated that the Treaty of Trianon still filled them with feelings of deep bitterness.

These national misfortunes—the disaster of Trianon, defeat in war, the fate of Hungarians living abroad and the psychosis of a nation in peril—have for generations been part and parcel of the traditions of the Christian middle classes, the very people identified by the Fidesz leadership as the potential core of a future great, national people's party. This doleful, historical factor has been especially strong in rural areas. When considering the deeds and choices made by the leading Fidesz politicians, the small group of its founding fathers, we should always remember that, with very few exceptions, they were first-generation intellectuals, coming from rural families, even if (and we have this on the best authority) they were atheist in inclination and the majority of them were not baptised.

During their flight from the provinces to the capital city, these young men forged their close ties and networks at the Bibó College rather than at university. It was not only their desire for independence that played an important role in their relationship with the Free Democrats. As already mentioned, in the personality-based interpretation of their political actions, the differences in social status and education among some of the important actors should not be overlooked. It was these differences, just as much as the superior behaviour of some Free Democrat notables, that must have given rise to the inferiority complexes of the young and then still inexperienced Fidesz politicians. The personal element was probably decisive in Orbán's chronic inability to make compromises and his recurring reflex reaction to political defeats or unconscious humiliations: political annihilation of his opponents and rivals.

Those who know him best emphasise again and again the immense importance of football not only in the origins of the political team called Fidesz but also in its tactics and strategy in politics. As a bitter opponent once put it, Orbán always wanted to be the referee, the lineman, the centre forward and the goalkeeper, all at one and the same time. He has never denied that he always wanted to be prime minister, comparing political struggle with a game of attacking football. He can only tolerate losing when he knows that, next time, his success-oriented team can, with hard training, grim determination and clever tactics exploiting the weaknesses of their opponents, and turn yesterday's defeat into a victory.

One of the most telling but barely known stories about the Hungarian prime minister concerns *Once Upon a Time in the West*, Sergio Leone's Spaghetti Western starring Claudia Cardinale, Henry Fonda and Charles Bronson. This 1968 film did not reach cinemas in communist Hungary until the 1970s. Over two-and-a-half hours it tells the story of a dramatic struggle over a piece of land that a railway company wants to buy, to build its line. As the family does not want to sell, it is slaughtered by a band of gangsters at the behest of the company. Only the wife survives. Then Charles Bronson appears on the scene as an avenging angel and shoots the leader of the gang, who had in the past murdered his older brother. Justice prevails.

According to his Polish biographer Igor Janke, Viktor Orbán has seen this film 'at least 15 times'. What so enthralled him about this film? Orbán:

> Everything! The heroic story. At the beginning everything seems hopeless. Night and day with little or no hope, nothing works. To persist and to emerge victorious, it is not enough that the hero can shoot and knows how to use his fists. He must also use his brain and show magnanimity. That is very important. You must know and understand your enemy, you must find out what in reality makes him tick and then, when things come to a head, you mustn't shrink from the fight but attack and win![2]

This credo has held true not only for Orbán's four years at the head of the opposition but also, in a deeper sense, for the whole life of this power-seeking politician. Depending on the situation, politics is for Orbán a mixture of a Western and a football match.

However, despite his professions to the contrary, after victory in his struggles with his political rivals he does not display magnanimity but ruthlessness. On every occasion, he demonstrated his assertiveness and resolve between 1994 and 1998 in the face of a seemingly all-powerful coalition government and a hopelessly divided opposition. With the election defeat, Fidesz was now freed of its liberal and doubting elements. From this time on, it formed under Orbán a tight-knit unit in the fight against the Socialist–Free Democrat government. The rise in its popularity and the applause it received in parliament from other parties on the opposition benches confirmed the impression that those groups that joined or cooperated with Orbán and his party could regain the initiative.

The political offensive of the small Fidesz team proved so surprisingly successful because the Gyula Horn government wasted its first eight months on fierce infighting within the Socialist Party. As so often before and since, this was over measures to avoid a threatening financial bankruptcy. Horn, the symbolic and convinced representative of the 'little man from the Kádár era', had initially believed that German Chancellor Helmut Kohl would, out of gratitude for the opening of the border in 1989, grant Hungary generous credits, thereby enabling him to avoid taking austerity measures. What the Germans were prepared to offer, however, fell well below his expectations. Thus Horn had to accept the most radical reforms to date, which included sweeping privatisations. He then, very grudgingly, had to push the measures through his party.

On 12 March 1995 and quite out of the blue, the new finance minister, Lajos Bokros, in close agreement with the governor of the National Bank György Surányi, announced together with Horn the notorious Bokros package. Taken together, the resulting abolition of social benefits, reductions in wages and pensions, introduction of student fees, sliding devaluation of the forint with an estimated annual exchange rate loss of 26–27 per cent as well as other changes in taxes and customs duties, all made deep inroads into the standard of living of the average Hungarian. In one year, 1995–6, real wages fell by 18 per cent (as against a fall of 20 per cent in 1990–4) and the purchasing power of pensions by 25 per cent. Two cabinet ministers resigned immediately in protest.

Yet, almost overnight, the Bokros package won back for Hungary the confidence of foreign capital and international financial institutions such as the IMF and the World Bank. By the beginning of 1998 the budget deficit had been reduced from 10 to 4.2 per cent of GDP and net indebtedness from 21 to 8.7 billion dollars. Hand in hand with this financial stabilisation, the Socialist–Free Democrat government carried out an ambitious privatisation of state property. The erstwhile reform communist Horn, for whom the very idea of selling off state assets had been anathema, bragged in parliament and at party meetings that his government had raised 1,007 billion forints ($5 billion) through its programme of privatisation between 1995 and 1997. The level of foreign investment in Hungary reached approximately 18 billion dollars (more than in every other transition country in Central and Eastern Europe) and the private sector was now responsible for 80 per cent of GDP, compared with only 20 per cent at the beginning of the government's period in office.

With hindsight, in economic terms this package was a breakthrough; politically, it was suicide. Although the reform programme was watered down after the forced resignation of the courageous finance minister in February 1996, the inexorable slide of the coalition government's fortunes may be dated to March 1995. At the beginning of 1996 the opposition was already 19 per cent ahead in the opinion polls. Then, on top of this massive collapse in the living standards of the 'little man', those whom Prime Minister Horn claimed to represent, came the infamous (though now almost risible, against the rampant corruption of the post-2010 Orbán era) Tocsik scandal. In the course of the privatisations, the two coalition partners each benefited from deals to dispose of real estate.[3] Other dubious financial transactions and the basic treaties with Romania and Slovakia (both perfectly correct from a public policy standpoint, but heavily criticised by representatives of Hungarians living abroad) were also grist to the mill of the opposition. Orbán attacked the government more and more fiercely on these questions too; and, despite the significant concessions secured in the government's wide-sweeping 1997 agreement with the Vatican on state financing,[4] he did so increasingly with the support of the Churches.

In an important policy declaration on the Day of the Civic Opposition, made at Budapest's Franz Liszt Academy of Music on 12 June 1997, Orbán stated (in words often quoted back at him by his critics): 'The Hungarian government is alien despite our constitutional law; it is not under national influence.' The national question was ever more starkly conflated with expression of bourgeois values. According to Debreczeni, in his speech to the Fidesz party congress in February 1998 Orbán used the word 'citizen' no fewer than eighty times in an eleven-page script. A circular of the Catholic Bishops Conference, read out in churches on Easter Sunday, was a clear declaration for the middle-class right-wing parties.

Four years after the fiasco of Fidesz's pitiful performance in the election of 1994, the opposition, now dominated more clearly than ever by Orbán, won a clear majority in the decisive second round of voting (though the Socialists had led in the first) in the distribution of seats in the individual parliamentary districts. The real sensation was the rise of Fidesz to become the main political force in Hungary, something that even shortly before had seemed inconceivable. Viktor Orbán, the power-seeking 'meteor in the political heavens' (Debreczeni), the most talented and the most controversial politician in Hungary, was to dominate the political stage for the next four years.

5

THE YOUNG COMET

Fidesz's surprising victory in 1998 opened the way to a restructuring of the state apparatus by the new ruling political party. Thanks to the support of other right-wing parties, Fidesz was able to increase its number of seats sevenfold to 148 in the second round of voting. Together with the revived Smallholders' Party (forty-eight seats) and the rump centre-right MDF (nineteen seats), Viktor Orbán was able to form a conservative coalition government with a large absolute majority. He was not, therefore, dependent on the support of the fourteen MPs of the extreme-right, anti-Semitic Hungarian Justice and Life Party (MÍEP) founded by István Csurka in 1993. József Debreczeni reminds us of a remark made by Orbán, albeit one dating from 1992: 'The Smallholders' Party is the furthest away from Fidesz ... Forming a coalition with it is something that must not happen even in our worst dreams.' The disappointed biographer added ironically: 'Dreams sometimes come true.' However, given the ease and frequency with which right- and left-wing parties even in the established democracies change course, the conclusion cannot be avoided that there is a political cynicism at large that respects values only as long as they do not clash with interests.

Two trends stand out from the four years of the first Orbán government (1998–2002): the determined and rapid expansion of the Prime Minister's Office as the assertive centre of decision-making, and the weakening of the parliamentary control mechanisms. Borrowing from American concepts of public relations, the prime minister became the central figure of government communications. Debreczeni describes with pertinent details a style of government dominated by a one-man leadership. Unlike his predecessors, Orbán, for example, took his oath of office as prime minister two days before all his ministers. Whenever the thirty-five-year-old head of government entered the room for a meeting of his cabinet, all the ministers (including men many years his senior) rose in greeting. Normally, there was no debate: proposals had been discussed and decided upon in the small circle around Orbán before the meeting. The fact that neither minutes were ever taken nor tape recordings made of the proceedings of a cabinet meeting was the subject of particular criticism. Only summaries were later compiled. This practice was without precedent, all the more so because during both the Dual Monarchy and the Horthy eras, and even during the four decades of communist rule, minutes of cabinet meetings were always taken.

The decision of the government to alter the order of business in parliament sparked widespread criticism. Instead of weekly meetings during ordinary or extraordinary parliamentary sessions, these were henceforth to be called every three weeks, thereby restricting the right of an immediate interpellation. In the expansion of the government machine directly subordinated to the head of government, a central role was played by István Stumpf, a reform communist who had been instrumental in the establishment of the Bibó College and in the emergence of the group of Fidesz's founding fathers. He was now made a minister of state in the Prime Minister's Office. In a very different but equally telling example, the celebrations for the thousandth-year anniversary of the crowning of St Stephen, the first king of Hungary, was stage-managed as a two-year national campaign and, in 2000, after a tour of all Hungary, the Crown of St Stephen was transferred from the National Museum to the parliament building.

Both at home and abroad, the image of the young, energetic and patriotic prime minister was very positive. In a television interview in March 2000 Orbán admitted that he always felt nervous both before and during official appearances and that he regarded these as the most difficult part of his duties. At the very beginning of his political career he revealed that he always analysed his interviews and speeches after having given them, to avoid future mistakes or slips of the tongue.

It was six years after his speech at the Institute for Human Sciences meeting in Vienna that I met Orbán again. This was at the international Europa-Forum held at the Göttweig Abbey in Lower Austria. At the invitation of the provincial governor, Erwin Pröll, I had been moderating events there from their inception in 1996. On Sunday, 6 June 1999, as one of the high-ranking foreign guests, Orbán gave a speech about Hungary and his European policies before an international audience. Afterwards at lunch I congratulated him on the fact that, in contrast to some prominent speakers, he had shown restraint and, as scheduled, spoken only for twenty minutes. To this he casually replied that he had read the text aloud several times in advance and where necessary shortened it in order not to exceed the time limit laid down by the organisers. He was already, back then, a political professional attentive to every detail.

The communications experts of the government manipulated the tabloid press and above all television to popularise the young prime minister and his family, something his (older) predecessors had not done. That Orbán played football in his local village team of Felcsút every Sunday was of course fully capitalised upon in TV and newspaper reports, as was his family life at Christmas or on summer holiday in Croatia. Media events, however, could not always be controlled. On 7 August 2001 a highly embarrassing episode took place in Mezőkövesd, a small and conservative town in the north of Hungary. Orbán, holding a bunch of flowers and a book in one hand, wanted to shake with the other the hand of an elderly woman, and could do nothing about it when she suddenly pulled his hand to her and in all servility kissed it. The photograph of this absurd scene, of which the politician was entirely innocent, was of course exploited to the hilt by the opposition and media. This incident aside, Orbán's weekly radio broadcasts and monthly TV appearances contributed significantly to the mobilisation of his supporters and to the successful dissemination of the political message of his government.

Even in this first period of office, the Orbán government promoted politically close individuals to key positions in the public service media and at newly founded daily and weekly newspapers. Moreover, the expiration of the terms of office of the state president, the supreme public prosecutor and the governor of the National Bank presented an opportunity to replace them with people totally loyal to the government. While Fidesz was consolidating its power and strengthening the personal authority of the prime minister, the media contributed to the creation of a scathing image of the government ministers of the Smallholders' Party, Orbán's coalition partners, as well as of the corrupt practices within the Socialist–Free Democrat government that had fallen in 1998. Eventually, though, Orbán had to distance himself from those of his ministers in the coalition parties who had been publicly exposed because of bribery.

The opaque transactions that accompanied the sale of the Fidesz headquarters in 1992–3 led indirectly to the resignation of Orbán's close friend Lajos Simicska as head of APEH, Hungary's internal revenue service. On the margins of this shady affair, details emerged in 1999 of another, this time involving Viktor Orbán's father Győző. Six years previously, prior to the acquisition of a quarry, Orbán Senior had benefited to the tune of 3.55 million forints ($17,000) through the purchase and sales transactions of a company founded by Simicska. Orbán confirmed this when questioned about it in 2002 by József Debreczeni. At the time his biographer came to the conclusion that 'In the West a similar scandal would have led to the fall of the head of government. He would have to resign. Not in Hungary. Here it is not necessary to stand down.'[1]

In 2001, and with a very clear eye on the forthcoming 2002 parliamentary elections, Orbán's government radically reversed its hitherto restrictive budgetary policy. The minimum wage for 750,000 employees was raised by first 50 per cent in 2001 and then by a further 25 per cent the following year; real incomes rose in the first half of 2001 by 4.5 per cent but almost doubled in the second two quarters to 8.4 per cent. In the course of the year pensions were raised twice, a nominal increase of 16 per cent and one of 5.8 per cent in real terms. Taking into account the special allowances for 120,000 civil servants, the 70 per cent increase in the salaries of professional soldiers, the augmented state interest rate credits for private loans for house building and the increased family allowances, as well as the special allowances for railway workers, doctors and nurses and so on, it is hardly surprising that for the first time since 1994 the 5.2 per cent growth in consumption was considerably higher than that of GDP, which stood at 4.3 per cent.

In the first quarter of the election year of 2002, the growth rate of real earnings was three times that of GDP. Industrial production stagnated whilst the balance-of-payments deficit and turnover in the retail trade doubled. Yet, apart from a nine per cent increase in private consumption, every other economic indicator showed the situation was deteriorating. The foundations for the subsequent and very grave economic crisis in Hungary, for which the successor Socialist–Free Democrat coalition (2002–10) was primarily responsible, were thus laid in the final phase of the first Orbán government.

Meanwhile, in the right-wing daily and weekly press, even on one of the most popular programmes on public service radio, the trivialisation, vindication and even glorification of the Nazi-allied Horthy regime was keenly pursued. The international media, NGOs and civil rights groups were increasingly preoccupied with the anti-Semitic and anti-Roma gaffes in public life. The calculated breaking of taboos, which was by no means restricted to the publications of István Csurka's far-right Justice and Life Party (MIÉP), and which influenced broad swathes of students, was strongly condemned in the publications of Jewish organisations abroad, especially in the USA. The fact that, after the 9/11 terrorist attacks, Orbán did not immediately and resolutely distance himself from Csurka's outrageous anti-Semitic and anti-American statements was, according to press reports, the reason why President Bush was not prepared to meet the Hungarian prime minister while he was in the USA in February 2002 for the award ceremony of an honorary degree from Boston University.

The inflammatory talk of Fidesz politicians on the right and the desire for autonomy among the Hungarian minorities in neighbouring countries won the enthusiastic support of most of the latter's representatives; however, it also provided political ammunition to the nationalist voices in those countries. That the Socialists were equally willing to engage in populist sloganeering to the detriment of the minorities when it suited their purposes was shown by their exploitation of an agreement that Orbán signed with the Romanian prime minister, Adrian Năstase, at the end of 2001. This was ambiguously worded and could be interpreted as granting a three-month work permit and social insurance to every Romanian citizen, i.e. not just to the ethnic Hungarians living in Romania. Although it was evident that in practice this would have involved a maximum of 81,000 people, that did not prevent the Socialists from launching a massive campaign of intimidation claiming that 'twenty-three million Romanians are at our door'.

To the very end of his first premiership, Orbán remained extremely popular. Yet, he surprisingly lost the 2002 election despite the stimulation of consumption and questionable wage increases. According to Debreczeni, there were two reasons for this: firstly, the unification of the right-wing camp by every available means, the price of which included the failure to clearly distance Fidesz from the extreme right-wingers hovering around the edges of the MIEP and associated with Csurka; secondly, Orbán's and Fidesz's extremely aggressive tone and their virulent but unproven allegations of corruption against the previous government. Though the tendency of the Socialist Party to fragment and split was all too apparent, it was its elegant and moderate candidate for the position of prime minister, Péter Medgyessy, who succeeded in winning over floating or undecided voters, not Orbán with his aggressive tactics.

In 2002, 72 per cent of the electorate went to the polls, the highest number since 1989. The centre-left won a narrow victory, achieved not least because the Free Democrats were able to leap over the 5 per cent vote share hurdle required for a party to enter parliament. The result, 198 seats for Fidesz, 188 for the Socialists and twenty for the Free Democrats, was without doubt a huge shock to Orbán and his team. Both in Budapest and as a participant in TV discussion programmes, I experienced those tense days myself, dominated as they were by the doubts and threats of the defeated right, which alleged election fraud. Thirsting for revenge, Orbán's media managers demanded retaliation for the 'stolen victory'. After the election, in a last extended interview with Jozsef Debreczeni held on 4 May 2002 to conclude the first biography, Orbán brusquely rejected any accusations of having been overly confrontational. On the contrary, he maintained he had not been sufficiently adept in the campaign and nowhere near tough enough in his managing of the government. More channels of information in new newspapers and the electronic media should have been created. His core message was that it was not the policies of the government that had failed; rather, the communication of its intentions and decisions had not been 'efficient enough, subtle enough and differentiated enough'.

In retrospect this curious interview indicates that the thirty-nine-year-old Orbán was not disheartened in the slightest by the shock of the defeat; on the contrary, it filled him with new vigour. In this context an episode from the time of the 2002 election, which only became known a decade later, must be related. In the Orbán biography generously supported by the Fidesz leadership and edited by Mária Schmidt (a controversial historian and adviser to the prime minister), the Polish journalist Igor Janke recounted the following scene which took place in the VIP room of the Millenáris Park in Buda.[2]

> In the late evening of 7 April 2002, after the announcement of the results of the first round of the elections and when the completely unexpected defeat of Fidesz was already evident, only some deeply shocked veteran party stalwarts remained with Orbán. Then the beaten prime minister said: 'Let us pray.' And the one-time anticlerical rebels, who in parliament had previously mocked the clergy and protested against the introduction of religious instruction in schools and the restitution of church property in 1992–3, now all prayed together.

The talk and stories about the public evolution of Orbán into a deeply religious man in the late 1990s were met with some derision by his political opponents. Both Orbán himself and the Calvinist pastor Zoltán Balog, the person who (apart from his wife, Anikó Lévai, a practising Catholic) most influenced him, have spoken several times in speeches and interviews about the prime minister's long path to belief. 'I didn't have a religious upbringing ... I grew up in a world of unbelievers,' confessed Orbán; he had been baptised but there was never any question of confirmation, the very symbol of Christian maturity and the personal profession of belief. He hadn't wanted a church wedding with Anikó; they had married in 1986, both still students, in a registry office.

Contacts and meetings with church dignitaries were intensified as liberalism was abandoned and growing attention paid to nationalist conservative ideas. Balog became Orbán's most important contact with the Catholic and Protestant Churches. Bishops now sat in the front row at the political gatherings for the presidential elections and at the Declaration for a Civic Hungary (2002). Balog told Igor Janke that after a meeting with the archbishop of Eger and the chairs of the Catholic Bishops Conference in 1992 Orbán had told him: 'I was not aware that the Church is so important, such an important part of Hungarian life. I cannot talk to the people about politics if I don't understand that!' Orbán's conversion was crowned with a church wedding with Anikó Lévai in 1997, ten years after their civil marriage.

One of his first foreign trips as prime minister took Orbán to the Vatican where he was granted an audience with Pope John Paul II. The next important step came in 2000, when the thirty-seven-year-old prime minister, after six months of weekly evening discussions with Balog on questions of faith, was confirmed by the pastor, who had in the meantime become his friend. But it was only some years later that he openly spoke about the power of faith. On the night of the election defeat Orbán is said to have spoken with Balog for a long time about the strength that comes with belief. Two weeks later, on 21 April 2002, he said at an event in the Millenáris Park in Budapest: 'He who carries within him faith, hope and love will see hardships as a salvation ... Only a person who has lost faith can be vanquished.' In 2007, at a public celebration of Advent in the small town of Kaposvár, he stated:

> We are of course constrained by laws. Parliament sets the boundaries, power is shared, but the ultimate barrier is nothing other than the fear of God. This is above all other laws, above the entire division of power and the constitution, the ultimate barrier of that dangerous activity that we call power.

Even Janke, who is generally very well disposed towards Orbán, says of his policies towards the Church that 'In his activities the weighing up of opportunity was, and still is, always present. Politics gave him the impulse for his rapprochement with the Church.' In his analysis of Orbán's evolution, Janke adds that it is rare today to find a politician who speaks with such openness as the Hungarian premier does about the role that belief plays in his activities and political struggles. However, in his comprehensive two-volume guide to Orbán's chequered political tactics and strategy, József Debreczeni comes to a different conclusion. 'Viktor Orbán is a man who almost automatically believes in the veracity of whatever he considers to be politically useful to him.'[3]

In 2010, a mere eight stormy years later, Hungary and an astonished Europe were to learn the lessons that this highly talented and complex personality had drawn from his temporary loss of power. After his unexpected and painful defeat in 2002, Viktor Orbán, capable of doing whatever it took as opposition leader to regain power, has contributed more than any other Hungarian politician since 1989 to the disastrous political, moral, economic and cultural polarisation of Hungarian society.

6

THE GRAVEDIGGER OF THE LEFT

The developments during the eight years of Hungary's second Socialist–Free Democrat government (2002–10) confirmed the observation of the German political scientist Wilhelm Hennis (1923–2012) that in order to maintain a system, the strength of institutions, the quality of the rulers and the virtue of citizens are required. Since 2010 Viktor Orbán and his team have almost effortlessly put in place, without any resistance worthy of the name, a skilfully veiled authoritarian system. This process would not have been possible without the moral bankruptcy of a system mired in corruption and increasingly discredited by political and economic incompetence, crowned by the all too evident failure of the centre-left elite. Finally, a deeply rooted mixture of frustration at the consequences of the system change of 1989 and nostalgia for the apparent stability of the Kádár era moulded not the virtues, but the disappointments, of Hungary's citizens. For this reason the failures of the Socialist–Free Democrat government must not be glossed over, regardless of the fact that since that time the Orbán regime has both quantitatively and qualitatively far exceeded the mismanagement and corrupt networks of the state bureaucracy during those years.

The series of scandals and upheavals began no more than three weeks after the Socialist–Free Democrat government had assumed office in the spring of 2002, when Prime Minister Péter Medgyessy was exposed in the opposition newspaper *Magyar Nemzet* as having been a counterintelligence officer (a 'D-209') of the communist secret services. This hitherto concealed detail in Medgyessy's otherwise glittering career in the Ministry of Finance and then after 1989 in the world of private banking deeply shocked the Hungarian public, as well as the Socialists' coalition partners, the Free Democrats. The leaders of the latter had of course been informed long before the election about this skeleton in the closet of their leading candidate, nominally an independent. The day the bombshell dropped, Free Democrat MPs moved to replace Medgyessy. But the very next day they caved in to Socialist pressure and, despite the scandal, expressed their confidence in the head of government. The mentor and former Free Democrat leader, the philosopher János Kis, promptly lamented the moral bankruptcy of his party, condemning the deception of the voting public and predicting serious, long-term political consequences.

The controversial and impenetrable 'D-209' affair was but one of several reasons for Péter Medgyessy's important place in recent Hungarian history. After all, two-thirds of respondents to a public opinion poll conducted soon after the affair was revealed had not seen this as sufficient cause to warrant his resignation. Given his previous career, his financial and economic policies have also remained a riddle to most observers. The new prime minister very much owed his slim victory over Orbán to his image as a self-confident, imperturbable, experienced and highly professional technocrat, an internationally accomplished expert with a veneer of statesmanship. He had worked for almost twenty-eight years in the Ministry of Finance, had been both before and after the collapse of the communist regime minister of finance and later the general director of the Budapest subsidiary of a large French bank. However, as head of government, he immediately began throwing money around in his much-cited '100-day programme'. As the internationally respected economist András Inotai has put it: 'His unforgivable crime was that, as a gentleman, he insisted on fulfilling all his election promises.'[1]

Perhaps never before had a Hungarian prime minister distributed so many electoral goodies in such a short time as Medgyessy did in the summer of 2002. The salaries of public sector employees (about 800,000 people) were raised by 50 per cent, scholarships and grants by 30 per cent, taxes on the minimum wage (already raised by Orbán), TV and radio licences were abolished, and from January 2003 the country's approximately 3 million pensioners received a thirteenth monthly pension. This generosity, for which there was no money, when taken together with the modernisation plans for the construction of new motorways and the continuation of the Orbán government's lavish subsidies on house-building loan interest rates, resulted in a budget deficit of 7.5 per cent of GDP in the first year of the programme. This was to put a great strain on the national budget in the coming years.

These and other measures of the Orbán and Medgyessy governments led to a 33 per cent increase in consumption by private households between 2002 and 2005, whilst GDP rose only by 18 per cent. In 2003 alone real earnings grew by 7.3 per cent in the private sector and 12.7 per cent in the public sector. While the Socialist–Free Democrat coalition partners, instead of reducing the deficit, were actually increasing it through enhanced expenditure on welfare and modernisation projects, the opposition, thirsting for revenge, was even demanding full implementation of the excessive electoral promises. Right up to 2009, no Socialist–Free Democrat government proved capable of escaping this vicious circle. There is unanimous agreement among all serious economists that the origins of this enormous burden placed on the public budget lay in the final years of the first Orbán government, a fatal policy continued with a vengeance by Medgyessy.

The reasons for Medgyessy's relatively rapid fall did not lie in his mistakes in financial policy, deluded though he was by his sudden and rapid popularity. Against the background of his government's evident lack of orientation and a Socialist Party paralysed by continuous internal bickering, Medgyessy, who had no party affiliation, did not radiate leadership and could not present ideas, let alone formulate a strategy against the revived forces of the opposition.

Measures taken to curtail the interest rate subsidies on housebuilding loans and to reduce or postpone various budgetary expenditures—cuts that were unavoidable but still relatively painless—led to an unprecedentedly swift deterioration in the mood of wide sections of the population during 2003. This was reflected in the prime minister's fall in popularity in opinion polls. By the beginning of 2004, the leadership in the Socialist Party was already discussing how and when it could rid itself of Péter Medgyessy, who had fulfilled his historical duty by winning the 2002 elections for the Socialists—albeit by a small margin—but was now expendable.

The final straw, however, was a controversial personal initiative by Medgyessy that alienated the governing parties. Upon the advice of American media specialists, he proposed the introduction of a second chamber in parliament, a reduction in the number of MPs and direct elections for the state presidency. Additionally, he floated the idea of a common list of all parties in the forthcoming elections to the European Parliament and hinted at the possibility of a referendum on these questions. These hastily presented ideas were criticised by both the left and the right, and eventually shelved by the government. The European elections on 13 June 2004 unsurprisingly proved to be a resounding slap in the face for Medgyessy's government and the

Socialists. Fidesz won twelve seats to the Socialists' nine, with two for the Free Democrats and one for the centre-right MDF. The Medgyessy era was thus condemned to be little more than a brief intermezzo, one characterised by its lack of transparency in the construction of motorways, mutual recriminations of corruption between the Socialists and the Free Democrats, and, above all, infighting within the Socialist Party itself.

The following years, from September 2004 to April 2009, were shaped by the successes and setbacks, the splendour and decline of Ferenc Gyurcsány. The most capable, controversial and unpredictable (and certainly the richest) politician on the left, he has gone down in Hungarian history as one of the very few prime ministers in Europe who has publicly and completely unnecessarily committed political suicide; and that just shortly after his greatest personal triumph.

I first met Ferenc Gyurcsány in April 2004 when he was the minister for children, youth and sport in the Socialist–Free Democrat coalition led by Péter Medgyessy. I had read some of his articles, such as those on the necessity of discarding the paralysing post-communist ideological ballast and of transforming the Socialist Party into a modern, open, social-democratic party along the lines of the British and German models. Friends whose opinions I respected saw in him a beacon of hope, whilst leading left-wing politicians made little attempt to conceal their opinions of the ambitious young man, calling him an 'enormously rich adventurer' and a loose cannon. Everything I had heard about him before our meeting made him look almost like a exotic bird of paradise amidst the grey suits and boring cadres of late Kádárism who were still in charge of the Socialist Party.

Our conversation in his ministerial office lasted well over an hour and was surprisingly frank. Without openly criticising Medgyessy, whom he had served as chief adviser from the beginning of 2003 until his elevation to government, he tore the

Socialist Party to pieces, deriding it as a party incapable of deciding whom and what it represented. Gyurcsány visited party organisations in various parts of the country two or three times a week. When asked what the point of all these activities was, he responded simply with a friendly smile: he just wanted to serve, to the best of his ability, the delayed but inevitable modernisation of the Hungarian left.

Gyurcsány is of unimpeachable proletarian origins, having grown up in abject poverty in the small provincial town of Pápa in southwest Hungary. By the time he was twenty-one this talented student had already moved to the top of the Hungarian Communist Youth Federation (KISZ) at the teacher training college in the city of Pécs.

Several months later Gyurcsány became a full-time secretary of the youth organisation at the local university merged with his college, earning a more than presentable salary for the time. The rise of the young party apparatchik within the Youth Federation was both rapid and smooth. By 1989 he had already moved to Budapest as a secretary of the Federation's National Committee. When he (temporarily) quit politics, Gyurcsány was the number two in the Democratic Youth League, which, though renamed, was still controlled by the Young Communists; it would soon disappear. At that time, Viktor Orbán, two years his junior, described him with uncanny intuition, in an oft-quoted remark, as the only interesting and capable representative in the Communist Youth Federation.

After 1989 this ambitious young man from the provinces, like so many others, blithely exploited the opportunities thrown up by privatisation and the transition from a command economy to a free market system. In the early 1990s Gyurcsány, by now the father of two boys, was already being regarded as an adroit and successful businessman. An affair with Klára Dobrev, the attractive, talented multilingual daughter of Piroska Apró, herself a top official and later successful businesswoman, led in the autumn of 1994 to divorce and, in turn, to his third marriage. It was to be the start of a new and exciting phase in his life.

That Ferenc Gyurcsány, the thirty-five-year-old son of a single working mother, could become a forint billionaire within just four years was little short of sensational. The media duly paid the requisite homage to his achievements. However, Gyurcsány's image in modern Hungarian history is more controversial than that of almost every other politician. This is primarily due to his family connection with his mother-in-law Piroska Apró, who was an influential businesswoman and previously also a top civil servant. How else could even a young man as talented as Gyurcsány have turned 3 million forints into 3 billion—€10,000 into €10 million—in just a few years? When a journalist asked him in the autumn of 1996 whether he had always wanted to be a businessman, Gyurcsány replied, 'No ... I thought that I'd make a very good politician, I thought one day I'd be prime minister. My poor country—as if it doesn't have enough problems without me! ... Today, I'd laugh at myself, but then I quite seriously believed in all of this.'[2]

Eight years later the apparently modest entrepreneur had indeed become prime minister of Hungary. József Debreczeni correctly observes that Gyurcsány's career was unprecedented in Hungarian history; it was in fact a phenomenon. In the post-1989 era, Gyurcsány was the first billionaire to become a top politician. Not only that, nobody had ever risen so quickly to the very summit of power: in 2002, Gyurcsány was not even in parliament; by 2004 he was prime minister. How did this almost inconceivable stroke of luck even become possible?

For an understanding of Gyurcsány's dramatic rise, we have to recall the consequences of the fall of the sympathetic but politically weak prime minister, Péter Medgyessy. After the 'D-209' affair, the Socialist Party reacted with lightning speed to topple the victor of the 2002 election, a man who had become a liability overnight, and to designate as his successor the uncharismatic but dependable Péter Kiss, chief minister in the Prime Minister's Office. The vote in the party presidium in favour of Kiss went off smoothly, without opposition. Within twenty-four hours, however, the party grandees were confronted with a grassroots revolt among the party members. Representatives of the various factions, its youth wing, supporters in the provinces and activists forced the calling of an extraordinary party congress to choose a new prime minister.

Communications experts gave the stolid Kiss no chance whatsoever against the charismatic Viktor Orbán in the parliamentary elections due two years later, in 2006. In this situation Gyurcsány's friends and soon Gyurcsány himself sensed an opportunity for his own candidature. Under normal circumstances this would have been an enormous risk: he had after all only joined the Socialist Party four years previously. However, in just a week's intensive campaigning on the telephone, Gyurcsány and his closest advisers were able to turn everything around and win over the support, above all, of the representatives from the provinces. In the parliamentary party's preliminary vote, Kiss was still ahead and Gyurcsány came third behind the future finance minister János Veres. But from the party executive Kiss received just a few more votes than Gyurcsány, and both had to be nominated by a reluctant party leadership as candidates for the party congress to be held the next day, 25 August 2004.

Although the hapless Kiss was supported by a number of members of the party presidium and also by the former prime minister, Gyula Horn, he suffered a crushing defeat. Of the 623 delegates, 453 (73 per cent) voted for the outsider, Ferenc Gyurcsány, who had become the symbol of a rank-and-file revolt unheard of in the history of the Hungarian Socialist Party. In the German daily *Die Welt* I wrote, 'Now the political future of the Socialist–Liberal coalition depends on whether Ferenc Gyurcsány, this fascinating and polarising figure, will turn out in the end to be the gravedigger or the reformer of the Hungarian left.'[3]

It was primarily due to Gyurcsány that the Socialist–Free Democrat coalition was able to win the April 2006 parliamentary elections and increase its majority from ten to thirty-six seats. Despite a speech impediment (since overcome), he was a brilliant speaker, though at times he was barely able to conceal his arrogance in debates with his political opponents. In a decisive television debate broadcast on 5 April 2006, he succeeded in trouncing his opponent Viktor Orbán. According to the polls conducted afterwards, 54 per cent of viewers put Gyurcsány as the winner of the debate, against just 23 per cent for Orbán.

The man who at the time of his rise to the political top ranked sixtieth on the list of the 100 richest entrepreneurs in Hungary possessed a fortune of 3.5 billion forints (approximately €14 million at the 2004 exchange rate), in a country where approximately 20 per cent of the population was living below the poverty line. His marriage into the Apró family and taking up residence in an elegant three-storied villa in the fashionable hills of Buda contributed to the spiteful and recurring mythmaking surrounding him. Because of this, from the very beginning Gyurcsány was the target of vicious media attacks, many of which were often well below the belt.[4]

Ferenc Gyurcsány turned out to be (in the sense of Jacob Burckhardt's reflections on history) a 'man of momentary greatness', in which a short phase of history is intensified. He was above all the champion who, for the first time since the changes of 1989, led the left to victory in two consecutive elections. Victory—but to what purpose? Personally, Gyurcsány wanted to set 'social-democratic signals' in the market economy, as Bruno Kreisky had endeavoured to do in Austria in the 1970s, and Tony Blair and Gerhard Schröder also tried three decades later.

However, the seeds of the future defeat were already sown in this unprecedented victory.

The political honeymoon came to an abrupt end within a matter of months. Gyurcsány's popularity fell from 55 per cent in April 2006 to 34 per cent the following August. No other government had ever suffered such a rapid and huge decline in popularity. In the election campaign of 2006 both parties had promised, as in 2002, that things would only get better. Gyurcsány concealed the gravity of the economic situation and remained silent about the planned belt-tightening measures, whilst his opponent Orbán even promised a fourteen-month pension and radical tax cuts, as well as cheaper gas and electricity prices.

The disappointment of the public was that much greater than in 2003, for the simple reason that Gyurcsány had already been in office for two years and, after his many election promises, now unexpectedly set about consolidating an economy which had tumbled into crisis. It only added insult to injury when, after introducing a package of cuts that included increases in gas prices and taxes, he casually let slip the remark that 'they wouldn't really hurt'. At the same time Gyurcsány failed to convince his own party of the need to take courageous and unavoidable, but unpopular, measures, as well as to initiate necessary radical reforms to deal with the structural weaknesses of the ailing economy. The contemporary historian Zoltán Ripp has pertinently noted that the Socialist Party was not an organisation of people sharing the same opinions, but rather one of people concealing different views.

Gyurcsány's opponent in the April 2006 elections, Viktor Orbán, easily survived what was now, after 1994 and 2002, his third defeat. Following a three-week trip to the World Cup in South Korea he cold-bloodedly and dispassionately began, even during the summer break, to lay the foundations for the recapture of political power in Hungary.

THE GRAVEDIGGER OF THE LEFT

However, nobody could have foreseen that it would be Gyurcsány himself, so triumphant in 2006, who, in a secret speech bursting with wanton recklessness, would deliver the actual key to Orbán's brilliant victory in the spring of 2010.

7

A MEGA-SCANDAL

GYURCSÁNY'S 'LIE SPEECH'

At precisely 4 p.m. on 17 September 2006, a mild late summer Sunday, a 'political nuclear bomb'[1] exploded in Hungary. First the public service radio, then a little later every radio and TV channel as well as the Internet, started to broadcast excerpts from an audiotape on which could be heard the familiar voice of Ferenc Gyurcsány, who had been re-elected prime minister only the previous April. What he was saying was shocking; moreover, it was in words that were both passionate and peppered with coarse expletives, language that the proverbial man in the street would instantly recognise:

> We had almost no other choice [than the package of cuts] because we fucked up. Not just a little bit but totally. No other country in Europe has committed such stupidities as we have. It can be explained. Obviously we have been lying our heads off for the last one-and-a-half, two years. It was quite clear that what we were saying wasn't true ... And in the meantime, we have, by the way, been doing nothing for the past four years. Nothing. You can't name me one single important government measure we can be proud of, apart from pulling the government

out of the shit again in the end [that is after winning the elections]. If we were forced to give an account of what we've been doing in the past four years, what could we say?

... Reform or failure. There is nothing else. And when I say failure, then I'm speaking about Hungary, about the left and, to be quite honest, about myself ... It's fantastic to be the leader of a country. I've only been able to keep going the last one-and-a-half years because one thing has spurred me on: to give back to the left the belief that it could accomplish something and win! That you don't have to bow your head in this motherfucking country. That you don't have to shit yourself when you go face-to-face with Viktor Orbán and the right...

I've almost killed myself the last one-and-a-half years having to pretend that we were governing. Instead we've been lying morning, noon and night. And I don't want to do that anymore. Either we do something about it, and you have the man for this, or you carry on with somebody else ...

Gyurcsány's passionate, improvised and rousing speech was made in May 2006. His tirade, riddled with obscenities, was an attempt to convince the 190 newly elected MPs gathered in a government-owned building at Balatonöszöd (Öszöd) on Lake Balaton that some painful reforms were unavoidable. It was the climax of several hours of discussions. In stark contrast to this very emotional speech, some twenty-five minutes long, Gyurcsány had been very careful in his choice of words during his earlier one-hour introductory address, when he expressly asked all those attending to treat what he said as strictly confidential. Some think that his openness, in the long-term suicidal, and the almost repugnant vulgarity of the words had been prompted by the cynical indifference or exaggerated fears of some of the speakers during the meeting. Others present later hinted to Western journalists that the prime minister had drunk 'some glasses of whisky' before he gave the second speech. Gyurcsány himself denies this.

A MEGA-SCANDAL

For Gyurcsány it was obviously a question of making a conscious break with the politics of dishonest compromise, which he had also undoubtedly gone along with. Whatever the reason for this catastrophic own goal, his speech, which was quickly dubbed the 'lie speech' and repeatedly quoted from one end of the country to another, irrevocably destroyed the prime minister's credibility. Irrespective of his motives, it is with hindsight beyond dispute that Gyurcsány had committed an irreparable political mistake. It was an error that his determined opponent Viktor Orbán gleefully pounced upon and masterfully and ruthlessly exploited to unleash a full-scale media and political offensive against the discredited prime minister and his coalition government. The broadcasting of the audiocassette, quickly passed to media outlets throughout Hungary, was the prelude to an unprecedented wave of violence.

To this day it is not clear who first made this recording—of an internal meeting of the Socialists—available to Orbán's party before it was released to the media. Unconfirmed rumours still circulate about possible 'rats' from within the Socialist Party itself. Was it Gyurcsány's well-known opponent Imre Szekeres, party organiser and briefly minister of defence, together with the dubious party treasurer László Puch? Or was it, as the *Sunday Telegraph* maintained, the high-ranking Socialist functionary Ferenc Baja together with Katalin Szili, the speaker of parliament, who later changed sides and joined the Fidesz government?

I have repeatedly discussed the 'Öszöd affair' with Gyurcsány himself, both before and after his resignation. I also recall a lunch I had shortly afterwards with three leading Socialists: the former party chair and EU commissioner, László Kovács; the head of the parliamentary group and Gyurcsány's successor as party chair, Ildikó Lendvai; and the (now deceased) minister of state, Péter Kiss. They all tried to convince me that the explosive audiotape had reached Fidesz through careless handling by the immediate circle around the prime minister. However, this version is now considered unlikely by independent observers. The entire affair remains shrouded in mystery; even in 2016, a collection of interviews speculating on the source was published, for the tenth anniversary of the broadcast.

It remains a matter of conjecture as to when the Fidesz leadership first obtained the tape. Debreczeni is convinced, as are most Hungarian and foreign journalists, that this had happened probably as early as July. Such an assumption is confirmed by the timing of the campaign against 'Gyurcsány's lie government' personally directed by Viktor Orbán. On 22 July the signal for the declaration of open war against the government was given in an extraordinarily acerbic speech, at a major event held by the Hungarian minority at Băile Tuşnad in Romania. 'For the first time since 1989 Hungary has become the victim of an open, organised political lie,' declared Orbán, prophesying the premature end of the government. He continued the campaign in a series of articles in the Fidesz mouthpiece *Magyar Nemzet* (29 July, 5 August and 11 September), conjuring up an image of grave danger and casting doubt on the legitimacy of the government because it had won the election on lies:

> The real problem is the lying of the government, its deliberate distortion of facts, its lack of authority for its policies and the reality that Hungarian democracy has not been able to defend itself against any of this. The Gyurcsány package [of budget cuts] is not a democratically authorised government programme but an arbitrary diktat—not legitimate. The government has no right to implement the Gyurcsány package. By the time winter is upon us, the right and the left will no longer be talking each other but an embittered and angry country will be standing up to its illegitimate government.

In retrospect, the lie campaign, with its demands for the resignation of the government and the launching of a protest movement called 'Good morning, Hungary', appears to have been the carefully orchestrated prelude to a climax in which the media first cleverly inverted and then cynically transformed Gyurcsány's shockingly honest appeal to parliamentarians for candour into an appalling catalogue of lies to deceive the electorate. Orbán called the prime minister a 'chronic liar' and described his measures as a 'dilettante' package.

The highly effective media coverage of the most provocative short extracts from Gyurcsány's secret 'lie speech', as well as the massive and passionate opposition attacks, with Viktor Orbán leading the charge against the 'illegitimate' government, served as the prologue to weeks of unrest that were to destroy the image of Hungary as a solid, peaceful democracy based on consensus. The dramatic events of autumn 2006 opened the cold civil war of the following three-and-a-half years, a struggle that ultimately was to crush all of Orbán's left-wing, liberal and conservative rivals.

The same evening as the first explosive excerpts from the speech were broadcast, angry demonstrators assembled on Kossuth Square in front of the Hungarian parliament building, chanting their demands for the resignation of Gyurcsány and his despised government. They were quickly joined by right-wing extremists, skinheads in camouflage suits and violent supporters of the racist and anti-Semite Jobbik Party,[2] which at that time was still not represented in parliament. The next day an even larger, angrier crowd marched from the parliament to the nearby building of Hungarian TV, which was stormed and partly set on fire. In the days that followed far-right skinheads and rowdies clashed with the police. Ernst Gelegs, for many years the Budapest correspondent of the ORF (the Austrian public service broadcaster), reported not only on the rioting of the radical right, which was ready to use violence, but also on the police's all too free use of truncheons on peaceful demonstrators.

In his book on Hungary,[3] Gelegs writes that it is often evident that Fidesz has forged a silent alliance with the extra-parliamentary Jobbik ...

Viktor Orbán and his Fidesz party friends might have condemned the violence of the demonstrators but have consistently indicated their understanding for the criminal acts of the mob. In numerous interviews and public speeches, the same words were to be heard over and over again: the people were simply very frustrated and disappointed by the Gyurcsány government, which now had to resign so as to avoid even worse things happening. It was repeatedly emphasised that through his confession of having lied the prime minister had lost his political legitimacy; that he was thus illegally in power. It was therefore fully understandable if 'all Hungary' revolted. Such were the words opposition politicians insouciantly whispered in the ears of the world media.

In this tense atmosphere, thousands of people demonstrated daily in front of parliament and chanted 'Gyurcsány must go'. The Fidesz leadership bet everything on a successful mobilisation of the masses before the countrywide communal elections on 1 October. Orbán declared these a plebiscite on the government. The vote was for mayors, district and local councillors; and virtually everywhere candidates from the opposition won a majority. The night the polls closed, the opposition leadership demanded the resignation of the 'chronic liar' at the head of the government. Not once did the state president, László Sólyom, try to mediate during the crisis; on the contrary, he added fuel to the fire with several speeches highly critical of the government. Thus, shortly after polling stations had closed, he was on TV openly demanding Gyurcsány's replacement. After an overwhelming victory in the local elections, Orbán gave the governing parties a seventy-two-hour ultimatum to remove the head of government and called upon the masses to attend a huge meeting in front of the parliament building to reinforce the call for the prime minister's resignation.

Gyurcsány, however, had no intention of quitting. His response to Orbán's ultimatum was to call a parliamentary vote of confidence. Gyurcsány was unanimously supported by the two coalition partners, the Socialists and the Free Democrats (even if only very reluctantly on the part of some of his internal party foes), and easily won the vote by 207 to 165. There was little question of the public mood cooling as Orbán now embarked upon an all-out campaign. More than 100,000 people heeded his call, gathering in front of parliament to hear his fiery call to arms against the 'illegitimate dictatorial' government. Hungarian patriots should from now on demonstrate daily before parliament until the government resigned, declared Orbán, adding that Fidesz MPs would leave the chamber every time Prime Minister Gyurcsány rose to speak.

It was no coincidence that the protest demonstrations and clashes peaked on 23 October 2006. On this highly symbolic day, Hungary commemorated the fiftieth anniversary of the uprising bloodily suppressed by the Red Army. Over fifty heads of state and government took part in the official commemorations in parliament. But instead of a dignified ceremony for the freedom fighters, total chaos ruled on the streets of Budapest on that day, provoked by violent mass demonstrations against the government. The response of the poorly led police was disproportionately harsh. Thirsting for revenge after their failure during the assault on the TV centre a few weeks previously, they reacted with great brutality and in equal measure against both the far-right hooligans and the peaceful demonstrators as they made their way home. The international media widely reported on an extreme right-wing pensioner who seized control of an old Soviet tank that had been wheeled out as an exhibit for the commemorations, and for a short time drove it around the centre of Budapest.

To this day the background, course of events and the responsibility of the ringleaders and the police for the acts of violence, which, according to a commission set up by the government, caused damage amounting to €37 million during the weeks of rioting, are all the subject of dispute. All reports confirm the occasional brutality of the police. On this tragic day of unrest 326 civilians were injured (sixteen badly), as were 399 police officers (forty-seven seriously). There was particular outrage at the police's use of rubber bullets. These caused open wounds to the chest and stomach, with two demonstrators losing an eye each.[4] A decade later, the media close to Fidesz still speaks of 'state terror', of a 'police state with Ferenc Gyurcsány at its head'. At the time Viktor Orbán hardened his political line and intensified his anti-government rhetoric. In his speeches, even at international events such as a meeting of the European People's Party, he maintained that 'the government has begun a war against its own people'. The radicalisation of Hungarian politics was also reflected in the undermining of trust in democratic institutions. Independent observers generally concluded that the extreme right-wing Jobbik Party, as well as those on the margins of the hard right, profited from the unrest of that autumn, whilst the Socialist–Free Democrat coalition government was beset with helplessness, confusion and fear. The autumn of 2006 marked the beginning of the 'power of fear' in Hungarian politics. The phantoms unleashed by Gyurcsány's fatal 'secret speech', feeding Orbán's 'all or nothing' confrontational course, now spun out of control.

8

ORBÁN'S VICTORY IN THE COLD CIVIL WAR

The four years between 2006 and 2010 were characterised by three different, yet inextricably linked developments: the completely unexpected but inexorable decline of the Socialist–Free Democrat government after its apparently great electoral triumph in April 2006; the equally astonishing and rapid rise both of Orbán personally and of his party; and the radicalisation of the political climate in Hungary, in which anti-Semitic and Roma-phobic undercurrents in society, hitherto latent, now came to the fore.

The catastrophic gaffe of Ferenc Gyurcsány's May 2006 'secret speech', which once leaked was successfully instrumentalised into a political theme, kept constantly in the public eye as a 'lie speech', created the conditions for the protracted suicide of the left. That Gyurcsány succeeded at the beginning of 2007 in being voted chair of his party by 89 per cent of party delegates did little to alter the collective denial of reality prevailing among the ruling Socialists, even if it was pepped up with some left-wing rhetoric. It had proved impossible to deal convincingly with the baggage inherited from the Kádár regime, or to push through the reforms clearly recognised by Gyurcsány as necessary. As a self-made man and a multimillionaire, the leader of the party and government was all too often regarded with suspicion as an 'alien' by his own post-communist party functionaries.

In addition, influential members of the party elite, particularly in Budapest, were themselves mired in a swamp of corruption. My conversations with Gyurcsány, with his staffers and secret enemies, as well as with independent commentators, confirmed my suspicion that the Socialist Party was not one of common convictions, but rather a disgusting snake pit of old Communists and left-wing careerists posing as Social Democrats. The twelve years of left-of-centre governments led by the Socialists Horn, Medgyessy and finally Gyurcsány were frequently overshadowed by the incompetence, cowardice and rivalries of the ministers responsible for economic policy and their high-ranking civil servants. A sad footnote to this depressing spectacle was the corrosion of the Free Democrats, who through their role as a willing helper bringing the Socialists to power in 2002 and 2006, and their recurring internal disputes, lost all credibility they once might have had.

Seven years later, during a visit to Hungary in October 2014, Heinz Fischer, the Austrian president, deliberately emphasised in a private discussion with Viktor Orbán the importance of the role of the opposition in a parliamentary democracy. The Hungarian prime minister replied with a broad smile that 'he didn't need any lectures about opposition because no Hungarian politician had suffered so many defeats as he had!' He had endured three, in 1994, 2002 and 2006, and even in the upper ranks of the Fidesz hierarchy after 2002 there were some (including the now Hungarian president, János Áder) who expressed doubts that their party would ever regain power with Orbán at its head. Yet, though he assumed responsibility for the third loss, Orbán succeeded in retaining his position of power. To be consistently successful in politics, a party leader requires not only a certain degree of luck and high intelligence but also a character that, without a hint of any scruple, will pursue the stated goals of retaining power and excluding any possible rivals.

From the very beginning, and this was obvious as early as his reckoning with the liberal wing of the Fidesz leadership in 1992–3, Orbán observed the maxim of only trusting in his own strength. He always demonstrated a singular and uncanny nose for shifts in sentiment. Thus in May 1994, shortly after that election defeat, there appeared in the conservative *Magyar Nemzet*, a newspaper then close to Fidesz, an attack both harsh and anonymous on Zoltan Pokorni, the popular Fidesz vice-president, who was accused of seeking power within the party. Two weeks later Orbán defended the honour of his deputy. In January 2007 a long article published under a pseudonym, again in *Magyar Nemzet*, attacked Orbán's former chief adviser between 1998 and 2002, Mária Schmidt. A millionaire and director of the controversial House of Terror museum in Budapest, she was alleged to have hatched 'on behalf of big business' an internal party plot aimed at replacing Orbán with János Áder, then head of the parliamentary group and former speaker of parliament. Schmidt immediately denied this, challenging the pseudonymous author—who to this day remains unknown—to a TV debate. Two years later Áder became an MEP and left Hungary for Brussels. That Orbán can execute a masterly shot across the bows of his potential rivals was demonstrated by the 'fall and rise' of this old comrade in arms: in another about-turn of fortunes, he became state president in spring 2012, replacing Pál Schmitt, who had been compromised by the revelations that he had plagiarised his doctorate.[1]

Repeatedly, not only in his lightning media and political exploitation of Gyurcsány's 'lie speech' but also throughout his years in opposition, Viktor Orbán demonstrated that even in a seemingly hopeless position he would not be brought to his knees. The very day after his electoral defeat in the spring of 2006, he set decisively to work to rebuild Fidesz and ensure its return to office. Long before the Fidesz leadership finally emerged triumphant in 2010, it could rely on the unrelenting propaganda hostile to the Socialist–Free Democrat coalition and the support of a media empire calculatingly built up by one of Orbán's closest friends, Lajos Simicska. This comprised two daily newspapers, two weeklies, a free newspaper on the Budapest Metro, two TV and two radio stations. Additionally, there were various websites, TV and radio stations controlled by other groups favourably disposed towards Fidesz.

With the aid of the media, its ingenious connections and opaque networks, the opposition was able to dictate the political agenda in Hungary and repeatedly force the panic-stricken governing coalition onto the defensive. In stark contrast to the incessant internal battles among the Socialists and Free Democrats themselves, not to speak of the very public rifts about their education and health policies, Fidesz was always able to present a unified line, one supported by the Churches and by various other political old faithfuls such as citizens' fora and teachers' associations. At the heart of everything lay the permanent mobilisation of the people of Hungary and the collection of signatures for a referendum.

With hindsight, it is incontrovertible that the referendum of 9 March 2008 was the moment of truth for Gyurcsány's government. The electorate was asked three simple questions: should the charge of 300 forints (about €1) per visit to the doctor, the same charge for every day spent in hospital, and university tuition fees (about 100,000 forints annually) all be abolished? The Free Democrats had always been the driving force behind the privatisation and restructuring of the healthcare system. In spite of the misgivings of some constitutional lawyers, the constitutional court allowed these three questions to be put before the people. The result was, as anticipated, an unprecedented defeat for the government: approximately 82 per cent of those participating rejected the three charges. This outcome, of course, was entirely predictable. What voter anywhere would opt to retain such payments?

This huge vote of no confidence in the Socialist–Free Democrat coalition was, according to the journalist János Széky, tantamount to the collapse of the political order established in the aftermath of 1989, to the end of democracy in Hungary.[2] He sees two reasons for the demise of the democratic system. One is Hungary's continuing inability to come to terms with and draw a line under the national tragedy of Trianon (see Chapter 4). The second was the government's tendency to overlook the 'feel-good factor' of the Kádár era, when there was a massive and sustained rise in living standards not only for the working but also the middle classes. The complacent post-communist Socialists were only able to deploy social demagogy, Széky believes, as long as Fidesz played both this card and, to great effect, the nationalist card.

According to a poll conducted in 2009, 72 per cent of respondents expressed the opinion they had been better off under communism. These and similar polls formed the gloomy background to the unequal duel between Orbán's strong and dynamic one-man leadership of Fidesz and the divided government of Gyurcsány, a widely discredited prime minister. Only 46 per cent of respondents in the 2009 poll believed that the transition to capitalism after 1989 had been the correct course; in 1991 this figure had been about 80 per cent. 74 per cent had found the multi-party system desirable in 1991; this fell to 56 per cent by 2009. Developments after 2010—above all the collapse of the centre-left camp and the triumph of the idiosyncratic mishmash of ideas that characterises Orbán's ideology—can only be understood through this historical and deeply rooted disappointment at the consequences of the political upheavals following 1989.[3]

The opposition exulted in its victory in the March 2008 referendum on the healthcare system; the shocked Socialists beat a retreat. Gyurcsány began speaking about 'soft reforms'. Any ideas for the planned restructuring of the state social insurance system sank without a trace, as did the Free Democrat minister responsible. The conflict between the Socialists and the Free Democrats about the health system sparked a crisis within the coalition. All Free Democrat ministers quit the government, and from May 2008 onwards Gyurcsány led a minority government, though it was able to count on the support of a majority of Free Democrat MPs in important votes. However, he owed his survival only to the fear of Socialists and Free Democrats alike of a crushing defeat should early elections be called.

Like many other Hungarian commentators, I now believe that Gyurcsány should have resigned immediately after the referendum debacle. By clinging on for almost a year at the head of a minority government, fighting on many fronts, he reminded some journalists of the lead character played by Sean Penn in the 1995 Hollywood film *Dead Man Walking*. Gyurcsány maintains that he offered to go but only one member of the party presidium was prepared to accept his resignation.

The onset of the world economic crisis in September 2008 would have led to Hungary declaring bankruptcy had it not been for the immediate financial aid granted to the country by the IMF, the World Bank and the EU. For the first time since the Socialist–Free Democrat coalition had first taken office in 1994, and of course far too late, serious budgetary cuts were now implemented. State employees, for example (civil servants, teachers, railway workers etc.), lost their right to a thirteenth monthly salary. The cutbacks led to a 3.5 per cent fall in consumption and a reduction of 2.5 per cent in real wages. In spite of the crisis, Fidesz MPs persisted with their filibusters: on 20 December 2008, they asked 1,300 parliamentary questions, to prevent ministers and their staff from going on their Christmas holidays.[4]

Gyurcsány's impetuousness and his penchant for theatrical exaggeration again won the upper hand when in March 2009, one week after his triumphant re-election as head of his party with a majority of 85 per cent, he announced his resignation. Predictably, Orbán and his party vociferously demanded the immediate dissolution of parliament and the prompt calling of new elections. Yet, the survival instincts of the Socialist and Free Democrat MPs prevailed once more. However, Gyurcsány had no script for his succession in his pocket. He later told me that he had originally wanted to push the cause of Gordon Bajnai, the minister for economic affairs, but had held back 'for tactical reasons'. Whatever the case, the week-long, at times almost farcical, search for a crisis manager discredited the centre-left camp even more in the eyes of the Hungarians, not to speak of Gyurcsány himself.

There is no question that in the spring of 2009 Hungary stood on the edge of a precipice. The election of a forty-one-year-old economics expert, Gordon Bajnai, as prime minister was a stroke of good fortune for the country, one that was internationally recognised. Even though he had been minister for economic development in Gyurcsány's minority government, he had never belonged to the Socialist Party. The austerity measures taken by the politically independent Bajnai did indeed save Hungary from the precipice. But they also utterly and irretrievably destroyed the electoral prospects of both the Socialists and the Free Democrats, who had had to give him a written undertaking of their unconditional support. The most important and painful cuts included the cancellation of the thirteenth monthly pension and the thirteenth monthly salary, the raising of the retirement age from sixty-two to sixty-five, the reduction in numerous welfare payments and an increase in VAT from 20 to 25 per cent. The Fidesz opposition, of course, voted against such a rigorous austerity package, but in reality it was very much in Orbán's interest that the Bajnai government implement the painful programme without any significant opposition. Bajnai, who spoke far better English than his two predecessors, was a modest and likeable expert, accepting as his prime ministerial salary a symbolic €1 a month.

Gordon Bajnai's crisis management was rated very highly by the international media and financial institutions. In a little more than a year he and his colleagues succeeded in winning back the confidence of international investors and in making savings of approximately 5 per cent of GDP. That in this crisis situation Viktor Orbán rejected every single one of Bajnai's invitations to hold discussions, and in fact exchanged barely a word with the prime minister, reflected the poisoned political climate in the country. For the opposition, now so assured of victory, it was important to hammer home the continuity from Gyurcsány to Bajnai, indeed of all governments with a Socialist stamp, and to smear the technocrat Bajnai as his predecessor's clone.

In his inaugural speech in parliament, Bajnai emphasised that he had no political ambitions and was nobody's political rival. He had but one task, the management of the crisis. Two or three years later, he tried, albeit without any success, to unify the opposition. The circumstances of his resignation and withdrawal from politics in 2010 subsequently confirmed the opinion, even amongst commentators well disposed towards him, that despite his many talents, Gordon Bajnai was no politician.

And Gyurcsány? It is unlikely that his Democratic Coalition (Demokratikus Koalíció), which split off from the Socialist Party in 2011, will be able to win more than 8–10 per cent of the vote in the 2018 elections. In his book on Hungarian governments between 1978 and 2012, Tamás Sárközy has characterised him as follows:

> Gyurcsány has charisma. He cannot be ignored. Extraordinarily resilient, combative, never prepared to capitulate. Some say he is an adventurer, a gambler, others that he is a great strategist. I have always liked him. He

had more ideas than all the other leading MSzP [Socialist] politicians put together in 20 years.

However, Gyurcsány had to all intents and purposes already lost his great duel with Orbán, a man two years his junior, following the own goal of his 'lie speech'. Since his brilliant victory in the 'cold civil war' between 2006 and 2010, Viktor Orbán, this vengeful and determined power politician, has with boundless energy and boldness on the international stage built up a new and, in many ways, unique system, one very much shaped by his own personality. This will now be described in the following chapters.

9

THE EARTHQUAKE

On Thursday, 8 April 2010, on our way from Vienna to Budapest my wife and I stopped, as we often did, at a motorway service station about 40 miles short of the Hungarian capital to buy newspapers and mineral water. When I went to the cash desk to pay, I noticed two tall young men with earphones, the standard paraphernalia of bodyguards. And then, a few steps further on, I saw Viktor Orbán at the bar, where he was just finishing a beer. His minders ignored me as I went up to him and we greeted each other in a friendly manner. Ever since his appearance at the Europa-Forum at the Gottweig Abbey eleven years previously, we had been using the familiar form of address with one another. Orbán told me he was travelling to Vienna because 'Martens is getting an award there.' Wilfried Martens had been prime minister of Belgium for many years and was still, aged almost seventy-five, the chair of the European People's Party in the European Parliament. We exchanged a few words and then he set off in his convoy for Austria. This unexpected meeting took place just three days before the parliamentary elections in Hungary.

That an opposition leader would leave his country—even for a short period—on the eve of an election that he himself had repeatedly called fateful did not seem the least bit absurd to me; and for two reasons. Firstly, Martens (1936–2013) was a doyen among Christian Democrat politicians in Europe, still one of the most influential, and Orbán, both in power and in opposition, has always placed great value on close personal contacts with important conservative politicians from the West.

Orbán gave Helmut Kohl and Wolfgang Schüssel the full red-carpet treatment in Budapest in 2000 after the German head of government had had to resign following the 1999 revelations about party financing and the EU was boycotting the Austrian chancellor because of his formation of a coalition government with the extreme right-wing FPÖ. These carefully cultivated political friendships would prove especially useful to Orbán in his own subsequent acrimonious disputes in the EU. Secondly, Orbán knew, as did almost everybody else in Hungary, that he would win the election with a landslide and would very soon be prime minister.

A strange mood pervaded Budapest at the time. Even though the prospect deeply concerned them, Liberal intellectual circles were resigned to a clear victory for Fidesz. Knowledgeable commentators, foremost among them József Debreczeni, who has been quoted many times in this book, all warned of the consequences of Orbán's winning a two-thirds majority as many feared. Yet even left-wing opponents of Fidesz found Debreczeni's analysis and warnings unduly pessimistic. It should not be forgotten that for the previous eight years the Socialist–Free Democrat coalition had frequently been mired in sleaze, cronyism and political corruption. Some young commentators did not conceal their desire for a strong, ordering hand and mocked Debreczeni for his gloomy predictions. A well-known political scientist spoke of a 'changed Orbán', whilst moderate conservative supporters expressed their hope that a strong Fidesz government would indeed clean out the swamp of corruption and the system of clients that had fed off it. Nevertheless, even sharp critics of the Socialists remembered a speech by Orbán, held in a closed circle but later published in full in a Fidesz newspaper, in which he voiced his hope for the creation 'of a central political force field', in which a large, conservative party, i.e. Fidesz, could rule freely and unhindered by any opposition for the 'coming 15 to 20 years'.

We spent the evening of the election, 11 April 2010, with several dozen liberal and moderate conservative artists, academics and journalists at an election party given by an artist couple. Soon after the polling stations closed and the first exit polls came in, Fidesz was felt to have scored an overwhelming victory. That same evening, even before the final result was known, the jubilation in the right-wing camp was entirely comprehensible. Fidesz had won 57.2 per cent of the popular vote and 206 parliamentary seats—with 192 MPs required for a majority in parliament, Orbán already had a clear majority in the first round. At issue was not only his own personal triumph but also the alarming rise of the extreme right Jobbik Party, which had won 17 per cent of the vote. Approximately 75 per cent of the Hungarian electorate had opted for right or far right parties.

The collapse of the post-1989 era's two large moderate parties (the MDF, centre-right, and the Free Democrats, centre-left) facilitated Fidesz's sweeping victory in the single-member constituencies. Both parties failed to win 5 per cent of the vote, the prerequisite to enter parliament. The election was also a catastrophe for the governing Socialists, who received only 19 per cent of the vote, down from 43 per cent in 2006. Two weeks later, in the second round of voting, the defeat of the left was complete.[1] For the first time in the history of democratic Hungary, a political party had achieved a two-thirds majority: with a total of 263 MPs Fidesz held 68 per cent of the seats in parliament. The Socialists had a mere fifty-nine and Jobbik, in the first elections it had contested, forty-seven. Fidesz's achievement, extraordinary by

European standards, owed much to the Hungarian electoral system's tendency to generate clear but disproportionate majorities. For some of the guests, above all the younger ones, at the election party we were attending the gloom was relieved by the surprising success of the new LMP grouping ('Politics can be different'). Thanks to the appeal of its green and youth-oriented programme, this new party won 7.5 per cent of the popular vote (10 per cent in Budapest) and sixteen MPs. It had excluded any cooperation, even in local elections, with the Socialists. After the election and especially before its split in 2012–13 (when approximately half of its MPs quit the party), rumours circulated about a covert electoral manoeuvre by Fidesz to support the politically diverse LMP, with the aim of isolating the left. Almost all our friends had voted for the LMP and were happy about its unexpected success on election night.

The overwhelming Fidesz victory marked a turning point in the political history of Hungary. The Socialists had suffered a debacle in every voter group. This was confirmed in subsequent analyses by pollsters. The reasons were not hard to find: the Socialists' inability to act, their involvement in numerous corruption scandals and their almost constant factional struggles. The survey results among those aged between eighteen and twenty-nine were particularly ominous for the future of the party: only 10 per cent had voted for the Socialists, whereas the extremist Jobbik Party had attracted the support of 18–23 per cent of this age group.

The final result of the election was a clear and unequivocal message, one of great significance for Hungary. With 80 per cent of the right- and extreme right-wing MPs in parliament behind him following the 'successful revolution at the ballot box', Viktor Orbán could swiftly implement his vision of creating a 'central political force field'. Given the annihilation of the left, in his seizure of absolute power, the only threat for the foreseeable future—if there was one at all—was from the right. The years since 2010 have provided ample evidence that the new strongman of Hungary would not be held back on his path towards an authoritarian order, neither by the political opposition nor by a functioning civil society.

The man who probably knows the Fidesz leader best, his biographer József Debreczeni, had warned earlier than most other commentators about the consequences of Orbán's reckless opportunism and his insatiable greed for power and money. In the epilogue of his second book on Orbán, published in 2009, he wrote: 'Once he is in possession of a constitutional majority, he will turn this into an impregnable fortress of power ... Nobody should have any doubts that Orbán will recklessly and utterly exploit this power.' The recent shifts in the governing and social structures of Hungary, pushed through at breakneck speed following Orbán's brilliant electoral victory, have only confirmed Debreczeni's warnings, previously dismissed by some as alarmist.

After 'the Hungarian nation's historic deed' in delivering the 2010 election result, the pompous text of a 'Manifesto of National Cooperation' was approved by Fidesz's two-thirds majority in parliament and hung (in a 50 x 70cm glass frame) in all public offices. The overblown speeches of the prime minister and his followers, together with their unctuous declarations at national celebrations, were intended to make clear to the masses the meaning of the 'revolution at the ballot box', and to whip up their enthusiasm for the new system. With an iron fist, the democratic and constitutional checks and balances built into the system in 1989–90 were removed. In his final speech of the new parliament's first session, Prime Minister Orbán boasted that his 'national centre' had achieved more in fifty-six days than the Socialist–Free Democrat government had in eight years.[2]

Debreczeni has dismissed the lofty claims of a 'system of national cooperation' as a 'falsification of history based on lies, pure and simple'. The 2.7 million votes won by Fidesz in 2010 comprised in reality little more than half of the actual vote, approximately one third of the electorate and about a quarter of the population. It was therefore stretching credibility to describe Fidesz as the embodiment 'of the undivided will of the unified Hungarian nation'.[3] Despite this legitimate argument, one must also remember the fact that in 1994 the Socialist Party had won a comfortable majority of 54 per cent of the parliamentary seats with only 31.6 per cent of the popular vote; when the support of its Free Democrat coalition partner was added to this, the new government held 72 per cent of parliamentary seats with only 49.9 per cent of the popular vote.[4] In his reckoning with the taboos of the 1989 system change, the journalist János Széky came to the justified conclusion that the institutions created at that time bore within themselves the seeds of the subsequent abuses.

How was it possible for Fidesz to attain this two-thirds majority? One of the primary reasons was the explosive force of the national question in Hungary, banned from public discourse under the communists, then repressed or concealed for decades. Despite the eastern enlargement of the EU and the opportunity for over 2 million members of the Hungarian minority in Central Europe (with the exception of Serbia and Ukraine) to travel visa-free, the overwhelming significance of the trauma that has dominated everything else since the abusive Treaty of Trianon cannot be underestimated. No Hungarian reacts with indifference when it comes to the architectural gems and memorials, the graves of mighty kings and the birth houses of great poets, in the old Hungarian towns in Transylvania (Romania), 'Upper Hungary' (Slovakia) and Vojvodina (Serbia). Novels and poems, paintings and family histories keep alive the memories of a glorious but irrevocably lost past. One must always remember that Hungary lost more than two-thirds of its territory and three-fifths of its population; after 1920 more than three million Hungarians lived under foreign suzerainty.

The populist rhetoric of the right and the passivity of the left have combined to create an interpretative narrative of Trianon that is dominated by right- and extreme right-wing views. The failure of the 2004 initiative, conceived by the right-dominated World Union of Hungarians and supported by Fidesz, to grant Hungarian citizenship to ethnic Hungarians in neighbouring states had marked the beginning of the radicalisation of Hungarian policies on the minorities.[5] This was also shaped by the periodical stirring up of historical resentments by right-wing parties in Slovakia, Romania and Serbia. The apparently indifferent (at times even hostile) attitude of the Hungarians in the mother country towards the citizenship question left deep wounds in the ranks of the Hungarian minorities abroad struggling for equal rights in culture and education.

Orbán's statement in May 2009 about a 'unified nation extending beyond national borders, belonging together' caused outrage, as did the proposal to discuss the joint representation of the Hungarians from the Carpathian Basin in the European Parliament. Shortly after it assumed office in 2010, the Fidesz government rushed two laws through parliament: one on the right of all Hungarians living abroad to a Hungarian passport even if they did not have permanent residence in Hungary; and the other designating 4 June, the day the Treaty of Trianon was signed in 1920, as the 'Day of National Solidarity'. These lightning moves were of course also motivated by the desire to outflank the aggressively nationalistic Jobbik Party after its surprising success in the election. Despite criticism from abroad and the exaggerated reaction in some neighbouring states, the move to undermine the extreme right paid off completely. In 2014 those Hungarian citizens residing abroad exercised for the first time the right to vote in a Hungarian parliamentary election.

Reliable sources state that 95 per cent of this new electorate voted for Fidesz.[6]

Critical observers tend to recall a controversial remark made by the former health minister István Mikola before the elections of 2006: 'If we win for four years, and then, let's say, grant the 5 million Hungarians citizenship and allow them to vote, then everything would be decided for the next 20 years.' Mikola almost immediately denied ever having said this.

The promotion of the Christian-national unity of the Magyars in order to seize and maintain power, regardless of borders or hostile international reactions, has been one of the decisive ideological and political successes of Viktor Orbán. In the Manifesto of National Cooperation, 'work, home, family, health and order' are named as the pillars of the 'new system that has arisen through the will of the people' and 'of the connection between the members of the multifaceted Hungarian nation'. The preamble of the 2010 parliamentary declaration making 4 June the 'Day of National Solidarity' commemorating Trianon contains a telling phrase: 'God is the Lord of history'.

10

THE NEW CONQUEST

Since Fidesz's election victory in the spring of 2010, Hungary has lived in a new era. There is no longer any meaningful discussion, as there would be in other democratic countries, about whether and when this government could be replaced in an election. The tacit and general assumption is that after its two overwhelming electoral successes of 2010 and 2014 the Orbán regime cannot be defeated under 'normal' circumstances by any free and fair election in the foreseeable future. The bastion of power elaborately constructed since 2010 is, as far as it is humanly possible to tell, impregnable to external assault. The prospects of the opposition are so bleak and it is so hopelessly disunited that it offers no serious option for political change. It says everything that in all its brilliant essays, stretching to 1,750 pages, Bálint Magyar's three-volume *The Hungarian Octopus: The Post-Communist Mafia State*, the most ambitious project yet describing and analysing the regime, has barely a word to say on realistic alternatives or promising, let alone possible, opposition strategies. Nevertheless, it represents a singular and highly original combination of insightful studies on the disastrous legal, political, social and economic consequences of Fidesz rule.[1]

The views of Hungarian commentators (some of whom already speak of 'Orbánism') on the nature of the Orbán regime are far from unanimous. Bálint Magyar, the inventor of the expression 'Hungarian mafia state', describes the regime as 'the privatised form of a parasite state, an economic undertaking run by the family of the Godfather exploiting the political and public instruments of power'.

This viewpoint—whereby the state institutions within the framework of the system serve the interests of one political family, and primarily those of its boss—is, for example, disavowed by the legal scholar Tamás Sárközy, on the basis that it is not a sociological academic analysis.[2]

Opinion is divided as to whether the structures established after 2010 are still those of a democracy or have already morphed into a kind of authoritarian system; there is only agreement that the system may no longer be considered a liberal democracy. Some believe that it may indeed be seen as a democracy of some kind because there remains the theoretical possibility of removing the government. In contrast the academics János Kornai and Lajos Bokros, as well as Bálint Magyar, speak expressly of an authoritarian system.[3] Kornai cites 'the systematic demolition of the fundamental institutions of democracy', while Bokros believes that 'an authoritarian and strongly centralised political power, a state without limits, has arisen'. The author and journalist Rudolf Ungváry even believes the regime (though this is still not evident to the majority of its citizens) to be a manipulated 'fascistoid mutation'; the sociologist Ferenc Pataki defines it as 'a neo-collectivist, neo-communist experiment' and Erzsébet Szalai, also a sociologist, as a 'semi-dictatorship'. The political scientist and former education minister András Bozóki speaks of a 'hybrid regime', in which 'the features of an authoritarian system are stronger than those of a democracy'.

Tamás Bauer, an economist and professor emeritus at the University of Frankfurt, rejects the mafia-state interpretation because it ignores the societal basis of the regime. However, he judges the entire Orbán regime a tyranny, as the separation of powers has been abolished. For this reason he also considers any preparations the opposition may make for the elections due in 2018 a damaging illusion, citing here, as do many other commentators, Orbán's famous interview with the Austrian tabloid *Kronen Zeitung* from 10 June 2011. Responding to a question as to whether the laws created through the new constitution, which can only be amended by a two-thirds majority, would tie the hands of future governments, the prime minister replied: 'I will extend the two-thirds law only on one point: that of economic laws. And I make no secret of the fact that in this respect I would like to tie the hands of the next government. And not only the next one, but the next ten governments!'

As mentioned in Chapter 9, on 5 September 2009 at a private party in the village of Kötcse, Orbán had spoken openly for the first time about the creation of a 'central political force field, of a great political party', which would replace the dual system for 'fifteen to twenty years'.[4] At that point Orbán was only the leader of the opposition. However, by the time of his 2011 *Kronen Zeitung* interview he was the official head of a government speaking in a foreign newspaper. His casual remark laid bare two basic truths: little more than a year after winning power, Orbán could allow himself the frankness of a head of government at risk from nobody, whilst at the same time and without any scruple revealing to the world and to the Hungarian public his long-term plans to retain power. He provided further evidence of his self-confident handling of his power at a Fidesz party congress on 13 December 2015. Referring to the approaching thirtieth anniversary of Fidesz's founding, he said, 'We have been here for thirty years and we will also be here for the next thirty.' Fidesz was the most successful party in Europe and he was prepared, in two years' time, if the trust was still there, to lead the party into the election campaign and, should it win, to continue as prime minister from 2018.

There is scarcely a country in Europe where the head of government is able to display so blithely and confidently his projections for staying in power behind a democratic smokescreen. The victorious Fidesz leader is thus thinking in terms of ten legislative periods—fifteen to twenty, even thirty years in power. In light of what has happened in the country since the breakthrough of April 2010, this brings us to the now almost forgotten debate at the time of that victory, over two diametrically opposed scenarios. One theory presumed the existence of a cogent master plan for a radical rupture with liberal democracy and also with the rule of law protecting minority and individual rights. The other saw the events mainly as a consequence of irrational and/or dilettante actions.[5] Today, it is incontrovertible that what perhaps could most accurately be described as a new land conquest (a reference to the legendary conquest of the Danube basin by the Magyars in 896 AD) has been conducted following a precise script whilst, at the same time, the activities of the central administration have been characterised by improvised, non-ideological dabbling. The lightning-speed assault on the key institutions that traditionally served as a counterbalance to executive power and as a controlling mechanism had obviously long been prepared. It is no accident that Orbán's infamous remark from his time in the opposition is quoted so often: 'We have only to win once, but then properly.'

The ambitious undertaking of consolidating Fidesz, immediately and irrevocably, as the sole ruling factor of power in Hungary succeeded not least because of a fortunate coincidence. The presidency of László Sólyom officially came to an end in June 2010, just two months after the election. As the head of state is elected by parliament, Orbán had, thanks to his two-thirds majority, a completely free hand in the choice of his successor. Sólyom, following a senseless quarrel within Gyurcsány's coalition government, had been elected president in 2005 with the support of Fidesz and was, by all accounts, willing to serve a further five-year term in office. Orbán, however, quite correctly perceived him to be an unpredictable factor, because he was independent-minded.[6] What was needed at such a decisive moment, when the new course was being set, was not merely a distinguished personality occasionally independent yet well disposed towards Fidesz, but a man of predictable obedience, an acquiescent political lightweight. Orbán found an almost ideal accomplice in a two-time Olympic fencing champion. Pál Schmitt had faithfully served the communist system as a high-ranking sports functionary and Fidesz equally reliably since 2003, most recently as speaker of parliament after the 2010 election victory.

The Hungarian head of state has only limited powers, but one with a strong personality could in a crisis situation obstruct the will of the prime minister. This was something the country had already experienced once, during the 1993 media war between Prime Minister József Antall and President Árpád Göncz over the appointment of the head of the public service TV and radio. But, essentially, the president can only delay parliament's decision-making processes by refusing to sign a bill and sending it back for revision. He can also have enacted laws reviewed by the constitutional court. Parliament has the possibility of overriding any veto and reaffirming its original resolution through a second vote. In any case, during Schmitt's two years in office, this of course did not happen. The new president had made it clear in his first speech that he would neither control nor put any brake on parliament, but rather he would complement it. He did not want to be a hindrance but a motor of the government. In this spirit, Schmitt, who dismissed the entire legal staff of the president's office, signed without hesitation every bill placed before him, including the internationally highly controversial law establishing a national media authority with unprecedented oversight.

The truly seamless cooperation between Schmitt and Orbán was, however, abruptly interrupted in the spring of 2012 when *HVG*, a weekly magazine, revealed that the president had plagiarised almost completely (in 197 of 215 pages) his doctoral thesis from a study made by a Bulgarian sports academic about 'The Olympic Games of the New Era'. After some initial hesitation, Orbán had to sacrifice his willing helper after the Semmelweis University in Budapest stripped Schmitt of his doctorate. He quickly found a compliant successor in János Áder, a crony of many years, who had 'emigrated' to Brussels in 2009 as an MEP.[7] He was elected president in May 2012. In stark contrast to Schmitt, Áder has, despite, or perhaps because of, his thirty-year friendship with Orbán refused several times to sign certain heavily criticised bills. However, the significance of these occasional signals of independence should not be exaggerated. He did not, for instance, despite international criticism and the public warnings of his predecessor László Sólyom, veto the controversial fourth amendment of the 'Fundamental Law of Hungary', the new constitution that had been adopted barely a year previously. On the contrary, he signed it into law, thereby hamstringing the Constitutional Court, on 14 March 2013.

The nomination of a political lightweight such as Schmitt as head of state had served as the prelude to an unprecedented wave of personnel changes on all levels. From the public audit office to the financial supervision commission, the monetary and budgetary councils, from army generals to police chiefs, from the state lottery to the state railways, from disaster control to horseracing, from the social insurance institutions to the central statistical office, posts were given to Fidesz loyalists; in many cases top officials resigned of their own accord, jumping before they were pushed. A new law allowed the government to gratuitously fire civil servants at any time.

From the very beginning the leadership concentrated its efforts on setting the parliamentary voting mechanism in motion in order to prepare its frontal assault on the old constitution, the constitutional court and the independent judiciary. For that an accelerated system of legislation was necessary. In the nineteen months after the government entered office the constitution, usually following proposals tabled by individual MPs, was frequently amended using fast-track procedures without any debate; in this way twenty-six reforms were passed, in twelve constitutional amendments. Barely a month after the new parliament had assembled, arguably the most important amendment was agreed by the two-thirds majority, following a proposal made by an MP after a debate lasting a mere three days: the safeguard clause requiring preparation of a new constitution to be approved by four-fifths of MPs was abolished. Zsuzsa Kerekes, a constitutional expert, pertinently observed that:

> With this amendment the path to the liquidation of the republican constitution and the rule of law has been left wide open. There no longer exist any blocks to the use of different tactics for the restructuring of independent institutions such as the constitutional court, the public audit office, the National Bank, the legal system, the system of an ombudsman and the autonomous administrative units of government.[8]

Kerekes demonstrated how the rules of parliamentary procedure as amended on 1 January 2012 have enabled the adoption of urgent emergency legislation requiring no debate, through the abolition of the threshold clause requiring a four-fifths majority. With this measure, it is now possible in peacetime to rush a bill through parliament in less than forty-eight hours and to publish the adopted text as a 'law' in the official Gazette.

On Sunday, 28 April 2013, two MPs put forward an amendment to the law on freedom of information, which had replaced the earlier data protection law. The next day they proposed that it be considered by urgent decision, leaving only three hours for supplementary proposals; the final vote would be held the following day. The parliamentary constitutional committee decided on Monday morning, after twelve minutes of deliberation, to refer the proposal to the plenum. About two hours later, in the plenary session, the government majority accepted the initiative for urgent consideration and the MPs had 180 minutes to put forward amendments. The constitutional committee, still in session in the evening, then rejected within five minutes all the opposition amendments, and at 21.04 the bill went to the plenum for a full debate. This lasted a mere sixty-four minutes. After a short overnight break, early on Tuesday morning—less than forty-eight hours after the amendment had been tabled—the bill was passed into law by the government majority.

As the bill had been put forward by a single MP, there was no expert consultation, no discussion within civil society and also no administrative coordination. The latter would have been especially important as the amendment concerned a law regulating constitutional basic laws. Kerekes has also revealed that of the 1,026 laws enacted between 2010 and May 2015, 303 (37 per cent) were tabled by individual MPs, and not the government; in the case of constitutional amendments, the figure is even more startling: nine out twelve (75 per cent) passed between May 2010 and November 2011. All these new laws and amendments were fast-tracked through parliament without any genuine debate or scrutiny.

Within the space of two-and-a-half years, the two-thirds majority applied this urgent procedure twenty-six times. After the May 2014 election victory the two-thirds majority extended the regulations for extraordinary legislation. Henceforth, not six but ten laws could be boxed through in one session. In the following eighteen months, no fewer than eighteen laws were passed by means of such a fast-track procedure, seven through motions tabled by individual MPs.

THE NEW CONQUEST

On 1 January 2012 the new constitution, the Fundamental Law of Hungary, had come into force. The former president, Lászlo Sólyom, spoke of the instrumentalisation of the constitution in the service of day-to-day objectives. Orbán had all laws essential to the consolidation of Fidesz's power enacted as constitutional laws via his voting machine in parliament. Known as cardinal acts, these form the basis for the concentration of power in his government, as they can only be altered in the future by a two-thirds majority. They also ensure that, even in the unlikely event of the opposition parties ever achieving a majority in parliament, the key positions in the state will still, for nine years dating from the appointment, be occupied by Orbán's compliant cronies, who could, if necessary, form a Fidesz shadow government. For this reason we must now examine potentially the most important institutional and personnel consequence of the 'new land conquest' in the fields of justice, the media, the economy and the administration.

11

THE END OF THE SEPARATION OF POWERS

With the 'successful revolution at the ballot box' in 2010, Viktor Orbán proclaimed not only a new government programme but also both a system change and a new historical era. Though during the election campaign a year earlier not a single word had been uttered about any constitutional reform plans, he proudly announced in February 2011 the drafting of a new constitution to be called the 'Fundamental Law of Hungary'. Within two months, on 18 April 2011, this new constitution had been adopted in a fast-track procedure with the votes of the governing party. It entered into force on 1 January 2012. The Fundamental Law was rushed through parliament in nine days, without any previous national debate, any political or legal discussion, and of course without a plebiscite. In place of a popular consultation, a parliamentary debate or a referendum, questionnaires with completely irrelevant questions were sent to all 8 million Hungarians eligible to vote.[1] The sole purpose of this 'national consultation' was to serve (and not for the first time) as an expensive alibi action, one sharply criticised and ridiculed by all well-known Hungarian and international constitutional lawyers.[2]

The preamble of the 'Easter constitution', with its 'national confession' and the concept of the Holy Crown of Hungary, was intended to enshrine the completion of the change. A new interpretation of history was codified once and for all, the ethnic understanding of the nation was pronounced in the constitution and a central role was assigned to Christianity. Under the Fundamental Law, the Crown of St Stephen stands as a bearer of Hungarian sovereignty and is a holy symbol, the slandering of which is punishable by law. The historical revisionism of the preamble gave rise in the Holocaust memorial year of 2014 to passionate disputes and an international scandal about the monument to the 1944–5 German occupation.[3] Fidesz was consciously rewriting Hungarian history. According to the new interpretation, the country was not free but occupied for the entire period from March 1944 to the first free elections in 1990.

The preamble declares: 'We date the restoration of our country's self-determination, lost on the nineteenth day of March 1944, from the second day of May 1990, when the first freely elected organ of popular representation was formed. We shall consider this date to be the beginning of our country's new democracy and constitutional order'. Though German troops did march into the country on 19 March 1944, the fact remains that Regent Miklós Horthy remained nominally in power. He named and dismissed prime ministers and, even after his failed attempt to surrender to the Soviets and his resignation, appointed a fascist government under the Arrow Cross leader Ferenc Szálasi. Moreover, the Fidesz version of history denies the great responsibility of the whole state apparatus in the deportation and murder of 560,000 Hungarian Jews.[4] A number of generously endowed pseudo-academic institutions have been founded since 2010. These are re-interpreting the history of the Horthy era in terms congenial to Fidesz, in particular with regard to the discrimination and persecution of the Hungarian Jews before the Germans occupied the country.

THE END OF THE SEPARATION OF POWERS

Despite the grandiloquent phrasing about the meaning and importance of the Fundamental Law, parliament made no fewer than five significant amendments to the new constitution in the following two-and-a-half years, as well as passing a series of cardinal acts. Ignoring the international criticism (which will be considered below), the Orbán regime acted without any scruple and, as always, at lightning speed to tamper with and undermine the troublesome brake of the constitutional court and the institutions of the rule of law. The weak and divided opposition was now irrelevant. The main target of the massive Fidesz campaign to conquer and, should there be any resistance, to destroy the central authorities of the separation of powers was now the constitutional court, which since 1989 had time after time acted independently towards whichever government was in power.

Within weeks of his election victory, Orbán began to take action. First, the selection procedure for the justices of the constitutional court was altered. In the past an all-party parliamentary committee had proposed candidates who were then accepted or rejected in a parliamentary vote. Now their appointment became a decision of parliament, with its huge Fidesz majority. The governing faction nominated a candidate who was then submitted to a parliamentary vote. In order to achieve a pro-government majority on the court bench as quickly as possible, the prime minister increased the number of justices from eleven to fifteen. As one position was already vacant, the ruling party was able immediately to appoint five new justices, all men close to Fidesz. Their period of office was raised from nine to twelve years. Orbán's very first choice of constitutional judge in July 2010 caused considerable surprise. This was István Stumpf, a political scientist who had known the new prime minister closely since their student days and who had served as his minister of state between 1998 and 2002. He had no experience of legal practice. In the years that followed, other former Fidesz ministers and MPs, as well as lawyers who had not exactly had a glittering career but who were politically reliable, were advanced to the benches of the constitutional court. Previously, the judges themselves had voted for the president of the constitutional court; a new regulation passed this duty to the parliamentary majority. We shall see later how, even with these personnel changes, the jurisdiction of the constitutional court was radically restricted.

Beyond the constitutional court, staffing decisions were made immediately after the 2010 election—again, at breakneck speed—in order to bring the judiciary, the civil service, the media and the financial sector under Fidesz control. With the aid of its two-thirds parliamentary majority, the government decided on the compulsory retirement of all judges and prosecutors who had reached the age of sixty-two (as of 2012), thereby reducing their retirement age by eight years. This measure, implemented without any public debate, affected 274 judges. A new regulation formally abolished the Supreme Court and renamed it the Kuria. This was done to ease first the removal of András Baka, the Court's independent president, and then his replacement by a pro-Fidesz justice at the head of the new body. After his ejection from office, Baka challenged this arbitrary act and won his case in the European Court of Human Rights in Strasbourg. He received financial compensation but the decision was not reversed.

Outrage at home and abroad was provoked by the liquidation of the administrative autonomy of the courts and the creation of the National Judiciary Office, which was also anchored in the new constitution. In addition, Tünde Handó was named its president, with wide-ranging powers in the appointment of judges and the hearing of cases, in courts determined by her. The period in office of the chief justice, chosen by two-thirds majority, is now nine years. Handó, a friend of Orbán and his family for more than thirty years since their days at the Bibó College, will remain in office until 2020. She is also the wife of József Szájer, a Fidesz founder and MEP. That he is said to have written the text of the new constitution on the train from Brussels to Strasbourg on his iPad lends a certain piquancy to the promotion of his wife, something unimaginable in a state under the rule of law.

The new retirement age of sixty-two, however, was only applicable to judges, not other civil servants. Symbolic of Orbán's total dominance over his parliamentary majority is the fact that in stark contrast to the compulsory early retirement of judges, a special amendment to the retirement law was passed at the end of 2010 enabling the appointment of Orbán's then seventy-two-year-old financial adviser, György Szapáry, as the Hungarian ambassador to Washington.[5] Known as the Lex Szapáry, this was in line with a series of other arbitrary measures instigated by the prime minister, which have led to repeated conflicts with the constitutional court, the European Court of Justice and the Venice Commission of the Council of Europe (the European Commission for Democracy through Law).

A few examples illustrate how casually the Orbán regime has dealt with statutory provisions, and yet also how the constitutional court, despite pressure, has on occasion demonstrated its independence. The court declared unconstitutional a law, unique to Hungary, regulating its civil servants, whereby employees in public service could be fired without reason or notice and their severance pay taxed at 98 per cent, backdated five years. Before this, the judges had overruled sections of the controversial media law, which was pilloried by all significant international media (such as Reporters without Borders, the International Press Institute, the OSCE Representation on Freedom of the Media) as an unconstitutional restriction on press freedom. One of potentially the most important decisions of the post-2010 constitutional court has been the annulment of several paragraphs of the electoral law reform, which would have obliged eligible voters to register at a particular time prior to the election. Those citizens who did not have themselves registered would have immediately lost their right to vote on the most crucial constitutional amendments for four years.

In a study completed at the end of 2012, Jan-Werner Müller, a political scientist at Princeton University, identified the political strategy pursued by Fidesz as being aimed at:

a highly centralised, partially illiberal democracy which systematically undermines the structures of checks and balances, which intimidates or de facto directly controls the media, which weakens civil society—and which makes it very likely that Fidesz will win elections in the foreseeable future (or, should it actually lose an election, can continue to control the important state institutions) ... All this must in turn be seen in connection with a redrawing of parliamentary constituencies and local districts which creates enormous advantages for Fidesz so that it remains the strongest party. The parallels with Putin's 'guided democracy' simply cannot be avoided. Certainly, elections will continue to be held in Hungary, Orbán's opponents will be allowed to demonstrate in Budapest, critical voices will find a niche somewhere in the media. Power really changing hands, however, is increasingly unlikely—even in the case of opposition parties winning the next elections.[6]

These and similar court decisions, declaring sections of Fidesz laws null and void, were considered by the power-conscious Hungarian prime minister as intolerable humiliations, and he took his revenge for these embarrassments with a massive counter-attack. In March 2013 the parliamentary majority voted for a significant curbing of the constitutional court's competences. Any review of the constitutionality of those laws concerning state finances was prohibited, and all laws previously overturned by the constitutional court were made into constitutional law and written into the constitution. This means that senior judges can neither examine nor cancel them. László Sólyom, the long-serving first president of the court (1989–98) and later state president (2005–10), described this ominous withdrawal of competences as an 'act of revenge of the parliamentary majority', enabling it to 'liberate itself from the restrictions of the constitution and constitutional controls'.[7]

He also pointed out that, thanks to the two-thirds majority, parliament could enact any clause in the form of a constitutional amendment even if it diametrically contradicted other articles in the Hungarian Fundamental Law. The fourth amendment in March 2013 rescinded all decisions taken before the inception of the new constitution on 1 January 2012. With this, in Sólyom's view, a significant portion of valid Hungarian constitutional law lost its binding force.

Since this first rather cautious criticism of parliamentary manipulation, Hungarian and international lawyers and academics have continued, much more openly, to raise the alarm about the looming consequences. With the notorious cardinal acts, the Orbán government has been able to create one fait accompli after another. Thus, for example, the reformed Budget Council, now anchored in the constitution, is authorised to veto at will any budget decided by parliament. Its three members are proposed by the prime minister and sent to the Budget Council by the governor of the National Bank, the president of the Court of Auditors and the state president. Their period of office is nine years and they cannot be dismissed. Their veto of the budget automatically triggers the dissolution of parliament and new elections. It goes without saying that the three members, in office until 2020, are loyal partisans of Orbán, who through this instrument are furnished with unprecedented power and who, even in the unlikely event of an election defeat, would continue to have a crucially decisive voice in Hungarian politics.

Another attempt, admittedly one that has at the time of writing so far failed, was the amendment of the law on the National Bank. At the end of 2011 the Fidesz government wanted to merge the central bank and the financial market authority into a new super-body, with a new chair to be named by parliament. The then independent and autonomous governor of the National Bank, András Simor, would become one of three deputies to the president of the new super-authority, and would thus be stripped of power. Through the energetic protests of the European Central Bank and the EU Commission, this provocative proposal, without parallel in European banking, was finally blocked and Orbán had to withdraw the bill. There was, however, no let-up on the intense pressure on Simor. When I visited him in the National Bank during this period, he told me that there were no fewer than five different investigations being conducted against him by various government offices.

Even before this the Fidesz-controlled parliament had, as an act of revenge, reduced Simor's monthly salary by 75 per cent to 2 million forints (€8,000). At the end of his six-year term in office in March 2013, he was replaced by György Matolcsy, the former finance minister. Three years later Matolcsy's remuneration was, without any explanation, raised to five million forints a month. (In November 2013, despite the opposition of Fidesz, Simor was elected vice-president of the European Bank for Reconstruction and Development in London.) As far as monetary policy is concerned, Matolcsy has shown himself to be just as obedient an executioner of Orbán's policies at the head of the National Bank as in his previous position as minister of finance. However, within in two years of taking office, Matolcsy and the National Bank became, as will be described in Chapter 15, the focus of a major public corruption scandal.

Independently minded political scientists, legal experts and journalists have provided endless lists of names and details on how, in the filling of important positions, the rules on incompatibility have simply been thrown overboard.[8] Orbán had a law specially changed to enable a specific army officer to become an MP. For another minion he had a sports college hived off from a university in order to name him its rector. Another creature in a key position is the long-serving public prosecutor Péter Polt, whose obligation to retire was waived and whose period of office was extended to nine years; moreover, he can no longer be questioned in parliament and his successor can only be nominated by a two-thirds majority. The introduction of special penalty taxes for international banks and for foreign financial and trading companies, coupled with particularly generous preferential treatment for supermarket chains whose Hungarian owners are politically close to Fidesz, the large-scale eradication of private small tobacconists and the allotment of multiple licenses (National Tobacco Shops) to relatives of Fidesz politicians or trusted supporters are further characteristic examples of how Orbán has systematically cemented power.

The centralisation of the school system was enabled by granting the minister responsible the power to nominate the 5,000 school heads and by subordinating the entire school sector to a new central administrative authority (KLIK). In 2016 the desolate condition of middle and vocational schools triggered an open conflict between protesting teachers and the principal KLIK office. The financing of the universities was also placed under the control of chancellors named by the government, whilst university rectors would be directly nominated by the minister. It is also of significance that the shady foundations set up by the National Bank to propagate the government's unorthodox economic policies are alone equivalent in funds to the entire higher education sector's eighteen-month budget.

There have thus been numerous examples since Fidesz took office in the spring of 2010 of the trend towards a consistent, even if somewhat veiled, eradication of the separation of powers (legislature, judiciary and executive) that lies at the heart of a democratic state under the rule of law. Since the 2014 election victory, the dismantling of parliamentary controls has been accelerated. A comparison of the first years of the 2010 and 2014 governments shows, for example, that the time devoted to enacting individual pieces of legislation sank on average from 2 hours and 12 minutes to 1 hour and 15 minutes—that is, by almost 50 per cent. The number of votes held in parliament also fell by two thirds between 2011 and 2015. The approval of the internationally controversial erection of a fence along Hungary's southern border to keep out refugees, as well as the authorisation of the army's deployment to police it, was dealt with in barely two hours. The favourite trick of individual MPs introducing draft legislation without any previous substantial debate has continued to enable fast-track procedures. An administrative record in this case was achieved on 21 September 2013: the amendment of a law was passed, from its first oral proposal in parliament to a final vote, in a mere ten minutes. In April 2016 the parliamentary majority granted the government the authority to amend the budget without consulting parliament. This momentous decision was considered by observers as a further step along the path to government by decree.[9]

The fourth amendment to the Hungarian Fundamental Law referred to above means that any violation of the constitution identified as such by the constitutional court can have no practical consequences if the government simply incorporates the controversial law into the constitution by means of its two-thirds voting machine. For good reason the constitutional lawyer Imre Vörös (himself a member of the constitutional court between 1990 and 1999) and the former president László Sólyom have both observed that 'the end of the separation of powers means in reality' that between 2010 and 2014 the Orbán regime was able to effect 'an unconstitutional coup ... [under] the cover of constitutionality, with constitutional means'.[10]

12

THE NATIONAL LIBERATION STRUGGLE

In seizing and consolidating his hold on power Viktor Orbán has repeatedly demonstrated, especially when in difficult situations, an almost uncanny instinct for the mobilisation of Hungarians' deeply rooted nationalist sentiments. When describing in my previous books the path to the collapse of historical Hungary and the developments after the suppression of the October 1956 uprising, I referred to 'the sense of mission of an easily seducible nation' and to the experience of 'victory in defeat'.[1] The trait which the Magyars call *délibáb* literally means *fata morgana*, an illusion. The talent for wishful thinking, a tendency which the psychoanalyst Sándor Ferenczi describes as 'magical thought', this penchant for daydreaming has moulded the attitudes of the elite and the people in the repeated crises the nation has faced. In his standard work on the intellectual and social history of Austria-Hungary, the American historian William M. Johnson observes of *délibáb:*

> Readiness to see the world through rose-coloured glasses induced Magyars to exaggerate their grandeur, while they ignored the misery of subject peoples ... Capacity for dreaming has made Magyars superlative advocates, ever ready to defend Hungary as an exception among nations.[2]

As a consequence of the recurring misfortunes since the conquest of 896, fears of a slow death for a small nation and the loneliness of a people with a language unique across the Carpathian Basin have remained the decisive factors in Hungarian history. The interplay between openness and isolation, between lonely sentiments and a sense of mission, between fear of death and rebellion, has always had a marked influence on the changing times and culture of the Hungarians. Feelings of defencelessness ('We are the most forsaken of all peoples on the Earth' in the words of Sándor Petőfi, the national poet) have imbued almost every generation of Magyars with a deep-rooted pessimism.

The list of catastrophes is long: the devastation of a country left in the lurch by the Occident during the Mongol invasion in 1241, the defeat at Mohács in 1526, which resulted in a century-and-a-half of Turkish occupation, the crushing of the struggle for independence in 1848–9 by the combined forces of Austria and Russia, the destruction of historical Hungary with the diktat of the Treaty of Trianon in 1920, the four decades of communism after the Second World War and the bloody suppression of the October Uprising in 1956. Taken together, these misfortunes have exacerbated the national sense of abandonment. In spite of the centuries of foreign rule, however, the Hungarians have been able to preserve their national identity. It is their passionate love of their motherland which has always given them the strength to survive and to overcome all calamities, trapped, as they believe they are, between the Germans and the Slavs, without any kith or kin and separated by the 'Chinese Wall' of their language.

In the introduction to my book *The Hungarians: A Thousand Years Of Victory In Defeat* (Hurst and Princeton, 2003), I wrote that the survival of the Hungarians and their nation state is a miracle of European history; but I also pointed to the 'unresolved question of the conjunction of patriotism and liberalism, of the national idea and social progress', and characterised the bridging of this yawning gap between Hungarian political culture's two tendencies as the fateful question for the future of 'the victors in defeat', and for Hungary's place in a changing Europe. Almost two decades later, the seven years of new 'conquest' superbly orchestrated by Viktor Orbán's government apparatus have answered my question clearly and unambiguously, in favour of the pre-eminence of the nation. The nationalist-populist course charted since April 2010 confirms yet again the warnings of István Bibó, written in 1946 after the inferno of the Second World War: that democracy is threatened if, as a result of a catastrophe or an illusion, the cause of the nation is separated from that of liberty.[3]

These references to Hungarian history must always be considered in any analysis of the strategy and tactics of Orbán and his team in their major disputes with institutions like the European Commission, the Council of Europe, the IMF and the European Central Bank. This is not a question of individual cases but of the systematic character of a regime that violates the rules and values of the European Union. Fortunately, there is one reliable witness, one above suspicion, to the reasons behind the repeated conflicts between the Orbán government and the European Commission in 2010–14. This is Viviane Reding from Luxembourg, who in this period was vice-president of the European Commission for Justice, Basic Values and Citizenship. It is of significance that she also belongs to the European People's Party (EPP), the strongest faction in the European Parliament; Viktor Orbán has for many years been one of its ten vice-presidents. A journalist before she entered politics, Reding, despite much opposition from within the EPP and despite a brutal campaign conducted by the Fidesz media, has resolutely reprimanded the Hungarian government; she has also succeeded in compelling the Orbán regime to retreat in a number of important areas.[4]

The victorious Fidesz party always insists that its two-thirds majority justifies its key claim: we and we alone represent the people, the true Hungarians. In this context it should not be forgotten that Orbán, after surprisingly losing the premiership in the 2002 parliamentary elections, maintained that the nation (obviously embodied only by Fidesz) could not be in opposition. This claim to the sole ideological representation of the Hungarian nation, irreconcilable with the inherent concepts of democracy, runs like a thread through the deeds and declarations of Fidesz governments. From the first disputes with the IMF and the European Commission about Fidesz's financial, judicial and media policies, to the rejection of the international outcry against the treatment of refugees and the sealing off of borders, the struggle to protect 'hard-working Hungarians' against the domestic and foreign foes of the mother country has become a constant feature of Fidesz discourse. On 15 March 2011, the prime minister chose the traditional event held on the steps of the National Museum in Budapest to mark the national holiday to rebuke his critics in this unceasing struggle in defence of the homeland: Hungary is not a colony, he said, and, after the occupation of the country by the Turks, the Habsburgs and the Russians, will not let itself be oppressed by Brussels.

From the very beginning, the full-frontal assault on the EU, which provided financial aid to Hungary amounting to about €23 billion between 2007 and 2013, has formed the core of the rhetorical crisis management of the 'liberation struggle'.[5] Hence, the particular sensitivity to criticism when in the first half of 2011 Hungary was due to assume the revolving EU presidency (for the first time since joining the EU in 2004). The measures under attack, either already in force or announced, were aimed at seizing control of the state apparatus, the dismantling of the constitutional state, the introduction of special taxes against foreign banks and concerns, and above all the state control of the media.

The law on control of the media adopted on 20 December 2010 by the two-thirds majority (despite its draft being heavily criticised) immediately became the target of generally negative reporting in both the EU and the USA. Ever since his electoral defeat in 2002, Viktor Orbán has striven for a takeover of the public service media, in conjunction with building up a pro-Fidesz media empire run by friendly oligarchs. As a first step, the three public service TV stations (M1, M2 and Duna-TV), the three nationwide radio stations and even the official press agency (MTI) were amalgamated under the umbrella of the new Media Services and Support Trust Fund.[6] The twin tasks of this enormous conglomerate, in which Fidesz people control all important positions, were a weeding out of unreliable employees, and the administration by a single office of the huge state subsidies available for friendly media. A centralised media authority was created to oversee the political control of the central editorial department, which provided the news 'gratis' to all broadcasters; other functions included the selection of directors-general and the allocation of frequencies, as well as the control of 'balanced news reporting' and the imposition of sanctions. Orbán personally named a trusted Fidesz official as its head for nine years. All members of the new Media Council were appointed from within the ranks of Fidesz loyalists for the same period.

The vague formulation of the guidelines and the authority to compel journalists to reveal their sources, or impose draconian punishments on newspapers and journalists in cases of libel, led to a European-wide storm of protest. As early as September 2010, Dunja Mijatović, the OSCE Representative on Freedom of the Media, observed that 'Laws like these are actually only known in totalitarian countries where governments limit freedom of speech.' She added that the law did not comply with OSCE standards, which Hungary had pledged to keep.

In light of the government's casual approach to the rules of the EU, Jean Asselborn, the long-serving foreign minister of

Luxembourg, cast doubt on the suitability of Hungary to assume the EU presidency. The Venice Commission of the Council of Europe, the European Alliance of News Agencies (EANA), Reporters Without Borders, the European parliamentary leaders of the Liberals and Social Democrats, and the EU Commission have all criticised the media law. This is in addition to their negative observations on some cardinal acts and parts of the new constitution infringing the independence of the judiciary, of the data protection office and of the National Bank.

Orbán obviously underestimated the outrage of the international community at his attempt to keep the Hungarian media on a strict leash. His guiding principle of governance has remained unchanged to this day: *'reculer pour mieux sauter'*, take a step back to jump further. In a revealing phrase (revealing because it came impromptu in a speech given before a selected friendly audience on 31 May 2012, the second anniversary of the swearing in of the Fidesz government), Orbán characterised the virtuoso mastery of negotiation tactics with the EU as a 'dance of the peacock'. This is the art of employing double-speak with critics in the governing organs of the EU and then bamboozling them so adroitly that they get the (false) impression that the Hungarian side had yielded, although in reality it had stuck unswervingly to the Orbán course:

> Because of the diplomatic dance we must present the challenge in such a way as if we would like to make friends with them. Part of the skill of this dance is nodding our heads in agreement with two or three of their seven proposals (we had in any case already implemented them but they hadn't noticed) and the other two, which we don't want anyway, we reject so that we actually accept the majority. This complicated game is a type of dance of the peacock.[7]

Voluntarily admitting this in public was unprecedented. But it was also an arrogant confession as Orbán's belief in his personal ability to masterfully fool his simpleminded opponents without them even noticing.

THE NATIONAL LIBERATION STRUGGLE

The dispute over the media law gave Orbán an opportunity in Brussels and Strasbourg to engage in this double-talk for domestic and foreign consumption, and to strut his peacock dance. In the years of both public and secret disputes with the EU's institutions, as well as with critical media, the reactions of Orbán and his people have always followed the well-known steps of this dance. Before his trip to Strasbourg for his first official visit as the new EU president, he bragged on Hungarian TV: 'We don't even dream of changing the media law. Only a country that lacks self confidence would withdraw this law, and such a country we are not.' Accompanying music was provided, as always, in the form of furious outbursts against left-wing conspirators abroad, who, hand-in-hand with his perfidious Socialist–Free Democrat predecessors, would like to torpedo the nationalist conservative policies of the Orbán government.

The hostile international reaction in Strasbourg to the presentation of the Hungarian presidency's programme, then a year later to the negative statements of the Commission and, especially, to the July 2013 publication of the Taveres Report on Hungarian constitutional concerns (see below), were all accompanied by passionate and personal polemics traded between Orbán and his harshest critics. Among the latter were the former Liberal prime minister of Belgium, Guy Verhofstadt, the Austrian leader of the Social Democrats in the European Parliament, Hannes Swoboda, and the legendary French-German rebel of 1968 and co-chair of the Greens, Daniel Cohn-Bendit. During the Hungarian premier's inaugural visit to the European Parliament in January 2011, Green MEPs symbolically greeted him with their mouths taped over, waving banners on which the word 'censored' was plastered over the front pages of Hungarian newspapers. (Unfortunately, some pro-Fidesz newspapers with 'censored' all over them were also held up, a faux pas that unintentionally gave Orbán's propagandists the easy argument that Hungary's critics were very ill-informed.)

Under the pressure of international headlines, Orbán made a tactical withdrawal, not for the first time and certainly not for the last. Four points of the media law were amended. These cosmetic changes primarily affected the foreign media, no longer required to register with the media authorities or fined in cases of alleged violations of the media law. Among other concessions were the abolition of the obligation of 'balanced news reporting' and restrictions of the ambiguous rules on libelling individuals or groups. These minor adjustments left the essence of the media law, namely the restricting of press freedom by a media council stuffed full with Fidesz representatives, unscathed.

In a penetrating analysis, Mária Vásárhelyi,[8] a communications scientist and a critic of the regime, confirms that despite such cosmetic concessions on the contested media law Fidesz was indeed able to achieve its political goals unhindered: total control of the public service media sector and the rapid expansion of its own media empire by friendly oligarchs. After his own apparent Humiliation of Canossa[9] in Strasbourg, Orbán could with some justification boast before his domestic audience that 'We have successfully defended the media law and rendered the arguments of our opponents risible.'

The media authorities have placed loyal Fidesz henchmen in all key positions. Over 1,000 experienced employees (including one with five children and another in the late stages of pregnancy) were dismissed without notice; influential and popular programmes were simply cancelled. Fidesz's events manager was named director of the first TV channel (M1) whilst a man who was involved in two public scandals continued to be responsible as editor-in-chief for the news. On one occasion he had manipulated a report about a press conference given by Cohn-Bendit; on another, he had the face of the former president of the Supreme Court digitally removed from a TV report. Appearances by government members and other Fidesz politicians make up 70 per cent of the news on state TV and over 80 per cent of the daily pro-grammes on Kossuth Rádió, the national radio station; two out of three reports trumpet government triumphs, whilst two thirds of the news about the opposition deals with its failures or internal disputes.

With its total control over the public service media, the creation of a media empire run by oligarchs close to Fidesz, the intimidation of the commercial media and the government boycott on advertising in liberal and left-wing newspapers and radio stations, the governing party has succeeded in ensuring that 80 per cent of viewers and listeners receive only information provided directly or indirectly by the government. After the international storm of protest in 2011–12, the regime's approach towards the media was subtly changed. It no longer relies on relatively easily discernible legal levers but has turned to other means of manipulating the state broadcasters into becoming propagandists of the regime. This was achieved with the aid of the substantial Media Services and Support Trust Fund, whose budget was doubled to 80 billion forints (approximately €260 million) between 2010 and 2015. Light entertainment, shows and magazine programmes were purchased from pro-Fidesz media companies, primarily, at least until the beginning of 2015, from the empire set up by Orbán's close friend Lajos Simicska and his partners. Hungarians spend on average four hours a day in front of the TV, and for 80 per cent of the audience their main source of information comes from the two large commercial broadcasters RTL and TV2. Fidesz also succeeded (at least until RTL was saved by Chancellor Merkel and TV2 was taken over completely by Andy Vajna) in depoliticising these two private stations through indirect pressure, targeted interventions and discreet threats of increases in advertising taxes.

In the print media, right-wing daily and weekly newspapers supporting Fidesz have been massively subsidised by a rapid increase in public service announcements and state advertising campaigns. Thus, for example, the weekly *Heti Válasz*, founded by the spokesman of the first Orbán government, received six times as many state advertisements as the business magazine *HVG*, which has a circulation three times higher. The declining market for daily newspapers offers a similar picture. In the first half of 2012 alone, the then Fidesz mouthpiece *Magyar Nemzet* received 17 per cent of all state advertising expenditure whilst *Népszabadság*, its centre-left competitor (again with a higher circulation), had to content itself with a mere 1.5 per cent. Hír-TV, a news channel à la CNN, and Echo-TV, founded by a pro-Fidesz multimillionaire and offering content wholly defined by Fidesz programming, are likewise generously subsidised by the government. In light of the double hegemony of the state-owned media and the private empire directed by Simicska, it is understandable that the prime minister easily succeeded in presenting himself and his party as heroic representatives of the spirit of the nation, at war on all fronts.

A rich source of income has been discovered through the introduction of special taxes that flout the basic regulations of EU competition policy. These are aimed primarily at the dominant foreign banks, supermarket chains, and energy and telecommunications companies. Hungarian firms, especially those that are patrons of Fidesz, are spared such taxes. In order to bring down Hungary's deficit to under 3 per cent and reduce state indebtedness, the government has taken measures that primarily hit foreign investors and multinational concerns. The EU Commission's repeated threats of proceedings to protect democracy and the rule of law, as well as the temporary blocking of half-a-billion euros from the Cohesion Fund, only served as proof for regime propagandists of their complaints that the 'Brussels bureaucrats' have a double set of standards, one for larger states and one for smaller countries.

One of the 'unorthodox' laws most praised in the friendly media enabled the plundering of the private pension funds, which were nationalised overnight in December 2010, along with their assets of €10 billion (representing approximately 10 per cent of GDP), by the parliamentary majority. Economists point out that this money was used, without any oversight, partly to slash the budget deficit and partly for the (unsuccessful) reduction of foreign debts. The economist András Inotai has pertinently pointed to:

> the absence of or, at least, an insufficient democratic awareness in society ... The robbery of 3 million citizens would have led in any other state to mass protests and possibly to the removal (and criminal prosecution) of the government. The response of the Hungarian public was silence and apathy. From this Orbán could draw but one conclusion: if such a drastic step is possible without any counter reaction, then in such a society almost anything can be done.[10]

Inotai also points out that the anti-foreigner special taxes are supported by wide sections of society, poisoned by 'xenophobia', as well as by those domestic entrepreneurs who could not hold their own against foreign competition and who wanted to regain their lost market share. This is also the context of the 2014 land law with its retroactive provisions, which not only makes it difficult for foreigners to acquire agricultural land but also denies the existing property rights of foreign, above all Austrian, farmers.[11]

A side-effect of the nationalist-populist, right-wing course barely heeded abroad is the concerted campaign, both open and veiled, against critical reporting in foreign print and electronic media about the state of affairs in Hungary. This includes not only slanderous German language blogs and trolling in Internet fora but also regular direct interventions by Hungarian ambassadors with editors-in-chief and heads of TV stations in Germany, Austria, France and Sweden. Ernst Gelegs, the Budapest-based East European correspondent of the Austrian public broadcaster ORF, provides in his book many examples of these dubious practices.[12]

This pressure from the Orbán government on influential foreign newspapers and broadcasters has remained without effect. At home, however, between 2010 and 2014—that is, before Fidesz's latest election victory—the public service broadcasters, as well as those owned by Simicska, complacently and obediently sang paeans to the national liberation struggle, embodied as always by Viktor Orbán. Watching some of these newscasts in Budapest takes one's breath away: the degree of their similarity with the dishonest press and doctored TV reports of the communist era is chilling. The essence of news manipulation under authoritarian systems, and not only in dictatorships, is often primarily the power of silence, an invisible censorship.

The first of two examples: on the evening of 3 January 2012 the ceremony marking the introduction of the controversial Fundamental Law, which had come into force three days previously, was broadcast live on state TV from the Hungarian state opera house in Budapest. Outside, 10,000 people demonstrated on Andrássy Avenue with banners and loud chanting against the new constitution and against Orbán. Well-known artists and intellectuals gave short but passionate protest speeches. Yet, for hour after hour, public service TV showed only scenes from the official ceremony and interviews about the enormous significance of the Fundamental Law. The reporters mentioned, but almost as an aside, that 'some people' were demonstrating against the government, but there was not a single word about the protests of the EU, the USA and many international institutions at the Fundamental Law's demolition of constitutional checks and balances being celebrated with such pomp.

A second example was the total silence in the regime's media on the internationally recognised film director Béla Tarr when he won the Jury Grand Prix at the sixty-first Berlinale with his

2011 film *The Turin Horse*. The reason was simple: he had previously criticised government policy, particularly with regard to the centralisation of the film industry. Moreover, together with other famous artists such as the conductor Ádám Fischer and the pianist Sir András Schiff, Tarr had signed an 'open letter to the artists of Europe and the entire world' with an appeal to act against the media law, as well as against the growing anti-Semitism and nationalism in Hungary.[13]

From the very beginning, Orbán personally dictated the pace of the campaigns against his critics. Whether Liberals or Social Democrats, independent human rights activists or liberal artists, irrespective of their beliefs, everybody was herded into the 'left corner'. In his speeches, for instance to the European Parliament in January 2012, and in interviews, especially with German newspapers, he conjured up a major European *Kulturkampf* between, on the one hand, a left-wing International and, on the other, the champions of piety, of the traditional family model and of the nation; unsurprisingly, he identified himself with the latter. The new constitution emphasises Christianity, family and national pride as the basis of Hungarian society, hence 'the furious attacks from the camp of the international left'; Hungary is a country of freedom fighters: 'Whoever doubts our will for the rule of law and democracy, we will fight fiercely.' He is convinced that millions of EU citizens have had enough of thinking in old left-wing, ideological ways: 'They don't want to be forbidden to speak of values such as Christianity, the motherland, national pride or family. We stand for our values and our nation even if there is a headwind. And even if it reaches hurricane strength.'[14]

A year on from these 2012 interviews, a hurricane is exactly what grew in Brussels, and not only there, when the Fidesz government forced through the highly controversial fourth amendment to the constitution, clipping the wings of the constitutional court. EU Justice Commissioner Viviane Reding threatened the

Hungarian government with the invocation of Article 7 of the EU Treaty—with the withdrawal of voting rights. Then in July 2013, after a year of careful research, the Portuguese Green MEP Rui Tavares presented a devastating forty-three-page report on civil rights in Hungary to the plenum of the European Parliament. This confirmed all the accusations of the critics so blithely dismissed by Orbán as 'old left-wing conspirators'.[15]

The subsequent vote to condemn Hungary in light of the report, with 374 for, 244 against and eighty-two abstentions, represented a clear symbolic and moral defeat for Orbán, according to the American constitutional expert Kim Lane Scheppele. Only one third of MEPs were prepared to support Orbán even though the conservatives hold almost half the seats in the European Parliament.

Viviane Reding had warned in a series of interviews with Orbán that the constitution was 'not a toy', but noted with regret that the 'atom bomb' of the Article 7 withdrawal of voting rights was not applicable because opening proceedings required the approval of four-fifths of member states and a two-thirds majority in the European Parliament. The final decision would also have to be approved by all other EU member states. In a significant article published in September 2015, Reding (no longer a vice-president but still a member of the European Parliament) referred to the previous legal violations and condemned Orbán's 'fomentation of resentments', 'xenophobic stance' and 'intellectual poisoning of the well' during the refugee crisis of that summer. She concluded her passionate accusations with a call to revoke Orbán's membership of the European People's Party: 'For too long we have allowed Orbán to cross red lines. For too long we have tolerated the violation of our values. Enough is enough. Orbán's Fidesz should leave the EPP.'[16]

Nevertheless, such accusations—the counter-balance to the *Kulturkampf* unleashed by Orbán, as will be seen later in this book—is not unfavourable for his regime. In his weekly Friday broadcasts on Hungarian radio, Orbán can with some justification point to the fact that his anti-refugee measures aimed at sealing off Hungary are finding understanding in more and more countries, even being mimicked.[17] However, the price that the Hungarian people are paying for their national liberation struggle à la Orbán is high. Almost half a million (overwhelmingly young) people have emigrated to Great Britain, Germany or Austria since 2010, above all to seek better wages but also to escape the state of siege in their motherland, contrived and orchestrated by Orbán.

13

A QUESTIONABLE ELECTION VICTORY

On 6 April 2014, Prime Minister Viktor Orbán won what was by European standards an outstanding electoral victory, a renewal of his two-thirds majority. His loyalists quickly appeared on TV news and in discussion programmes where they displayed an almost provocative self-confidence whilst the Fidesz press virtually fell over itself in exultation. *Magyar Nemzet*, which was still at that time taking a pro-government line, ran the jubilant headline 'Hungary has been dipped in orange', a reference to the Fidesz Party colours.

In previous chapters we have seen how, in the years prior to his re-election, Orbán, unfazed by the justified warnings of a toothless EU, purposely set about laying the basis of an authoritarian system. The main features of this system after the first four years of Hungary's new era were: the unassailable hegemony of the right-wing print and electronic media, strengthened by the silence of private broadcasters all too anxious about their advertising revenues; direct state control of all financial and credit policy (including the National Bank) and blithe discrimination against Western investors; the politically motivated personnel purges of the judiciary, higher education and the research institutes, and growing pressures on cultural and educational policy. Against this background, the election result was undoubtedly a personal triumph for the then fifty-year-old head of government.

Nevertheless, the image of an overwhelming mandate for another four years in office deceived, for the government had actually lost about 600,000 votes since 2010, almost one quarter of its support. In that election, Orbán's party had won 53 per cent of the votes cast; in 2014 this dropped to 45 per cent. Yet despite this loss of eight percentage points (in an election where 40 per cent of the electorate abstained), Fidesz was still able to achieve exactly the number of parliamentary seats required to retain office with a two-thirds majority. Though Fidesz remained the most popular party in Hungary, Orbán was not satisfied with a simple parliamentary majority. Once again he had striven for the two thirds enabling him to make constitutional amendments at will.

How did Orbán and his party succeed in winning a two-thirds majority in parliament with the support of only one third of the electorate? This question was posed by Kim Lane Scheppele, a sociologist at Princeton University and one of the few foreign observers who can speak Hungarian. In the introduction to her study on the 2014 elections,[1] Scheppele refers first to the 'scathing' report of the OSCE (Organization for Security and Co-operation in Europe) election monitors. They noted that the Fidesz government had an 'undue advantage' in the whole election process, from writing the rules to conducting the campaign. The report documented a general failure to separate party and state, a strongly biased media landscape, a partisan electoral apparatus and an election framework pushed through parliament without any input from the opposition. The monitors found that the Hungarian government had violated a number of important OSCE standards in the way that the election was run.

Scheppele was far from alone in emphasising that the new election law, most recently amended just a year before the election, had been tailor-made solely for the benefit of Fidesz. First of all, the Fidesz majority in the 2010–14 parliament had dramatically reduced the number of MPs from the next parliament onwards from 386 to 199, and redrawn all the constituency boundaries. This gerrymandering was not a proposal discussed publicly by experts, but a policy determined exclusively by Fidesz officials. Calculations made by Political Capital, a Budapest think tank, suggest that with this redistribution of seats the left-wing alliance would have needed 300,000 more votes than Fidesz to win a majority.

The governing party both abolished the previous two-round system in the individual constituencies and facilitated the proposal of candidates by 'phantom parties' and splinter groups. This new regulation favoured the largest party, Fidesz, as the divided left-wing opposition parties had to rally in an uneasy alliance behind a common candidate in order to have any chance of winning a single constituency. Fidesz also benefited significantly from the decision of the tiny, liberal-Green LMP not to join this five-party alliance.[2] Scheppele calculates that the LMP's determination to go it alone helped the ruling party to win eleven additional seats.[3]

What cannot be disputed is the fact that with 45 per cent of the votes in the new electoral districts Fidesz won 90 per cent of the seats (96 out of 106). According to Scheppele, it secured for itself six additional seats through a transferable voting system unique in Europe. As we've seen, Hungary has a combined electoral system, in which voters cast one vote in their local constituency and another one for a party list. In most European countries, the party lists are compensated when the individual candidates of a party win votes but lose in their actual constituency. Instead of offsetting the distorting effects of the first-past-the-post system, in Hungary it is the winning parties in the individual constituencies who are also assigned the transferable votes for the party list seats. This perverse winner compensation system, peculiar to Hungary, completely undermines proportional representation.

Scheppele's judgement[4] leaves no doubt about the dubious nature of the fudged Hungarian electoral system: 'The combined effect of the gerrymander, the first-past-the-post system and the winner compensation rules, makes the Hungarian electoral system one of the most disproportionate in Europe. It turned a plurality into a supermajority.' She also points out that this is by no means the end of 'Fidesz's tricks'. There is also the question of the foreign-based vote, composed of those ethnic Hungarians resident in neighbouring countries who, on account of the 2010 law (see Chapter 9), have acquired citizenship without actually living or paying taxes in Hungary. Of 500,000 such new citizens, approximately 200,000 have registered to vote—though in fact only about 90,000 actually went to the polls in 2014. According to official but unverifiable data, 95 per cent of these votes went to Fidesz. 'Such a result is normally only achieved in countries such as North Korea,' observed Scheppele, who, like other commentators, has emphasised the curious circumstances of the hasty registration process, the postal vote and the lack of oversight in the counting procedures. At any rate these 'over-the-border' voters added about 1.5 seats to the Fidesz list, just enough to secure Orbán his two-thirds majority.[5]

In stark contrast to the generous and unregulated[6] treatment of the new 'over-the-border' citizens, the over half-a-million Hungarians working abroad in non-neighbouring countries often encountered (and still encounter) difficulties in dealing with Hungarian embassies and consulates. For those in countries such as Great Britain or Germany, voting often requires much time and money because of the difficult eligibility requirements. There is no postal vote—Hungarian citizens living abroad are only allowed to vote in person at embassies and consulates. For this reason, in 2014 only 30,000 Hungarians resident outside the country were able to register to vote. Most commentators see this as a deliberate tactic, because many of these primarily young Hungarians are critical of the regime.

The picture of this altogether bizarre election would not be complete without brief reference to the enormous preponderance of the government in the election advertising on TV and radio, in the print media and, not least, on giant billboards. Nobody who was in Hungary during the months and weeks before the election could have failed to recognise the oppressive hegemony of the right-wing media.

The absurdity of this manipulated election, organised by a 'constitutional dictatorship' (Scheppele), becomes particularly obvious when considering the simple fact, repeatedly stressed by Hungarian commentators, that Fidesz actually received fewer votes in 2014 (2.14 million) than it had in 2002 (2.31 million) and in 2006 (2.27 million). Fidesz had lost both of those elections, but following its electoral reforms was able in 2014 to gain a parliamentary supermajority with fewer votes—'by rigging the rules,' in Scheppele's words.

However, it has to be conceded that in the election Fidesz was most effectively aided by the left, specifically by the Socialist opposition. The explosive news, revealed just before election day and of course massively played up by the Fidesz media, that the party's number two, Gábor Simon, had about €800,000 stashed away in a secret bank account in Vienna utterly and finally discredited the Socialists. Neither they nor their liberal and left-wing allies were capable of presenting a clear and credible programme to win over the many voters disillusioned with Orbán. The Left Alliance, hastily cobbled together, received only 25.5 per cent of the vote, ahead of the hard right Jobbik (20.2 per cent) and the LMP (5.3 per cent).

In the four years between the two parliamentary elections, the internal struggles for power in the centre-left camp dominated media reports. Many liberal and left-wing intellectuals had seen a beacon of hope in Gordon Bajnai, who had been a successful prime minister in 2009–10—but his political activity had lasted less than two years. In the 2014 election the crowning achievement of Attila Mesterházy, the hapless head of the Socialist Party, was preventing the timely merger of the opposition groups under Bajnai's leadership. Despite his great promise and international respect, after the disappointing performance of his group Bajnai quit politics on the eve of the local elections in the autumn of 2014.

In the European Parliament elections of May 2014, just after the Hungarian parliamentary elections in April, Fidesz increased its share of the vote to 57 per cent and won twelve seats. The extreme right-wing Jobbik Party gained almost 15 per cent of the vote and three seats. The Socialists and Gyurcsány's Democratic Coalition each won two seats, whilst the Bajnai group had to content itself with just one. This surprising high-profile success of the far right—particularly in the year marking the seventieth anniversary of the mass murder of Hungarian Jews—raised concerns, and not only in Hungary itself.

The third set of elections in 2014 was the nationwide local elections, another resounding success for Fidesz. In twenty-one of the twenty-three most important towns in the country a Fidesz party member was elected mayor; in the capital Budapest, the sitting Fidesz mayor was re-elected with an increased majority. Whilst these superlative majorities were undoubtedly favoured by the election law and some shady tricks (as for example in Budapest), the scale of victory also owed much to the apathy of the population.

This unprecedented series of election victories gave rise to feelings of resignation and fear in the left-wing and liberal camps. Presenting his new government,[7] Orbán, exuding self-confidence, announced a 'new and hopeful epoch ... The next four years will be not an epoch of great ideas but one of great deeds.' Orbán had been highly successful in selling himself and his policies, by means of a kind of perpetual communications process aimed at both his domestic audience and the international public. He wanted to anchor in the public consciousness the idea that Fidesz's assumption of power was not just a normal change of government, but something that had revolutionary dimensions. Many of his voters now expected the promised and long overdue reforms of the health and education systems, and confidently looked forward to a bright new future. They were soon to get the shock of their lives.

14

THE PRICE OF 'ORBÁNISATION'

Despite the successful establishment of a centrally directed authoritarian system, Hungary remains a country of surprises. Within a few months of the 2014 election triumph there was a rapid reversal in the general mood. Many reasons lay behind this: serious misjudgements on taxation and domestic policies; murky corruption affairs; the dramatic split between Viktor Orbán and his oldest friend, the media mogul Lajos Simicska; tensions in relations with the USA and, to cap it all, the Hungarian premier ingratiating himself with Vladimir Putin. Even before the end of 2014 pollsters were unanimous that Orbán, the 'strongman of Central Europe', could no longer get his own way in everything.

An unparalleled wave of protests began at the end of October 2014 after the prime minister, evidently blinded by his recent election success, announced that his minister for economic affairs had submitted a draft law for the introduction of a new Internet tax (as always, without any prior or wider discussion in public). In the country with the highest rate of VAT in Europe (27 per cent), the initiative led to passionate protests by young urban Internet users. More than 10,000 angry people took to the streets holding candles and waving banners or EU flags. The anti-government demonstrators had been quickly and efficiently organised not by one of the opposition parties but by a spontaneously organised independent Facebook group (Hundred Thousand Against the Internet Tax). In view of the surprisingly resilient mass demonstrations and the promise of further protests, Orbán personally withdrew the controversial bill three days after it was proposed on 28 October.

The revolt against the Internet tax coincided with an unusual scandal in the relations between Washington and Budapest. It became known through a deliberate leak in a pro-Fidesz newspaper that the USA had imposed a travel ban on six high-ranking government civil servants and businessmen close to Orbán because of their involvement in corrupt practices that were damaging to American investors. Among those banned was Ildikó Vida, the head of the National Tax and Customs Administration since 2010, along with members of her staff.[1] The reports about this strange affair strengthened the feeling among Hungarians that groups of oligarchs in receipt of state favours were orbiting around Orbán and Simicska, like cancer tumours eating their way slowly but surely into the tissues of society and the state. Almost weekly until the end of the year, thousands demonstrated on the streets, mobilised through Facebook and buoyed up by their victory against the failed experiment of an Internet tax.

Pollsters were all in agreement that, in the course of just two months (October and November 2014), Fidesz lost twelve percentage points—the support of around 900,000 voters. Orbán's popularity plummeted from 48 to 32 per cent. Leading foreign newspapers wrote of 'nervousness and cracks' in the Fidesz camp.[2] On 17 November in Budapest and other cities, over 25,000 people participated in demonstrations under the banner of a 'day of general outrage' against corruption, welfare cuts and the growing arrogance of the new power elite. The demonstrators demanded Orbán's resignation, and continued their protests into December and January 2015. At the beginning of February, thousands protested in front of parliament, calling on the German chancellor, Angela Merkel, to exhort Orbán to defend European values during her visit to Budapest the following day. The pro-Russian policy was also attacked at many demonstrations. President Vladimir Putin's visit to Budapest, just two weeks after Merkel's, symbolised the Fidesz government's demonstrative rapprochement with Russia. The individual initiatives were coordinated on social media, via email, Twitter and Facebook, by young students, trade unionists and, often, hitherto apolitical citizens.

In just five months, between December 2014 and April 2015, Orbán's party lost nine out of eleven regional and communal elections. The most serious setback was the loss of the precarious two-thirds parliamentary majority after the surprising byelection victory of independent opposition candidate Zoltán Kész in the west Hungarian town of Veszprém; the standing MP, Tibor Navracsics, had been named EU Commissioner. The supermajority, decisive for constitutional amendments, had depended on a single vote, lost simply because during the February byelection one in two former Fidesz voters stayed at home.[3] In other words, the government's defeat in no way represented the recovery of the opposition, which remained as divided as ever, but reflected its own declining popularity.

Then, just eight weeks after this major unexpected setback for Fidesz, the Orbán regime suffered what a foreign correspondent called a second 'slap in the face'. In a byelection in the western town of Tapolca following the death of its MP, a candidate of the extreme right-wing Jobbik Party (founded in 2003) won a direct parliamentary seat with a clear majority. Thus for the first time since the Second World War in a free democratic election the candidate of a party which, following a court ruling,[4] can be called neo-Nazi, entered the Hungarian parliament after a free democratic election.

During a visit to Budapest in those weeks I perceived a deep sense of despair on the left, helplessness amongst liberals, secret anxiety in the Jewish community and an almost astonishing change of mood in some hitherto pro-Fidesz media. In the smaller towns and villages particularly, a series of corruption scandals had often lain behind the clear shift towards Jobbik. After its 'historic victory', the thirty-six-year-old leader of the party, Gábor Vona, quickly distanced himself from right-wing extremism and openly called upon anti-Semitic and anti-Roma members to leave the party. As with Marine Le Pen and the Front National in France or the Freedom Party (FPÖ) in Austria, Vona wants to play down the right-wing extremist messages and present Jobbik as a respectable alternative for middle-class voters disillusioned by rampant state and party corruption. The writer and journalist Rudolf Ungváry has observed that 'right-wing extremist elements, fascists, [form] the basis of Jobbik, even if these are far fewer than the number of [Jobbik] voters'. The broad mass of people only sees them as young men who have not lied. And for them this suffices as a political standard.

After an unfortunate spring for the ruling party, with a string of corruption and financial scandals and the wanton recklessness of certain Orbán loyalists, some opinion pollsters and sociologists began to anticipate an unstoppable rise in Jobbik's popularity. The petty corruption, promoted and politically instrumentalised by the state, and ranging from the carefully regulated allocation of lucrative concessions for the National Tobacco Shops to the distribution of leases of state-owned land, only excited attention within Hungary itself. However, the collapse of several financial services providers (Buda Cash and Hungaria), above all the brokerage firm Quaestor (which was closely associated with the Foreign Ministry), was already attracting interna-

tional interest. Almost 100,000 savers and investors were estimated to have been affected by the failure of Quaestor, which
had launched fictitious bonds amounting to half-a-billion euros.
Several ministries, in particular the Foreign Ministry, had deposits with the firm, some of which were withdrawn a few hours
before its insolvency became public. There were contradictory
statements about the total failure of the financial supervisory
authorities and even about the exact point in time of the direct
intervention by the prime minister, who had instructed government departments to remove their deposits from the brokerage
firm. Orbán stated that he had ordered the withdrawal of public
money after the insolvency of Buda Cash. The public had not
been informed to avoid panic breaking out. The arrest of
Quaestor's boss, his wife and his closest associate, all of whom
had a good relationship with Fidesz, only took place three weeks
after the announcement of the bankruptcy.[5]

The government had to retreat not only on the Internet tax
but also in the battle about the discriminatory top marginal tax
rate on advertising revenues. As with the banking taxes, special
taxes and other regulations for supermarket chains, this primarily affected foreign firms. The maximum top rate, retrospectively
imposed on the private broadcaster RTL-Klub (a subsidiary of
the German RTL group) in the summer of 2014 and raised to
50 per cent that November, not only sparked off strong protests
by the company itself but also led to sharply critical comments in
the international media. It was an open secret that Fidesz politicians considered RTL's regular main evening news coverage of
the numerous financial and corruption scandals involving government departments or high-ranking officials to be the single most
important reason for the party's election defeats and the government's precipitous fall in popularity. The German broadcaster
(majority-owned by the giant Bertelsmann corporation) has by
far the largest audience in the country, due to the quality of its
entertainment programming.

RTL filed a complaint with the EU Commission, which launched an investigation on the grounds of suspicion of discrimination. During her flying visit to Budapest Chancellor Merkel met with representatives of the most important German companies, including the RTL group, and discussed their complaints regarding the discriminatory special taxes. This, together with the intervention of the EU, contributed to the abolition of the controversial tax by parliament at the end of May 2015 and the introduction of a uniform tax rate of 5.3 per cent. The RTL group withdrew its complaint from the EU Commission. Rumours of a horse trade—a watering down of political news reporting in exchange for a relaxation of the tax laws—have not been substantiated.

These political developments provide the framework for the changes, staggering even to experienced observers, described here. But our main focus is the figure behind it all, Viktor Orbán. 'Our freedom is as great as our power,' Orbán said during his first period in office.[6] In possession of the two-thirds majority between April 2010 and February 2015, his actions reflected the unmistakable characteristics that have shaped his entire political career. Gregor Mayer, the seasoned Budapest correspondent for a number of Austrian and German media organisations, identified very clearly both during the demonstrations and before the election defeats the reasons for the change in mood in the late autumn of 2014. 'The steam roller's motor is sputtering, because after his election triumph in the spring, instead of consolidating his gains, Orbán has opened up new battlefronts in the political war.'[7] Most other politicians in the recent history of Hungary, after such unprecedented successes, would have rested on their well-deserved laurels. This, however, would have been almost inconceivable for the victorious but highly emotional Orbán.

At the end of July 2014 he had delivered a public speech at the usual summer meeting of young ethnic Hungarians in Romania.

THE PRICE OF 'ORBÁNISATION'

This address gained notoriety worldwide for its strident and undisguised tone, as Orbán threw off the mask of a democrat and finally revealed his true colours as an admirer of nationalistic, populist and authoritarian regimes. In it Orbán declared his total rejection of liberal democracy and announced his aim of establishing an 'illiberal state'. He mentioned Russia, Turkey and China as shining examples of success.[8] The dramatic shift towards Putin's Russia and the attacks on Washington for its travel ban on Hungarian civil servants—a conspiracy, the Orbán regime claimed, aimed at 'regime change' in Hungary—led to sharp rebukes in both the EU and the USA.

For Orbán, as a rule, personal admonitions and attacks are never an occasion for reflection, but rather for an aggressive reaction. According to Tamás Sárközy, he is courageous and remorseless. 'He never asks for mercy and he never gives it.' Like many other observers Sárközy admires Orbán's tremendous fighting spirit. He is always to be found on the front line; a long-term weighing up of the risks in the heat of battle is not his strong point. Exaggerations, at times the gravest violations of any sense of proportion, are recurring features of his sweeping declarations.[9] A similar conclusion is reached by the publisher and author János Gyurgyák, who has known the prime minister since they worked together on the Bibó College magazine *Századvég* in the mid-1980s, and considers Orbán 'the greatest political talent of his generation'. One discrepancy is characteristic:

> He acts very well in situations coming to a head, in the solving of conflicts, through strength, in election campaigns; yet, how vulnerable and how unsuccessful he is in daily events, in the minutiae of government, in the selection of his staff, in the motivation of an efficient and well cooperating team, in assigning tasks.[10]

These mild words of criticism came from the mouth of the man who had rewritten and shaped the famous speech Orbán delivered at Heroes' Square in 1989. Three years after this 2013 interview, Gyurgyák was far more sceptical about Orbán's fundamental ideas of establishing a total political hegemony of the right, stressing that the attempt to completely eliminate the Hungarian left, which has always been one of the faces of the nation, would almost certainly fail. Ultimately, this was a battle that could not be won. At the same time Gyurgyák rejected the assertion that, by exploiting its huge majority, Fidesz would like to restore the Horthy regime of the interwar years. Orbán's practice of government had a modern character and it followed no historical example. Gyurgyák noted: 'Although his practice of government undoubtedly strives for the concentration of power and although some autocratic features are undeniable, in my opinion these spring from the personality of the head of government, from his impatience, his loneliness, from his by no means unfounded grievances and his extreme mistrust.'[11]

These characteristics complement possibly the most important quality of a born political leader—namely, his effective force to carry something through, without which there is nothing. Orbán is not a team player, but a leader who trusts only in his own strength and demands absolute loyalty from his friends and associates. That even in power he has remained a fighter at heart is shown by his words in an off-the-record and very revealing speech given to students at the Bibó College, in the very hall where thirty years previously Fidesz had been founded. The students asked him for his opinion about the prime ministers of the future. Orbán replied:

Politics is a battle. The most important quality of the premier of the country would have to be the ability to cope with smears. You have to put up with them or ward them off or strike back even harder. Whoever takes their opponents' attacks personally or translates them into their own personal moral catalogue of values is a loser and that doesn't work in a battle. The leader who cannot put up with slanders, who suffers from them, who is emotionally offended or who makes a moral dilemma out of them is unsuitable. If I stand in the field with a big sword in my hand and three people attack me, then I cannot start moralising or arguing; then there is only one task, slaughter all three of them. To endure all that is a talent that cannot be learned.[12]

In the course of this dialogue with the students Orbán repeatedly returned to the themes of character assassination and vilification. This, he said, was why he did not have women in his government, because they would not be able to bear such attacks. He further mentioned personal attacks aimed at him in the past as an example of how election campaigns and smear campaigns are two different things. His wife had had to appear and smile before the TV cameras because the communists had spread a story in all media outlets that he had hit her so hard that she had bled. There had been a book published about him to coincide with the elections in 2002. About 90 per cent of the text was given over to how he, Orbán, had allegedly raped women at the Bibó College. The aim, according to Orbán, had been 'the destruction of the moral basis of your very existence ... That you can never again appear before the people as a trustworthy, honest citizen.'[13]

Orbán also returned several times to the theme of the perils for women in politics. That such patriarchal attitudes can be turned seamlessly into exaggerated macho claims of male superiority is demonstrated by a distasteful speech given by the speaker of parliament, László Kövér, at a Fidesz party congress, which caused a great deal of offence. 'The crowning of the personal fulfilment of women is that they give birth to as many grandchildren as possible for us.'[14] It is therefore no wonder that there are no female ministers to be found in the Fidesz government and that the percentage of women in the Fidesz-dominated Hungarian parliament, a mere 9.5 per cent, is the lowest in the EU. Among the 133 Fidesz MPs there are only nine women.

During this relaxed informal meeting with students at his old college, Orbán, at the time only fifty-two, willingly replied to their questions about the ideal character traits of a future prime minister. But he left no doubt that he still saw 'enormous possibilities' for himself and that he wanted to remain active 'for quite a few years' yet. Indeed, his speeches and interviews in recent years have radiated an exaggerated self-confidence, complacency and conceit. An interview given in *The Wall Street Journal Europe* on 13 July 2013, notable for the prime minister's choice of words, revealed that success had not left him untouched:

People like me would like to do something meaningful, something extraordinary. History grants me this opportunity ... In the leadership position I have always been confronted with historic challenges ... In a crisis you don't need governance by institutions. What is needed is somebody who tells the people that risky decisions must be taken ... and who says to them follow me ... Now strong national leaders are required.

Two-and-a-half years later, in the middle of the refugee crisis in Europe (and after his second victory at the polls in April 2014), Orbán stated with unmistakable hubris in a Christmas interview with the new Fidesz newspaper *Magyar Idők* that 'In the great crisis Europe made a bad choice, under the illusion that the era of personalities such as Kohl, Aznar, Sarkozy etc. has passed. That is the root of the problem. If something goes in the wrong direction, bureaucracies can no longer react. Then you need strong personalities.' He did not add 'one like me', but his meaning was crystal clear. He, Viktor Orbán, is such a strong man, one whose time has not passed but who, on the contrary, is only now maturing for his great deeds.

For a man with such ambitions and such an unprecedented personal concentration of power, the second electoral triumph in 2014 made it increasingly intolerable for Orbán to share decision-making in economic, personnel and media policy decisions (not to speak of the division of spoils) and to cooperate with Lajos Simicska, his oldest and most reliable friend of thirty-five years. Despite Orbán's indisputable political talents, Fidesz as a party would long since have sunk into oblivion without, in the words of the political scientist László Lengyel, the 'brilliant mafioso' Lajos Simicska. Without Simicska, Orbán would never have become prime minister and without Orbán, Simicska would never have become a billionaire. It was an alliance, a tried and tested male friendship between two equals.

This was the conclusion reached by Lengyel after the open rupture between the two men: Orbán and Simicska had broken a cardinal rule, and had turned on each other. There was no longer any honour among the rogues. And in this rift Lengyel also saw the end of strength through unity, of the unitary Fidesz centre—from now on, within Fidesz, everybody can rob everybody else, and anybody can put anybody under pressure. According to Lengyel, Orbán lost two of his best friends within six months: László Kövér and Lajos Simicska. They were the last two people who could speak openly with him—but nobody is allowed to be on an equal footing with Orbán, nobody may be completely frank. Though this analysis may well be correct, at the time of writing (2017), Kövér, at least to all appearances, remains in power and in office.[15]

What had happened? Why, after thirty-five years, did this friendship between two men once as thick as thieves, who had gone through everything together, fall apart? Lajos Simicska, after all, was the man who was always in the background and who, as the architect of the pro-Fidesz financial, construction and media empires, had made possible the development of Orbán's unlimited power. Simicska was also a man who never gave interviews and of whom there were scarcely any photographs. The political earthquake within the Orbán regime was thus all the greater and unexpected when, on 6 February 2015, he levelled virulent personal attacks against the prime minister in a series of TV and media interviews using some of the most vulgar verbal abuse possible in the Hungarian language.[16]

In a long interview with the liberal weekly *Magyar Narancs*, Simicska accused Orbán of wanting to establish a new dictatorship. 'My alliance with Orbán proceeded from the assumption that we wanted to tear down the dictatorship and the post-communist system. But in this alliance there was never, damn it, any idea that we would instead set up a new dictatorship. I am not a partner to this.' Simicska bitterly rejected Orbán's pro-Russian foreign and energy policies, his media policy and the planned advertising tax on all media companies. For him, Orbán had proved a great personal disappointment: 'He is not a statesman.' Simicska also made it clear that he could barely discern any real difference between the behaviour of the Soviets in the past and that of present-day Russia. He revealed that the perceptible cooling of his relationship with Orbán went back to a conversation in April 2014 after the election victory, in which the prime minister outlined to him unspecified ideas for the future. Simicska did not like these and told Orbán that he did not want to be his partner in them.[17]

Despite Simicska's assertions, this all-out war between the former closest of friends was not—or not primarily—a question of differing values, but of concrete conflicts of interest. Even shortly before the 2014 election, there were rumours of a deep split in the structures of the Orbán regime. The minister for development, a Simicska loyalist of many years standing, was removed. In the new appointments to both the central and regional administrations, of those responsible for the allocation of public contracts and the distribution of EU money, Fidesz officials not loyal to Simicska were given jobs. In the Ministry for Development alone, 200 people were replaced. The prime minister more or less openly indicated to friendly politicians and oligarchs that Simicska had become too mighty for him. He is reported once to have said in an informal conversation with foreign ambassadors, 'I have learnt. If you have an opportunity to eliminate your rivals, then don't think about it, do it.'[18] After Simicska's media (the daily *Magyar Nemzet*, the news channel HírTV, Lánchíd Radio and the weekly *Heti Válasz*) had begun to criticise individual government measures, Orbán hit back with his announcement that they could no longer count on receiving advertising from state-owned and state-affiliated enterprises.

Simicska's unprecedented outburst against Orbán was provoked by the simultaneous and totally unexpected resignation of his six top media managers and editors-in-chief for 'reasons of conscience', announced on 6 February 2015. This pincer movement against the Simicska empire was planned well in advance and ruthlessly executed. Its consequences were not limited to an upheaval in the media world. On the one hand, a new media empire, completely controlled by Orbán's people, was set up, in part with the aid of these 'traitors' (Simicska's description) who had jumped ship; on the other, there were to be no more public contracts, not only for Simicska's media empire but also for his construction company Közgép. Thanks to his contacts within government, it is estimated that since 2010 Simicska and his partners had won about 40 per cent of all tenders in which EU transfers to Hungary were awarded; these amounted to several billion euros.[19]

Orbán now set about restructuring the Hungarian economy by calling on oligarchs dependent on his favour, as well as enlisting some new ones. In this he was aided by two men personally loyal to him, the ministers János Lázár and Antal Rogán, at the head of the hugely expanded Prime Minister's Office. They worked hand-in-hand with his loyal supporter in the central bank, the former finance minister György Matolcsy, in politically and financially destroying the shady empire of the brilliant financial juggler, Simicska. This reorganisation executed through his subordinates, at times quite brutally, was not without its problems for Orbán. For the moment, at the height of his tirades against

Orbán, Simicska remained combative. 'I have known Orbán for thirty-five years. Yes, I know a lot about him,' he told *Magyar Narancs*. To the reporters' question as to whether that did not imply a political risk for the prime minister, his answer was: 'And if somebody shoots me for this? [Laughs.] Let's hope it won't come to that.' That the media mogul even mentioned the possibility of an assassination attempt in several interviews highlights Hungarian realities. Today, Simicska's construction and media empire is in inexorable decline. Nevertheless, with his intimate knowledge of Orbán's career and the financial circumstances of his family, Lajos Simicska, a man who likes to drink, remains a potential danger for Hungary's strongman.

The three elections defeats of 1994, 2002 and 2006 failed to rock the unity of the small group of men who founded Fidesz, but in 2014 its epochal second victory did. Its paradoxical consequence has been the combination of the open rift between Orbán and Simicska, the two strongest personalities in the erstwhile leadership circle, and the gradual stripping of power and influence from other well-known members of the Fidesz old guard.

The deceptive unity that endured after the earlier electoral defeats ultimately cracked because the architect of the later victories claimed absolute power. Viktor Orbán is today no longer *primus inter pares*, but the uncontested leader of the country. There has certainly never, in the history of Hungary since the collapse of the Dual Monarchy in 1918, been another figure who has concentrated so much power within himself in such a relatively short time, virtually unchallenged. By international standards, Orbán is still a relatively young man. This personal concentration of power, unique in the EU, is shaping the emergence of a new elite, which—as in medieval times—is in part built on the feudal rights conferred by Orbán; moreover, it is entirely moulding Hungary's foreign, economic and social policies.

15

POWER, GREED AND CORRUPTION

Viktor Orbán himself once said, 'In politics everything is possible.' This he has demonstrated with his own staggering rise from utter poverty in Felcsút to his supreme and unchallenged position in Budapest. However, the warning given in the House of Lords by the Earl of Chatham, William Pitt (1708–78), is more pertinent than ever in modern Hungary: 'Unlimited power is apt to corrupt the minds of those who possess it.' Almost a century later the British historian Lord Acton (1834–1902) put it even more succinctly in his oft quoted letter to Bishop Mandell Creighton: 'Power tends to corrupt and absolute power corrupts absolutely.'[1] The personal attacks of opposition spokesmen and the independent media against the Hungarian prime minister on account of his family's alleged fabulous enrichment and the notable number of privileged oligarchs among his friends underscore the doubts as to whether Orbán can still learn how to deal with power without succumbing to it completely.

The order that has evolved in the last seven years under Orbán is a system sui generis. Before the election in 2010, for example, Orbán personally vetted and handpicked every candidate (in other words, the subsequent Fidesz MPs) at his home at Felcsút. He leads the party alone, with lightweights as deputies, and without any controlling body. One of his oldest but intellectually shallowest friends serves him as the nominal leader of the Fidesz group in parliament. The annual lists of the most influential Hungarians reflect the ups and downs in the careers of former and current figures in politics, business and the media. Their rise or fall depends not on talent or performance but primarily on their personal relationships with, as well as absolute loyalty to, Orbán. The revolt of his powerful and potentially most dangerous former friend and ally, the impetuous Lajos Simicska, has merely served to increase the prime minister's general sense of mistrust of associates who have become too powerful or too ambitious. This conflict and the subsequent purge of Simicska's people from the bureaucracy have without doubt strengthened Orbán's tendency to skilfully play the strongest figures in his immediate circle off against each other. Even before the 2014 election triumph the Polish author Igor Janke,[2] himself a genuine admirer of Orbán, cited unnamed staff members who claimed that the Hungarian head of government is:

> a ruthless chess player of power politics, who has concentrated immense power in his own hands, power that he is unwilling to share, and that is extraordinarily dangerous ... Inwardly, he is full of passions which are not visible on the outside ... He plays chess with the people around him but in such a way that they cannot endanger his own position ... He takes good care that all substantive decisions remain in his hands and he is not choosy about his methods.

Quoting off-the-record remarks from other Fidesz insiders, Janke illustrates how Orbán has, step by step, deprived his deputy and former parliamentary leader Tibor Navracsics of power, in favour of the emerging young talent János Lázár, as well as insidiously promoting the rivalry between the two finance ministers György Matolcsy and Mihály Varga.[3]

These characteristics, pronounced ever more strongly in the course of the seven years in power, have shaped not only the methods employed by the Fidesz apparatus in the struggle against the disloyal Simicska but also the selection, promotion and, if necessary, punishment of favourites suspected of similar disloyalty. There is no better evidence for the impotence of the current opposition parties than the fact that, with very few exceptions, the corruption scandals linked to the Orbán regime have primarily been uncovered by courageous journalists or persistent, independent local politicians.

Everything that has taken place since 2010 within the ranks of the regime elite recalls the famous saying of the French premier François Guizot (1787–1874), who, instead of lowering the income threshold required to vote, formulated the cynical maxim of the July Monarchy by exhorting the French people to 'enrich' themselves. Orbán, of course, has not expressed himself in such words. Yet, András Lánczi, a so-called theorist close to him, has provided a profoundly cynical explanation matching Guizot's for the nature of the regime's policy, one that has been frequently quoted during subsequent political controversies in Hungary. 'What is called corruption is actually Fidesz's supreme policy. What I mean by this is that the government has set for itself goals such as the establishment of a group of domestic entrepreneurs, the building of the pillars of a strong Hungary.'[4] Lánczi, president of the controversial Fidesz think tank Századvég, which has received billions from the government propaganda machine, added that 'if something is done in the national interest, then it is not corruption. For Fidesz it is a matter of strengthening the domestic entrepreneurial class. About this they say that it is corruption itself. This is a political perspective, what has happened here is that the word corruption has become mythical.' In another interview Lánczi took as an example the post-1948 nationalisations and the post-1989 privatisations, which were not defined as theft. 'Now too there is a system which may be criticised as corruption, but I maintain that that is the attainment of a political idea.'⁵

This is also very much the case of the Hungarian National Bank, which has become the focus of alleged scandals barely conceivable in the West. The main responsibility is borne by its governor, György Matolcsy, a man Orbán has never had any hesitation in promoting to new top positions.

Who would ever have thought that, of all institutions, a central bank—the supposedly unimpeachable custodian of sound finances and the strict controller of banking—would in 2015 become the centre of a scandal that raised eyebrows abroad, caused by the adventurous initiatives and activities of its governor? At the heart of the affair lay the assets of six foundations established by the National Bank worth 260 billion forints (more than €830 million). What aroused the suspicions of the media and opposition was the secrecy shrouding the whole business, made possible by a piece of legislation smoothly enacted by the Fidesz majority in parliament. The government and the Bank's governor Matolcsy argued that the foundations were private institutions not subject to public scrutiny. After the resulting uproar, President Áder passed the matter to the constitutional court for an assessment. This was one of the rare occasions when he refused to sign a law without any further ado. The court ruled that the foundations' finances must be made public. They had to publish lists of their bizarre subsidies and curious business transactions. Thus, thanks to some enterprising journalists and the protests of the opposition, the wider public came to learn of some hair-raising details about the way taxpayers' money is handled in Hungary.⁶

The six foundations and five further subsidiaries were managed exclusively, hence without any external scrutiny, by National Bank governor György Matolcsy, his confidants and by trusted high-ranking officials of the bank. Particular outrage was caused by Matolcsy's personal involvement. NHB, a previously insignificant banking house owned by his cousin Tamás Szemerey, became the greatest beneficiary of bond purchases and securities accounts. Szemerey ranks as number fifty in the list of the richest Hungarians. His wife is the CEO of the biggest foundation, of which Matolcsy himself is president. Another son worked for a longer period in a bank owned by the National Bank. Further details have also emerged about the lucrative and often obscure transactions of the far-flung Szemerey family, while Matolcsy has claimed in an interview to have over 100 cousins worldwide.

Public reaction was even more hostile when it was revealed that the book written by Matolcsy's former secretary about the wondrous policies of her boss as finance minister, together with the foreign language version of a publication from one of the foundations, had received substantial subsidies. Additionally, the foundation of which Matolcsy is president purchased a printed selection of his own newspaper articles at an inflated price. The book incidentally lacked an ISBN number and failed to identify either its publisher or printer.

Much money flowed into the acquisition and renovation of real estate such as office blocks, villas and hotels; the purchase of wine cellars was also considered. Moreover, the foundations turned out to be generous patrons of those authors and journalists who churned out sycophantic articles about Orbán and his government policies, mixed with poisonous attacks on his opponents. The lists of grant recipients also featured an Internet news site, TV stations, construction companies and advertising agencies of the cronies around Matolcsy and Orbán.

It is very unlikely that the protests and complaints about this abuse of public money and the concerns expressed by the European Central Bank in its annual report on the lavish spending of the foundations will be crowned with any success. The wife of

Hungary's chief prosecutor Péter Polt was made director of human resources in the National Bank in 2014; Polt himself, a close confidant of the prime minister for many years, is on the boards of two foundations, one of them as chairman. Confident in his total backing by the prime minister, Matolcsy could allow himself to mock the attacks as 'blah blah'. Orbán was quick on this and subsequent occasions to declare his unwavering trust in Matolcsy: 'heaven and earth would have to collide' before he would condemn the governor. Thus, Matolcsy remains unchallenged in his position as the regime's number four and can, with the complaisant support of his boss, continue to freely dispose of the parked government securities and the interest earned from them.

The Fidesz ideologue András Lánczi has maintained that the activities of the National Bank regarding the foundations are 'part of a political concept and do not belong to the world of immorality'. Such a statement is in no way astonishing, but rather quite natural and even logical. The Századvég Foundation, of which Lánczi was until recently president, is said, with its various subsidies, to be the transmission belt for the Orbán regime's covert communications and lobbying activities. Here too an attempt has been made to keep commissions and documents secret; only after a decision of the Supreme Court did Századvég deign belatedly, and only partially, to publish them. The previous incarnation and forerunner of this think tank (whose name literally means 'end of the century') was the student magazine founded by István Stumpf in 1985, which became seven years later an 'intellectual workshop where research, education, and publication are done simultaneously'.[7]

After the Fidesz victory in 2010, Századvég evolved, as a private company, into the government's central planning and communications office. Since then, together with two other sister institutions for economic research and planning (Strategopolis) it has received, according to the estimates of *atlatszo.hu*, public contracts worth €40 million from the National Bank, the Ministry for National Development, the Ministry for International Development and the Prime Minister's Office. By the summer of 2016, after the Supreme Court decision on disclosure, contracts to the value of €15 million had been made public. After the all-too-familiar delaying tactics of an appeal, documents of first 30,000 and eventually 70,000 pages were published—far beyond the anticipated 1,600. Critics assume that the projects were usually determined only after the money had been transferred.[8] The National Bank, for example, concluded a €6 million contract with Századvég for the provision of various studies, despite the fact that the think tank has at its disposal a large number of experts, and that another prestigious institute had submitted a considerably lower offer of €4 million.

These lucrative institutions maintain a close relationship with the government. A former research director shuttles between the foundation and the government as its official speaker, the vice-president was named the Hungarian ambassador to London and the Fidesz visionary Lánczi was elected rector of the respected Corvinus University in Budapest. His son Tamás remains in a key function as a research director at Századvég. After the purchase of the economic weekly *Figyelö* by a Fidesz oligarch and the resignation of its senior editors, Lánczi Jnr was appointed its editor-in-chief in February 2017.

One of the most mysterious figures in Orbán's court, Árpád Habony, is said to have played the key role in the 'informal control' of the whole group.[9] This forty-nine-year-old communications expert is said to be perhaps the prime minister's closest and without any doubt most influential personal media adviser. More than ever since the rift with Simicska and the government boycott of his media empire, Habony, a man shrouded in secrecy, has been the central and secret controller of all government communications, answerable only to Orbán personally. Nevertheless, he never appears at public events, refuses all requests for interviews and has absolutely no official position. In reply to journalists' questions, Orbán himself has more than once said that 'this person' is not employed in any government post and for this reason he cannot give any information about him. Absurdly, Habony's activities are treated by Orbán himself and by all government spokespersons as a kind of classified state secret, even though there are photographs and videos of this invariably casually dressed man in the presence of the prime minister. In the list of the most influential people in Hungary, Habony, this 'not official person' is to be found in sixth place, ahead of most ministers; among the country's most important media figures, he is ranked third.

A man who has Orbán's ear, he has also become a media entrepreneur. Together with the controversial American media guru Arthur J. Finkelstein,[10] he recently founded a joint venture in London, Danube Business Consulting Ltd. Its director is Tamás Lánczi, the same Tamás Lánczi who is research director of the Századvég Foundation, which is fed millions of forints by Hungarian government bodies. Almost at the same time, in May 2016, Habony showed up together as co-owner, with a former secretary of state, of a new media concern in Budapest, Modern Media Group.[11] This group runs the Internet portal *888.hu* and, since the beginning of June 2016, has published a new free daily and weekly newspaper called *Lokál* with an initial circulation of 300,000. This replaces *Metropol*, another free newspaper, which was closed following the withdrawal of government advertising. Like its predecessor, *Lokál* is supported by large advertising contracts from government bodies and from firms headed by Fidesz supporters.

Independent commentators have speculated as to the source of Habony's money for the funding of the new company: officially he has no demonstrable income. Between 2009 and 2013 the film and media mogul Andy Vajna is supposed to have lent him two instalments totalling $150,000, and another pro-Fidesz businessman $70,000, interest-free for seven years. Habony is doubtless the most colourful personality in Orbán's orbit. In contrast to the almost pathological secrecy surrounding his true activities as the *éminence grise*, he has been photographed in a nightclub in Ibiza; his ex-wife, incidentally, set up Orbán's website. Habony has a weakness for expensive sports clothes and for fast cars. He was three times the Hungarian champion in kendo, the modern version of Japanese sword fighting. He also demonstrated his aggressive propensities in a rather unusual way in 2012 when he attacked a married couple allegedly walking too slowly in front of his car, knocking down the man and hitting the woman in the stomach. A Budapest municipal court gave him a suspended sentence of two years in prison for disorderly conduct. This incident did not prevent his friend, the director of Budapest's Museum of Fine Arts, from not only acting as a witness at Habony's wedding but also allowing him to celebrate it in the museum. He also loaned Habony, free of any charge, a number of valuable paintings from the museum's collection to hang in a flat that he used.[12]

Even more impressive has been the stellar career of the seventy-two-year-old former film producer Andy Vajna, who today is ranked the fifth most influential Hungarian and the second most important media personality; his estimated wealth of approximately €150 million puts him sixteenth on the list of the hundred richest Hungarians. He left Hungary with his parents in 1956 and grew up in Los Angeles. After an eventful early career as a photographer and hairdresser, he produced wigs and blue jeans with a partner in Hong Kong. Since the mid-1970s, Vajna has been a successful film producer in Hollywood; his action films *Rambo* and *Total Recall* were major box office hits. His close personal relationship with Orbán goes back to the

1990s when the young Fidesz MP stayed with him during a trip to the USA.

Though he had founded a number of companies in Hungary in the years following 1989, Vajna's meteoric ascent into the ranks of Hungary's oligarchs began only after Orbán's 2010 election victory. As government commissioner for the entire film industry with practically unlimited powers since 2011, Vajna contributed to the financing (and thereby to the Oscar triumph) of *Son of Saul*, the shocking Holocaust film made by the young director László Nemes Jeles. After this success, the prime minister described Vajna, himself a Jew, as 'one of the most courageous Hungarians'.

In 2013 Vajna succeeded in obtaining (without the necessity of any tendering process) five out of seven concessions for casinos from the Orbán government. His first, Las Vegas Casino Kft., alone brought him a dividend of €10 million. His five casinos are estimated to have earned him total profits of €50 million in 2015, money which, via various offshore companies including some in London, landed in the accounts of the Andrew G. Vajna Revocable Trust, which he controls. Together with his Hungarian wife, Vajna is also (via a financing group registered in Budapest) involved in the purchase of diamonds, in the hospitality industry and in the organisation of beauty contests.

But to date Vajna's most important and politically explosive project was the taking over of the second largest TV channel, TV2, on 15 October 2015 by his company Magyar Broadcasting Co. Kft., which he had founded only just before this. This transaction seems to confirm the observation that the difference between Silvio Berlusconi and Viktor Orbán is that Berlusconi gained political power through his media empire, while Orbán used his political predominance to set up his own reliable media apparatus (with the active support of compliant oligarchs).

The TV2 affair was primarily a battle with the weakened but still active Simicska group, which Vajna won with the help of vast financial means. He admitted himself that TV2 would face a loss of €15 million in 2015, adding that it would first make a profit in three to five years. Nevertheless, at the end of November 2015 Vajna had been granted a credit amounting to €22 million for the purchase of the loss-making channel, and then, in April 2016, a further injection of €4 million for the current programme budget. These sums of money, enormous by Hungarian standards, had been made available to him by the state-owned Export-Import Bank. As this bank is principally intended to promote foreign trade and the exports of domestic entrepreneurs, this more than generous support for TV2 caused a political scandal. However, the government pointed to a 2013 change in the law whereby the state bank is allowed to finance domestic investments if the companies receiving the support are able to use them to improve their international competitiveness. A mere 2 per cent of TV2 revenues come from exports.

With these huge amounts of state money, TV2 proceeded to set up ten new entertainment and sports channels. The dumbed down programming is, however, mixed with hard propaganda and personal attacks on critics of the regime. Typical of TV2's selective news reporting was, as many media commentators have noted, its evening news devoting just forty-two seconds to the large protest demonstrations attended by thousands of teachers in June 2016.

The new pro-Fidesz media empire is being established with public money and with the aid of massive advertising by firms and organisations close to the party. Thus, for example, the biggest Internet portal, Origo, has been bought from a Fidesz loyalist with the aid of a €4 million credit guaranteed by one of the financial institutions belonging to the National Bank. Another portal, VS.hu, received almost €2 million from one of the foundations connected to the National Bank. (A group of its journalists resigned in protest, saying they had not known about the grants.) Independent media observers point out that the entre-preneurs engaged since the Orbán–Simicska breakup in estab-lishing and financing the new Fidesz media empire are running no risks; they are the recipients of generous credits from state banks and are able to count on revenues from advertising placed by both government institutions and private firms associated with Fidesz. In 2015, for instance, TV2 received 18.2 per cent of the total sum spent by the state on advertising.

The public service and state media must also not be over-looked: these comprise six TV channels, six radio stations and the MTI press agency. According to the communications expert Mária Vásárhelyi, the government pumped approximately €400 million into state TV and radio in 2015, a sum that, together with state advertising, almost equals that of the entire budget for higher education in Hungary.[13]

Despite his fall from grace, the media controlled by Lajos Simicska still plays a particular role. Though he has fallen on the list of most influential Hungarians from third place in 2014 to ninth in 2015 and sixteenth in 2016, he still remains the ninth richest man in Hungary, with a fortune of €280 million. Politically, it is important that HírTV, a CNN clone, the daily *Magyar Nemzet*, the weekly *Heti Válasz* and his radio station, all of which had shamelessly and aggressively spread pro-Fidesz propaganda for years, have often, since the February 2015 breach, broadcast and published more interesting news than the centre-left media. In light of the all-out mobilisation to create a media apparatus unquestioningly loyal to Fidesz, the future prospects of Simicska's empire are more than doubtful. Thus, in autumn 2016 the frequency license for his highly successful commercial radio, Class FM, which had 2 million listeners, was not renewed and its place was taken nationwide by Radio 1, which belongs to Andy Vajna's media empire; meanwhile, view-ers with non-digital subscriptions can no longer receive HirTV from the UPS cable network.

POWER, GREED AND CORRUPTION

2016 was the year of a decisive breakthrough in the consolidation of the Fidesz regime's near total hegemony in the Hungarian media world, guaranteeing the smooth functioning of the 'illiberal democracy' propagated by Viktor Orbán and strengthening the prestige of his 'national liberation struggle' on the international stage. The most crucial blow struck against the freedom of the press was the overnight closure of what was by far the most influential left-liberal independent daily, *Népszabadság*. Once the central organ of the ruling communist regime, it became after 1989 a respected and critical voice in its reporting on political, economic and cultural life. Majority ownership was held first by the German Bertelsmann group and subsequently by the Swiss Ringier group. A merger of the subsidiaries of Ringier and the German Springer concerns was allowed in 2014 by the media and competition authorities only on condition that *Népszabadsag* was sold to Vienna Capital Partners, a private equity firm owned by the Austrian speculator Heinrich Pecina. He was also involved in shady deals in connection with the biggest postwar banking scandal, around the collapse of the Hypo Alpen Adria of Klagenfurt. In mid-2015 Pecina took over the 27.7 per cent stake in *Népszabadsag* previously held by the Socialist Party.

On Wednesday 8 June 2016, the parent company, Mediaworks, abruptly closed the newspaper over the weekend without informing the editor or the staff's union representatives. Access to email and to the website, including the newspaper's archive, was blocked. The eighty staff, journalists and employees were denied entry to the newsroom that Sunday. Mediaworks replaced the content on the paper's website with a brief announcement that it was suspending publication immediately because of sharp falls in circulation, amounting to 'more than 100,000 copies in the past ten years'. Nevertheless, the paper still had a circulation of 43,000 and the losses incurred were considerably reduced. On the Saturday night, several thousand people protested in front of parliament against what the paper's journalists called a 'coup'. The foreign press and international insitutions protecting press freedom condemned the 'contract execution' of the most important liberal newspaper in Hungary without any attempt at seeking a viable business model. The reference to the deficit, which had been public knowledge for years and was actually declining, was regarded as little more than a smokescreen, coming as it did just days after the paper had published allegations of corruption against Antal Rogán (the head of Orbán's cabinet office and the regime's number three) and revealed new lurid details about the luxurious life style of the National Bank governor, Matolcsy.

Two weeks later, Mediaworks, which ran twelve regional dailies and the national sports newspaper, was sold for an undisclosed sum to the Opimus Group, which is said to belong through middlemen to one of Orbán's closest friends, the wealthy oligarch, Lőrinc Mészáros, whose fantastic career is described in the following chapter. The editors of six important regional dailies and the sports paper were quickly replaced by reliable Fidesz scribblers. Following this sale the management of Mediaworks was acquired by the director of *Magyar Idők*, the Fidesz paper founded after the rupture with Simicska. Soon afterwards Echo TV, founded and financed by an industrialist close to Fidesz, was also purchased by Mészáros media holding.[14]

An editorial in the *Frankfurter Allgemeine Zeitung* made it plain that nobody should take seriously the claims of the Hungarian government that it had nothing to do with the liquidation of Hungary's foremost liberal paper. Attacking Orbán by name, it added: 'The authoritarian rulers of today do not ban media, they take them over or divest them of their economic basis. They start with television and radio, and only then move on to deal with the newspapers and, like every proper evil-doer, take great care to erase all traces.'[15]

There are unmistakable signs that Habony, Vajna and others operating on Orbán's behalf also intend to put growing pressure on the hitherto critical TV channel ATV, operated by an evangelical group. They are also prepared to acquire popular dailies that occasionally unmask the scramble for unlimited enrichment within the ranks of Fidesz dignitaries. The few remaining left-liberal dailies and weeklies, as well as Internet news portals, serve only a relatively small segment of the population. The leftist Klub Radio has managed to survive despite the lack of advertising, but can only be heard in and near Budapest. The summary execution of *Népszabadság*, and the devastating echo from the international media and institutions fighting for press freedom, make it almost impossible for the Orbán regime now to provide any credible 'evidence' that the freedom of the media is not endangered in Hungary.

16

THE GREAT AND GOOD OF THE COURT

'Orbán wanted and wants to be at one and the same time the most powerful and the richest man in Hungary,' concludes economist László Lengyel in his latest book.[1] He offers no sources to substantiate his claim, but since the mid-2015 conflict with Simicska (who was, it should be recalled, the architect of Fidesz's finances) Orbán's and his family's enrichment has been openly and frequently discussed in the media and even in parliament. One such occasion was during the parliamentary questions hour on 21 March 2016. The leader of the extreme right-wing Jobbik Party, Gábor Vona, demanded the appointment of a committee of inquiry to investigate the financial affairs of the prime minister; he also accused Lőrinc Mészáros, the mayor of Felcsút, the small village where Orbán had grown up, of having become rich at a breathtaking pace over the last few years and of being nothing more than a strawman for the prime minister. Vona further alleged at a public meeting that media mogul Andy Vajna and Árpád Habony, the 'unofficial' communications adviser, were also strawmen for Orbán.

The Fidesz leader rejected Vona's repeated questions: 'I have never had and I do not now have a strawman and I will never have one.' He added that, like many other MPs, he had signed a declaration of assets every year for the past twenty-six. He had never been a wealthy man, he wasn't one now and wouldn't be one. As in every such situation, Orbán immediately went on the attack, accusing Jobbik of being involved in dubious dealings and of not paying taxes. Some weeks later, the MP Viktor Szigetvári, leader of the centre-left Együtt Party (*együtt* means together), alleged that the prime minister's estimated fortune of €650 million made him the richest Hungarian, richer than the nominal number one, OTP banker Sándor Csányi.[2] He added that while politicians may formulate what is publicly known of these 'strawman contracts', journalists are unable to do so because of the lack of concrete evidence: 'Just as Putin is known to be the richest Russian alive, we believe Orbán is Hungary's richest man, but is using strawmen to distribute his wealth.'

'Is Viktor Orbán, the man who governs [Hungary] single-handedly and at will as lord of the manor, corrupt?' In his description of 'corruption as the glue holding together the Orbán regime', Zoltán Kovács, the editor-in-chief of *Élet és Irodalom*, refers to two cases in connection with Orbán's family going back to Fidesz's early years and Orbán's first premiership, which were uncovered by the newspaper and led to a whole series of court cases. These concerned the preferential treatment given to Orbán's father in the acquisition of a quarry[3] and a 1999 remark by the prime minister concerning the degree of state support for a vineyard partly owned by his wife.

Since 2010 the scandalous turn of events at Orbán's home village of Felcsút have become a focus of media attention both in Hungary and abroad. The quarry company owned by his father and his two younger brothers generated a net profit of more than €4 million in 2015. The Orbán family appears in the Forbes report on the most influential Hungarians with a worth of €23 million.[4] In response to a parliamentary question on the almost fairy tale acquisition of wealth by Fidesz clients, Orbán casually replied that he had looked at the list of the ten richest Hungarians and could not find the name of a single Fidesz representative on it. To this a columnist from *Népszabadság* responded that Gábor Széles, the fourth richest entrepreneur with a fortune of €330 million, might not be a Fidesz man on paper, but did finance extreme right-wing pro-Fidesz newspapers and TV stations.

For several reasons, the real star among the nouveau riche and Orbán cronies is Lőrinc Mészáros, who became mayor of Felcsút in 2010. The one-time gas fitter, three years younger than Orbán himself, went to the same primary school. According to Mészáros they only met again in 1999 though it was through playing football that he actually got to know Orbán well. The close connection was first cemented during the construction of the huge new football stadium opposite Orbán's house and reinforced after Mészáros' election as mayor. The turnover of the company owned by the mayor and his wife, registered as MM, has increased tenfold since 2010, the year of the Fidesz election victory. In 2015–16 alone Mészáros was able to triple his personal fortune to €80 million. In 2013 the village mayor appeared for the first time on the list of the hundred richest Hungarians, at number eighty-eight; only three years later he was number thirty-one. At the same time he was ranked as the tenth most influential Hungarian. His explanation for this dizzying career is quite simple: 'The good Lord, good luck and the person of Viktor Orbán have certainly all played a role that I have come so far. But I have never privatised, never taken anything, I have acquired everything with my own work and with my own brains.'⁵

The list of state contracts that have come Mészáros' way have encompassed a multitude of activities, ranging from the construction of a large riding school and horse racing track to the rebuilding of a Danube harbour and the erection of flood defences. Always in consortium with other firms, Mészáros has undertaken the electrification of railway lines, the production of equipment for air conditioning and large agricultural enterprises. In 2015 he acquired a majority shareholding in a Croatian football team (NK Osijek). In addition to his varied activities as an industrialist, he has also become the most powerful landowner in the Fejér region. As private individuals can only hold a maximum of 300 hectares of agricultural land, Mészáros' wife and three children (the entire family) had by the end of 2015 purchased a total of 1,425 hectares of land for approximately €6.5 million.

Following extensive research, the economic and political magazine *HVG* concluded that by the end of 2016 Lőrinc Mészáros had built up directly or indirectly a network of twenty firms, which had won (in consortium) orders and contracts worth over €1 billion. Additionally, more than a dozen hotels belong to his rapidly expanding empire. The thirty-year-old István Tiborcz, who in 2013 married Orbán's eldest daughter Rachel, has also become a highly successful entrepreneur. In just a couple of years his company Elios has received public orders worth €65 million for installing LED street lighting in a number of towns and communities. As these contracts were in part financed from EU transfers, the European Anti-Fraud Office is said to have started an investigation. Tiborcz sold his holdings in Elios and then invested in real estate, acquiring some extremely valuable properties. After he paid the stamp duty on a major deal involving a famous castle, reporters alleged that the Orbán family and their business associates were using proxies so that the real owners remain hidden. Close relatives of Orbán's wife, Anikó Lévai, have also been involved in profitable business transactions. Losses incurred by her close relatives, amounting to £10 million, were also settled by Lőrinc Mészáros. Moreover, press reports and photos have documented the contacts between the prime minister's family and Adnan Polat, a Turkish millionaire and football club president, and with Ghaith Pharaon, a highly controversial Saudi investor on the FBI's wanted list, whose dealings with Orbán were also the subject of heated parliamentary debates before his death in January 2017.[6]

When in 1972 the young avant-garde film director Gyula Gazdag made a now famous regime-critical documentary called *The Resolution*, about a power struggle in an agricultural cooperative in the back of beyond, nobody could have thought that the sleepy little village in which the action took place, Felcsút, and its surrounding area would four decades later become the centre of Hungarian and world media attention, sometimes even heated parliamentary debates. Only somebody who knows of Orbán's tough childhood and the gruelling ascent of his family[7] can understand why Orbán gives free rein both to his fervent passion for football and to his much criticised national megalomania, shaped by nostalgia. How else is it to be explained that the largest and most expensive stadium in Hungary has been built on the very spot of the small football pitch where he had once played as a centre forward? When in the autumn of 2014 I viewed the large arena with its carefully tended grass, I was, like every visitor, amazed by the contrast. The equation is well known: Felcsút has 1,800 inhabitants and its football stadium a capacity of 3,800. With its arched facades of wood, stone and copper, it is the most beautiful stadium in the country. The style of the interior is also elegant, even if it is overwhelmed by the sheer quantity of photographs, panels and memorabilia of the wonder team—the Golden Eleven captained by Ferenc Puskás, the greatest and most famous footballer in Hungarian history. Next to the €13 million stadium is the large building of the Puskás Academy for young players. There, almost 100 talented boys are educated and trained.

Not only did Orbán's crony Mészáros play a key role as developer in the construction of this splendid edifice but he is also the president of the foundation supporting talented young players, supervised by the Ferenc Puskás Football Academy. It is said in the village that Orbán, who during his first premiership still played football himself and once postponed a cabinet meeting because of a training match in Poreč, Croatia, had the magnificent stadium built on his own initiative exactly opposite his own little farmhouse with its neat garden.

Football, the prime minister's lifelong passion, also lies behind the generous tax breaks given to companies that directly support team sports. Between 2011 and 2016, large domestic and foreign firms donated a total of about €1 billion for football, handball, water polo, ice hockey and basketball. About half of this sum went to football. In these five years, through the agency of the Hungarian Football Association 1,200 sports clubs have received over €300 million, of which more than €30 million landed with the Felcsút foundation for young players headed by Lőrinc Mészáros. The legal regulations for this favourable tax regime have been in force since June 2011 and companies are not obliged to make public any information about how much money they transfer from their corporate taxes, or to which clubs. Critics point out that in this way the state loses revenues equivalent to the two-year budget for higher education.[8]

All this, of course, goes well beyond the hyperactive Mészáros. A whole line-up of entrepreneurs, above all those close to the prime minister, is building lavish and expensive football stadia in the towns where their largest factories are located. Sooner or later they profit from large public contracts. The president of the Hungarian Football Association, for example, is Sándor Csányi, chairman of Hungary's biggest bank and for years the absolute number one on the list of the richest people in Hungary. The seating arrangements and facial expressions of the entrepreneurs and Fidesz politicians sat with Orbán in the VIP lounge for a football match in Felcsút or neighbouring

Székesfehérvár are watched and analysed almost as carefully as János Kádár's favourites in the past, at a hunt or on the May Day parade tribune in Budapest.

Orbán is often to be seen in the company of the particularly successful businessman István Garancsi, owner of the Videoton football club from Székesfehérvár. According to media reports, the fifty-year-old former broker has also achieved his position as a close confidant of the prime minister through their common passion for football. In 2015 alone his real estate and construction companies received public contracts worth more than €150 million. Garancsi landed in the headlines at the end of 2015, when it was reported that between 2011 and 2014 the state-owned energy company MVM had bought gas from the Hungaro–Russian MET Group (registered in Switzerland) at a higher price than from its Western partners. MET, in which Garancsi has a 10 per cent shareholding, made a profit of at least €70 million on this deal. At the beginning of 2016, his company was able to launch a huge real estate project in Budapest with a €55 million credit from the state-owned Eximbank. It is no wonder that this football and Orbán enthusiast has, since Fidesz took office in 2010, been able to almost triple his fortune to €80 million, rising on the list of most influential Hungarians from fourteenth to eighth place.[9]

Garancsi is not the only entrepreneur or Fidesz politician pushing the construction of stadia in small provincial towns following the example of Felcsút. Yet, in spite of the enormous investment, the number of spectators has not grown in recent years. On the other hand, opinion pollsters note that the government and, without doubt, Orbán personally have been able to profit from the recent international successes of Hungarian football. In 2016, for the first time in forty-four years, the Hungarian national team not only qualified for the European Championship but also reached the last sixteen as undefeated group leaders. Despite then losing against Belgium, the team was given a triumphant reception at Heroes' Square upon their return to Budapest.

Whilst on the subject of Felcsút, one more story should be mentioned: the reconstruction of a 6-kilometre-long narrow gauge railway with subsidies worth €2 million from the EU. On 1 May 2016 Orbán rode with Mayor Mészáros on the relaunched train from the restored station in Felcsút to the park with its arboretum in the neighbouring village of Alcsútdoboz. For the project, built of course by one of the mayor's companies, the state provided a further €1 million. The journey between the three stations takes about twenty-five minutes. At the reopening Orbán said that as a child he had always dreamed of working a hand-operated draisine. He rejected any criticism of this tourist project as pure cynicism, and then announced the extension of the railway to the nearby small town of Bicske by 2019.[10]

In any analysis of the beneficiaries of the Orbán regime and the social consequences of this cronyism, it is the overall dimension of the corruption, and not just the individual cases blown up by the media, that must be taken into consideration. In the reports about the richest people in Hungary, a correspondent on the online portal *444.hu* noted that, of the hundred persons on the list, one in seven is associated with the Fidesz regime. These forint billionaires have been able to amass their fortunes considerably more quickly than average. This 'unreal sphere' (*Napi.hu*) of the rich means that these people have primarily become wealthy not through competition but thanks to winning tenders, to state auctions and, in fact, to not having any real competition at all. It has been calculated that more than half of the credits granted by the state Export-Import Bank have flowed in the direction of pro-government companies.[11]

Claims that the awarding of these large public contracts may be seen as the equivalent of legal theft have been corroborated by an investigation of the Research Centre for Corruption, an NGO in Budapest.[12] 120,000 contracts were concluded with government bodies between 2009 and 2015. The result: in the case of 25 to 40 per cent of public tenders (depending on the year), only one offer was received, meaning the bidder won automatically; approximately 62 per cent of public contracts were awarded without any official announcement—that is, only those who had been informed in advance by the tender issuing body could participate, rendering impossible any open competition; in the tenders for projects financed with EU money (approximately 60 per cent of the total) the risk of corruption was much greater, sometimes reaching 80 to 90 per cent of cases.

However, it must be strongly emphasised that the corruption prevalent in daily life, in the economy and in society is in no way a product of the Orbán era. Numerous great novels, famous films and plays by Hungarian authors from the nineteenth century onwards have dealt with the deeply rooted traditions and varied practices of bribery, nepotism and moral collapse in Hungary. Scholarly investigations and contemporary works alike point out that the roots in part go back to the time of the Turkish occupation,[13] but above all to the early years of the Dual Monarchy following the Compromise of 1867.[14] The results of comparative surveys show that in Hungary 30 per cent of those questioned would report a case of corruption to the authorities; in Germany and the UK this figure rises to about 90 per cent, and even in Romania it is 59 per cent. Hungary's position on Transparency International's Corruption Perceptions Index has consistently worsened, slipping seven places to fiftieth of 176 countries (surpassed only by Bulgaria in the region), while the country finds itself in an especially lowly position on the OECD index on corruption in government departments. It is no wonder that 69 per cent of Hungarians regarded their government as corrupt in 2014.

Researchers point out that corruption in Hungary is now veiled behind a complex system of contracts and organisations; it is also being conducted in a much subtler manner. 'People see no great difference in whether an investment project costs nine instead of eight billion forints.' Researchers estimate that inflated invoices amount annually to €1.3 billion.[15] Many opponents of the regime are amazed that the flood of reports on the corrupt cronyism of Fidesz people has not had any serious impact on the party's popularity in opinion polls. Yet, ironically, in 2010 it was the allegations of bribery made against the Socialists that contributed significantly to Fidesz's victory. This allows its supporters to console themselves with the fact that 'the Socialists also stole, those [in power] today do it too, but at least we now have a true national government and a strong leader'.[16] The silence in the state and Fidesz-controlled media about the most explosive cases is also an important factor. However, we must also recognise the positive consequences of the recent metamorphosis of Simicska's newspapers and radio stations into critics of the Orbán regime. Some of the juiciest corruption stories, including those about Orbán's own family, were first reported in *Magyar Nemzet* or on HírTV, once blindly loyal to the government.[17]

The sobering reality that, after seven years in office, wide sections of society are not alienated by the Orbán regime or outraged by the corruption scandals it tolerates, that people are not turning significantly against the governing party, may largely be ascribed to the fact that Socialist politicians are still very much compromised. It is an irony of fate that to date in Hungary only functionaries of the Socialist Party, which lost office in 2010, have been named in the Panama Papers.[18] The former chief financial officer of the party, László Boldvai, was for example the first active Hungarian politician forced to admit to the existence of an undeclared company abroad, as well as a bank account in Switzerland held under his wife's name. As Socialist Party treasurer he had already been involved in a huge bribery scandal in 1996. There was particular indignation at the report that this owner of a luxury villa and other real estate, not to speak of a number of expensive cars, had taken part in a 'hunger march' for minimum wage earners organised by his regional party executive. Moreover, the party chairman (replaced in June 2016) had asked him to help in cleaning up the financial affairs of the party. His influential successor as financial officer, László Puch—said for years to be a symbol of internal party corruption—has been indicted as the holder of an account worth millions in a Viennese bank. In the meantime he has been able to pay, out of unknown sources, back taxes amounting to €300,000. In June 2016 a new Socialist Party chair was elected after unsavoury intrigues and public squabbles, a man who was also involved in several financial criminal proceedings—though he was ultimately acquitted of them all.

There are more than enough indications that the mutually beneficial cooperation between the Socialist and Fidesz financial chiefs dates back a very long way. As Orbán's biographer József Debreczeni put it in 2011, the only difference between the two parties in their conversion of public assets into private ones lay in the fact that Fidesz was much the better organised. Quite correctly, a scandalised reader of *Népszabadság* wrote after the revelations about Boldvai that, next to Fidesz figures, the Socialists were amateurs when it came to corruption.[19] In the meantime, the breathtaking financial careers of Mészáros, Vajna, Garancsi and the rest of Orbán's cronies and proxies confirm assessments by critical observers that Hungary has moved onto a qualitatively higher plane of state and personal corruption since Fidesz's seizure of executive power in 2010.

17

HUNGARY'S 'FÜHRER DEMOCRACY'

After seven continuous years of Fidesz rule and in light of all opinion polls, even Viktor Orbán's fiercest critics concede that at the age of fifty-three his position appears impregnable. His unlimited personal power is virtually unchallenged within Hungary, nor is it under threat from the EU. In an essay published to mark the halfway point of the 2014–18 Orbán government, the legal scholar Tamás Sárközy speaks of a

> government of what has become a permanent national liberation struggle ... It is not a conservative Christian Democratic government but a politically very successful radical half-bourgeois administration governing right and left of the centre, headed by parvenus, ambitious upstarts of the first generation, who govern on the one hand with semi-feudal patriarchal, partisan order elements; and on the other, with post-modern tendencies, often aligned with the much reviled globalisation. At the heart of this regime, devoted almost exclusively to power politics, has stood since 2014 the retention of power at any price.[1]

What could be described as the nationalisation of politics in the face of an almost paralysed civil society has at its centre a de facto presidential and centralised government, with Viktor Orbán

177

as its sole and arbitrary head. The number of ministers has remained unaltered at eight since 2010, but that of secretaries of state has mushroomed to fifty and of deputy secretaries of state to over 100, many of whom are at one and the same time MPs. The approximately fifty government commissars should also not be forgotten. Though Zsolt Semjén, the leader of Orbán's small coalition partner, the sixteen-MP-strong Christian Democratic People's Party (KDNP), is the (nominal) deputy prime minister, more than ever the actual centre of power is the Prime Minister's Office with its eleven secretaries of state, eighteen deputy secretaries of state, approximately two dozen commissars and altogether 800 civil servants. The executive minister is János Lázár, forty-two, the former head of the Fidesz parliamentary group, who at the time of writing (2017) is regarded as the regime's number two. However, in the autumn of 2015, Orbán made Anton Rogán, forty-five, another former parliamentary party leader, his chef de cabinet with the rank of minister. Rogán, number seven on the list of most influential Hungarians, is seen by the media as Lázár's rival.

One of the more bizarre features of the Orbán regime is that political reporting in the media primarily revolves around gossip or leaked information about supposed or real power struggles and intrigues in the court of the supreme leader. These rumours have spread especially since Rogán was installed as a minister with four secretaries of state, two deputy secretaries of state and his own bureaucratic machine in the Prime Minister's Office; he is now ranked equal with Lázár and answerable only to Orbán. Though Rogán retains the prime minister's backing, a spate of press reports in the autumn of 2016 about his alleged abuse of power seriously undermined his reputation. A few months previously, in July 2016, Orbán carried out a surgical division of the government into a strategic cabinet, headed by János Lázár, and an economic cabinet, chaired by finance minister Mihály Varga. This has been regarded as a major step towards a semi-presidential system, which, through the appointment of three commissioners responsible only to Orbán, curtails the competences of the executive minister Lázár, particularly with regard to the supervision of key financial institutions.

László Lengyel, who has an intimate knowledge of the career of Hungary's 'strongman', suggests that Orbán, basing himself loosely on the ideas of Carl Schmitt,[2] wants to have the right and power to decide who is a friend and who is a foe. Lengyel believes that Orbán accepts the fundamental precepts of Schmitt, whereby the person who decides on a state of emergency is sovereign, and concludes:

> Both in his domestic and foreign policy [Orbán] suspends the liberal democratic institutions, principles and relevant practices in order to build up his illiberal/autocratic system based on unity against the enemies of the nation, on the Führer principle, on autocratic authority, on the basis of a permanent state of emergency and political legislation, and in order to spread this model internationally.[3]

Speculation flourishes not only in the media but also among the opposition about the methods and relative strengths of the rival cliques in Orbán's court, about their respective options and aims, and also about the shifts in the personality of the *vezér*. This translates literally as the supreme leader or Führer. It is also how Orbán is obliquely but frequently referred to by critical analysts and commentators in independent publications.

In a discussion on the phenomenon of Viktor Orbán and his government hosted by the left-wing monthly *Mozgó Világ* in Budapest in January 2016, all participants, for example, rejected the claim of a well-known psychologist that he would, at most, have trusted the 'very mediocre' Orbán with the management of a leather goods warehouse or a sports shop. András Bozóki, founder and editor-in-chief of *Magyar Narancs*, the first Fidesz newspaper (1989–92) and today Professor of Political Science at the Central European University in Budapest, has emphasised:

... politics is not only a question of education or intellect. Orbán was from the very beginning driven by an astonishing absolute will to win.

Not a statesman, but a 'good politician', in his understanding of the mechanics of power, of intrigues, of competence, of political instinct and with the ability to keep himself in power for a long time. He has also only been able to achieve this because he has violated the rules and not respected the democratic order. In reality there are only three things in which Viktor Orbán is still truly interested: power, money and football. And in that order. There is no substance, the goal is to stay in power, and that is going well. Slowly, Orbán is following in the footsteps of Kálmán Tisza.[4]

The successful build-up of a new pro-Fidesz socioeconomic elite with a relatively broad-based clientele in both the central and regional administrations has also been promoted by measures such as the flat income tax rate, child allowances and reductions in gas and electricity prices. The incomes of the upper two deciles of the population grew by 22 per cent between 2010 and 2014. The sledgehammer propaganda proclaiming the successes of the regime has also been facilitated by the close coordination of budgetary and monetary policy, by the stabilisation of the deficit under the 3 per cent level set by the EU, and the repayment of IMF loans. The fall in unemployment trumpeted by the government is partly due to the fivefold increase in the number of those who receive wages paid by the local or state authorities for so-called community service instead of unemployment benefits. An especially important factor in reducing unemployment is, of course, the fact that between 350,000 and 500,000 people are estimated to have found employment abroad, mostly in Great Britain, Germany and Austria. Their money transfers home have contributed to the improvement of the balance of payments.

The boastful announcement of the controversial governor of the National Bank, György Matolscsy, that on the basis of the economic successes of recent years the 'historical goal' (that of over-taking Austria) is realistic within twenty-five years caused a great deal of amusement amongst experts in both Budapest and Vienna. At present, the per capita economic output in Austria is still about double that in Hungary. The Hungarian economy would have to grow annually by 3 per cent more than the Austrian economy just to catch up with its neighbour within twenty-five years. 'With annual 2-per-cent faster growth this catching up process would take forty years and with 1 per cent it would take seventy!'[5] Matolcsy's prediction reminded a Vienna-based economist of 'comrade Khrushchev's announcement in 1959 during a visit to an American exhibition in Moscow that the Soviet Union would catch up with the USA within seven years ...'.

If we compare the government's enormously expensive advertising campaigns blaring out the fantastic results of the Orbán years with the actual performance of the economy, and the doleful consequences for Hungary's education and healthcare systems, and contrast this with the achievements of the neighbouring countries, then we should heed the warning of the incorruptible István Bibó (1911–79): 'In contrast to the widely spread view we can only observe that there must be no lying in politics. Put more precisely: now and then it is permissible to lie but it is impossible to build a political construct, a political programme on lies.'[6]

Citing Bibó, the economist István Csillag concludes that it is only the annual transfers from the EU cohesion fund, amounting to €2.5–5 billion, which have enabled the maintenance of the facade of a positively growing economy. Without the EU, without the transfers, which make up 2.5 to 5 per cent of GDP, the collapse of the Hungarian economy would be unavoidable. In the decade preceding 2014, Hungary experienced an annual growth rate of a mere 0.9 per cent whilst in the Czech Republic GDP rose by 125 per cent, in Slovakia by almost 150 per cent and in

Poland by 170 per cent. All these countries joined the EU at the same time as Hungary in 2004. The much hyped 3.7 per cent rise in economic performance in 2014 was, according to Csillag, an exception, due to a particularly high rate of transfers amounting to €5.4 billion (5.2 per cent of GDP); additionally, there was a record performance in the agricultural sector. Without the transfers from the EU, Csillag notes, the economy would be stagnating or suffering a mild recession. The facts that the much vilified foreign banks, despite the special taxes, have also contributed to economic stabilisation by raising their capital by €4.8 billion, and that the equally despised multinationals have paid taxes of €5.8 billion (three times the amount paid by domestic enterprises), is often overlooked or deliberately ignored. Overcentralisation, dependency on the state, and a nation marching in the direction of a dictatorship with voluntarist economic policy-making, are all, in Csillag's opinion, stifling the Hungarian economy. It lacks decentralised economic actors, predictability, honesty and credibility, as a result of the demolition of the rule of law and constitutional checks and balances.[7]

The extremely harsh observations of those respected economists who had occupied important positions in the first Orbán government have attracted particular attention in recent years. One of them is Attila Chikán, the director of the Research Institute for Competitiveness at Corvinus University and Orbán's minister for economic affairs between 1998 and 2000. In a series of disparaging interviews given to opposition newspapers and magazines he did not mince his words:

> Government propaganda about successful reforms has little to do with reality. A series of statistics reveal that we are falling more and more behind developed countries. In 2001 we were ranked number twenty-nine on the global competitive listing of the World Economic Forum; today we are number sixty-nine. Even worse is the fact that among the former Socialist member states we were the best; today we are one of the

stragglers. Most of all, corruption paralyses the performance of our entrepreneurs, for wherever cronyism or bribery and not entrepreneurship are rewarded, there is no incentive to work harder and at the same time there is no trust. That does not mean that everybody [in Hungary] is corrupt but the influence of those who are in the key positions of the economy is so strong that this colours everything else ... The runner who always begins the 100-metre race with a 20-metre lead at a domestic track meet is hardly likely to break the world record at an international competition.[8]

Whilst Chikán fully acknowledges the prime minister's political success, he is very negative about the consequences of Orbán's financial and economic policies:

The illiberal democracy and the unorthodox economic policies go hand-in-hand. Four factors determine economic policy: the central role of the state; the priority of short-term political factors; the predominance of political and of power interests at the expense of economic rationality; [finally] social questions are pushed strongly into the background and are solved not by economic but by political means.'

Chikán repeatedly points out that the observance of internationally required monetary obligations has not been achieved by the promotion of investments, of small and medium-sized enterprises or of production, but at the expense of the social sphere, primarily the healthcare and education systems. It is intolerable that Hungarian productivity is only 50 per cent that of the European average. Chikán does not foresee the danger of an economic collapse but rather of a steady decline of the economy.

That the ever-growing corruption, whether tolerated by or originating from those 'up there', is destroying the moral fibre of the nation is becoming a major source of concern in Hungary. It is not the enrichment of individuals that is interesting, but rather the structures of cronyism and nepotism; equally of concern is the fact that it is always the same groups or individuals that are awarded the lion's share of public contracts. All this eats away at competition and causes incalculable moral damage, says Chikán. An even harsher and more comprehensive critique of government policy comes from Tamás Mellár, a professor of economics and a man who had held a leading position in Orbán's first government.[9] He does not believe that economic and social policy is conservative or right-wing but is rather a hodgepodge, partially recalling the communist era in Hungary and in many ways the Horthy regime of the 1930s. Mellár speaks of the establishment of a semi-feudal regime, of a concentration of land ownership unprecedented in modern Europe. 'The only thing that is missing,' he writes, 'is the feudal *droit du seigneur* for the new landowners'; he also mentions the fact that the several-thousand-hectare estate of the head of the OTP Bank, Sándor Csányi, has been declared a model farm by the government. The regime has done nothing for small and medium enterprises or for agriculture in the successful manner of Holland and Denmark. Mellár, a conservative thinker, finds utterly disgusting the politics of the strong hand, the cant about illiberal democracy and the shocking extent of corruption.

Mellár, who was president of the Central Statistical Office from 1998 to 2003, has on more than one occasion heavily criticised the ending (in mid-2015) of the publication of official data about poverty and subsistence levels in Hungary, observing that 'As someone who is aware of the non-manipulated data, it is no exaggeration to observe that Hungary is once again a country of 3 million beggars' (a reference to the conditions in the Horthy era). The poverty and hopelessness in the lowest third of society has reached unprecedented levels. Mellár estimates that the number of poor people has reached 4 million, and in a number of interviews he has castigated the yawning gap in living standards. 'Health conditions and life expectations in the second district in Budapest correspond to the average achieved by the Scandinavian countries, while those for the inhabitants of the villages in Szabolcs county [situated in northeast Hungary, bordering on Romania and Ukraine] barely reach the average of central African countries.' Novelists such as Krisztina Tóth and Ferenc Barnás or the playwright György Spiró have described in their works the collapse of living standards and the consequent moral degradation of the lower middle classes, of those families without employment or homes, of pensioners living in the countryside or even in the suburbs of Budapest, all of whom are hardly ever seen by foreign visitors.

The recurring demonstrations of teachers and nurses are also a warning. They reflect a growing dissatisfaction with the consequences of increasing economic hardships and considerable discontent due to the grotesque contrasts between the conspicuous consumption of the nouveaux riches and the general impoverishment of wide segments of society. These miserable conditions are all too evident in the areas of northern and eastern Hungary where the Roma live. Like so many other cleverly packaged Fidesz programmes, the measures presented in 2011 (during Hungary's EU presidency) for a qualitative improvement in the position of the country's estimated 800,000 Roma have proven a pipedream.

Leading economists and sociologists believe that the Fidesz regime is living on borrowed time. If the estimates that the transfers from the EU and foreign capital are financing 90 per cent of industrial and infrastructure investments and that the subsidiaries of foreign concerns account for 80 per cent of exports are indeed correct, then it is evident that in the run-up to the 2018 elections the government will seek to generate as many as possible of the transfers from Brussels foreseen for the period up to 2020, in order to finance wage and salary increases, as well as other projects popular with the electorate.

Critical economic experts such as Tamás Mellár, Attila Chikán or János Kornai believe that the huge sums from abroad, as well as the 2010–11 state expropriation of the €3 billion reserves of the private pension funds, a de facto 'legalised robbery' (see Chapter 12), have not been invested systematically but, against all economic common sense, stuffed into the pockets of a chosen few oligarchs.

Those who have been disgraced or who have voluntarily drawn back from the circle around Orbán whisper of the considerable rifts in the Fidesz camp, of the jealousies among the forint billionaires and their retinues. It would, however, be wrong to underestimate Orbán's political instincts and his determination to use his powers of decision-making. His speedy withdrawal of the Internet tax after the wave of protests in 2014, the abolition of the ban on Sunday opening by retail businesses in 2016 as a response to the suddenly strong public support for a referendum on the matter, the cancellation in February 2017 of Budapest's bid to host the 2024 Olympic Games after a new opposition group, Memento, had collected 266,000 signatures for a referendum, and the successful restructuring of Fidesz's financial and media empires after the breach with Simicska, provide convincing evidence that Orbán remains a nimble and experienced technician of power despite his numerous critics' prophecies of doom. He is only too conscious of his unique position as the head of the government, the leader of the parliamentary majority and of his party; in a crisis situation he can take decisions, alone if necessary. Thus most commentators, whether pro- or anti-Fidesz, agree that power rises and falls with the person of Viktor Orbán.

Even after thirty years of toiling on behalf of his party, Orbán's perception of politics remains one of conflict rather than consent, battle instead of compromise. The political scientist and director of the Institute for Political Science at the Hungarian Academy of Sciences, András Körösényi, the man who coined the phrase *vezérdemokrácia* (Führer democracy), sees no 'Orbán system, only an Orbán regime' because a system is predictable, stable and lasting:

HUNGARY'S 'FÜHRER DEMOCRACY'

The most important feature of the Orbán regime is the unprecedented concentration of power and the manner in which power is exercised. The assertion of political will and power interests have priority over the constitutional state and concrete issues. A certain tinkering with the policies of the regime is characteristic because its narrative has been assembled from elements stolen from here, there and everywhere. The new post-2010 regime has endeavoured to legitimise its power with the person of Orbán and for this reason it presents him as a leader of extraordinary capabilities.

Körösényi believes that the survival of the regime after Orbán is questionable.[10]

The stocktaking of this political scientist, who regards himself as a conservative, stands of course in stark contrast to Orbán's own claims and those of his pseudo-academic lackeys such as Gyula Tellér and other highly paid propagandists.[11] This debate illustrates, not for the first time, the truth that it is sometimes more difficult to create or to craft an ideology to justify personal rule than it is to achieve and enjoy power. Here the biography of Mussolini is enlightening.[12] Regardless of how we assess the rifts in the power structures of Fidesz and possible incipient power struggles within the circle around Orbán, now three-quarters of the way through his third period in office, nothing but question marks hang over the economic and social policies of the regime. A balance cannot yet be drawn.

18

'THE MOST DANGEROUS MAN IN THE EU'

Three times in the last sixty years refugees have played a special role in Hungarian history. In 1956 the world watched with a mixture of admiration and sympathy as almost 200,000 Hungarians fled to Austria after the bloody suppression of the October Uprising. More than three decades later the reform communist government removed the first brick in the Berlin Wall by allowing East German citizens to leave Hungary, thereby making a significant contribution to the reunification of Germany. On the third occasion, it was TV pictures of tens of thousands of refugees, mostly from Syria and Iraq. Their harrowing situation at Budapest's Keleti (East) railway station, at the southern refugee camp at Röszke on the Serbian border, and finally during the long march to the Austrian border, once again put the focus on Hungary in the autumn of 2015.

Astonishing things were happening in Germany and Austria in those weeks, as well as in other West European countries. Opinion on the whole issue of asylum shifted: dismay, compassion and a desire to help temporarily replaced fear, rejection and mistrust. The public perception of asylum seekers changed, even in the tabloid press and in the political world. The speedy reaction of the German and Austrian governments to the issue of opening their borders to approximately 20,000 (later hundreds of thousands) refugees would have been unthinkable a few weeks earlier. The response was primarily due to the power of the image. The photographs of the drowned three-year-old boy washed up on the Turkish coast, of the father with his wife and child who threw themselves onto the railway tracks and began crying and screaming amidst Hungarian policemen, or of the asylum seekers who were dragged off the Hungarian train bound for Germany—it was these dramatic TV reports about people who had nothing to lose that shook the governments in Berlin and Vienna.

On 4 September 2015, as a direct consequence of the patent failure of the Hungarian authorities and their chaotic crisis management, thousands of refugees set off on foot for the Austrian border from Keleti station in Budapest. On what was, for me personally, this unforgettable Friday, I witnessed the mood in Hungary at first hand. Travelling from Vienna to Budapest for a friend's birthday party, I was unexpectedly phoned by the editor of the Austrian public TV channel (ORF) and asked to give a live interview on the situation in Hungary for its 10 p.m. news bulletin, as the resident correspondent was out of the capital reporting on events on the border. However, it was impossible to find a free studio in Budapest and so I had to make my way to the front of Keleti railway station, where Eurovision technicians would set up a line to Vienna for the interview. There I met a truly international team: a Serb producer, a Slovak sound engineer and an Irish cameraman.

As I waited for more than half an hour on that mild summer evening for the transmission to begin, I saw all around me a world of unbelievable contrasts. In the lower part of the station there were still thousands of refugees, among them many families with children, sitting or standing out in the open with blankets and the food they had been given by volunteers. Above, looking down from the street, Budapesters, in their hundreds, gawked at the extraordinary goings-on in the heart of the city, at times with loud comments. Meanwhile, other groups and interested people had gathered in front of the station entrance, which was crammed with the cameras and equipment of TV teams from all over Europe reporting directly on the refugee drama.

Waiting for the link to Vienna, I could hear a cacophony of voices; near me a Finnish journalist was describing her impressions to the camera whilst a little further away a German colleague was interviewing a Hungarian woman. Groups of curious passers-by immediately formed around interviews or wherever a camera team popped up. Nearby, there also stood a handful of dubious looking men waving the Árpád flag with its five red and five white stripes. This had been used by the national socialist Arrow Cross Party and is associated with its reign of terror from mid-October 1944 to the end of the war in 1945. Historically rooted in the medieval Árpád dynasty (ninth to fourteenth centuries), today the flag is usually brandished by extreme right-wing activists.

The old man who recognised me had probably come from this group: he hurled abuse at me non-stop even during the live interview with the anchor in Vienna. Standing just a few metres away from me, in Hungarian he very loudly called me an 'enemy of Hungary' and a 'Mossad agent'. Despite the presence of a couple of policeman at the entrance to the station, this was an unpleasant situation, a mood that—I later learned back in Vienna—was conveyed to the viewers and listeners, perhaps through my facial expressions or my repeated references to the tense atmosphere in Budapest. In any case I was lucky. The loudmouth, who went away still shouting insults at me after I finished my live report, failed to get anybody else interested in me.

It was already evident on that first day, as well as subsequently from both personal conversations and media reports, that the majority of the population had no empathy for these people in need. To this day they support the government position: the 175-kilometre-long fence along the border with Serbia (and the later one with Croatia), as well as the deportation or punishment of refugees, protects not only Hungary but all of Western Europe from the masses of foreign people who, in the words of Orbán, 'are overrunning us and threatening our civilisation'. In stark contrast, the cultural philosopher Sándor Radnóti expressed the feelings of shame among the intellectual elite in the liberal magazine *Magyar Narancs*: 'The Orbán regime with its ruthlessness and barbarity is the embodiment of everything that is bad in Europe.'

Lurid scenes abounded that autumn on the border with Serbia as tens of thousands of refugees were transported to the Austrian frontier from the reception camps there in special trains. A spokesperson of the Hungarian Helsinki Committee complained that the Hungarian government and authorities were totally panic-stricken and simply wanted to get rid of the refugees. Responding to the huge media campaigns and the urgent need to deal with the refugee question, the constitutional scholar Gábor Halmai pointed to the absurdity of the government's attempts to portray Hungary as an acutely endangered frontline state. Just two comparisons: the proportion of foreign citizens among the Hungarian population amounts to 1.4 per cent, while in Austria it is 13.3 per cent; only 4.5 per cent of Hungarians were born abroad (and these are overwhelmingly ethnic Hungarian immigrants from Romania), whereas in Austria the equivalent figure is 16 per cent.[1] Yet according to a poll conducted between 11 and 15 September 2015, two thirds of those questioned in Hungary supported the building of the fence along the Serbian border, 79 per cent argued for even harsher treatment of asylum seekers and 41 per cent were even for using weapons to defend the border against illegal immigrants. Between June and September 2015 Fidesz's poll ratings rose by the equivalent of 300,000 votes and Viktor Orbán's popularity ratings rose from 43 to 48 per cent.

The developments in Hungary in 2015–16 confirmed yet again the well-known maxim of the French psychologist Gustave Le Bon (1841–1931): 'People in masses are like children, easy to influence and even easier to steer if the message is well packaged and repeated often enough.'[2] Opinion polls leave no doubt that Viktor Orbán has once again succeeded in exploiting a single issue, in this case immigrants and refugees, to achieve a turn-around in his support. In the summer of 2016 a representative poll conducted by the American Pew Research Center in ten European countries[3] ascertained that the fear of a terrorist attack by refugees was strongest in Hungary: 76 per cent of those questioned agreed with this, compared with a statistical average of 59 per cent for the ten polled countries. Even greater was the fear of refugees taking jobs at the expense of Hungarians: 82 per cent of Hungarians were of this opinion as against an average of 50 per cent elsewhere. Hungary also topped the list in the expression of anti-Muslim sentiment (76 per cent): on anti-Semitic (32 per cent) and anti-Roma feelings (64 per cent) it was beaten only by Greece.

In all of these comparisons, it must be borne in mind that in contrast to countries like Germany (over 1 million asylum seekers) and Austria (90,000 refugees in 2015) Hungary has had practically no refugees in the current crisis, since they have been quickly transferred to third countries or threatened with jail. There are hardly any Muslims in the country. Regardless of political setbacks to the regime, such as the loss of the migrant quota referendum in the autumn of 2016, all opinion polls confirm the deeply rooted anti-foreign attitudes present in Hungarian society: a February 2017 survey, for example, revealed that 60 per cent of respondents regarded migrants as a serious threat to the EU. The one-time liberal leader, then Fidesz MP and now independent conservative political analyst Péter Tölgyessy observes that since the Treaty of Trianon Hungarian society has been one of the least solidarity-minded societies in Europe, and is still one of the most closed and culturally least colourful.

How, with this single issue, was Orbán able to dictate the narrative about refugees, initially in Hungary and subsequently across the post-communist states of Central and Eastern Europe? Here the national tradition of the 'victor in defeat', together with two predominant elements of Hungarian self-image—the victim myth and the will to survive—must always be considered. The notion of Hungarian exceptionalism, of Hungary's superiority to other nations and of a special mission flowing from this, was official state doctrine from the Compromise of 1867 (and despite the diktat of Trianon in 1920), save of course for the four decades of communist rule. Since the mid-1990s, Fidesz has presented itself as a type of national liberation movement feeding on the deep collective sentiments of secular humiliation and affront. Once in power Fidesz exploited its huge communications apparatus to promote the notion of mobilising all forces to liberate Hungary from its political and economic dependency on foreign powers. The desire no longer to be deluded or told what to do by the mighty EU (despite the enormous transfer payments from the cohesion fund) has been the watchword of all three Fidesz governments. The denunciation of ideas of European integration, liberalism, social democracy and enlightened conservatism as both obsolete and yet detrimental has gathered momentum, especially since Orbán's controversial stand in favour of the 'illiberal state' and 'illiberal democracy'.

Following the terrorist attack on the French satirical weekly *Charlie Hebdo* in January 2015, Viktor Orbán, alongside numerous other heads of states and governments, participated in the huge solidarity march in Paris. Perversely, it was during this event that, for the very first time, he publicly and demonstratively announced

> zero tolerance against immigrants ... As long as I am prime minister and as long as this government is in power, we will not allow Hungary to become the destination of immigrants by planned actions steered from Brussels. We do not want to see in our midst any minorities whose cultural background differs from our own. We want to keep Hungary for the Hungarians.[4]

The fact that the Hungarian prime minister chose precisely the occasion of an impressive solidarity demonstration in Paris to express words of xenophobia instead of sympathy or unity was condemned as outrageous by representatives of civil society and the liberal media. However, Orbán's emerging strategy was politically much more decisive. His declaration in Paris was the signal for major campaigns based on national and Christian roots, spreading fears of being swamped by foreigners and terrorists, and calling for the right to seal Hungary off. This costly propaganda operation launched by the government, with huge posters and signs all over the country, was ostensibly aimed at foreign migrants: 'If you come to Hungary, you must not take jobs away from Hungarians!'; 'If you come to Hungary, you must respect Hungarian culture!' But all the billboards and the government-sponsored advertisements were in Hungarian. What Syrian or Afghan migrant who had by chance ended up in Hungary on their way from the Balkans to Western Europe would be able to understand them? It is no wonder this grotesque and profoundly unethical exercise was mocked and condemned in equal measure abroad. Yet, what cannot be denied is the reality that this transparent and crude attempt to rouse public opinion against foreign refugees was a great public relations success for the Orbán regime.

The far right Jobbik Party was no longer able to outflank the Fidesz steamroller of panic-making; the challenge from the other end of the spectrum also vanished into thin air. The divided and disheartened left fell silent in the face of callous government propaganda deliberately conflating economic migrants with potential terrorists, and asylum seekers with illegal immigrants. The response of the weak Socialist Party's leadership, still reeling from internal power struggles, was to sit on the fence.

On the other hand, Orbán has been proved correct with his early assessment of the refugee crisis as social cement for communal and national cohesion—as a unifying bogeyman. This was a particularly seductive message in ethnically and religiously homogenous countries such as Hungary and Poland without any tradition of immigration, countries with deeply rooted nationalistic and racist prejudices, which were swept under the carpet in communist times and which since 1989 have again become virulent. It is no accident that the ethnic and religious marginalisation of 'the other', by no means restricted to Muslim immigrants, practised in Hungary and Poland remind the billionaire and philanthropist George Soros (and in this he is far from alone) of the regimes of Admiral Horthy in Hungary and Marshall Piłsudski in Poland in the interwar years.[5]

In one of my weekly columns in the liberal Austrian daily *Der Standard* (28 December 2015), entitled 'Orbán's year', I described the prime minister, purely in terms of his accumulation of power, as the most successful politician in Europe. This was hyped in *Index*, a Hungarian online news site, presumably without any knowledge of the entire text, as a hymn of praise for Orbán by one of his sharpest critics.[6] This, of course, was a wildly exaggerated interpretation even if, for example, the liberal thinker János Kis and *Der Spiegel* had in essence reached exactly the same conclusion. 'The Hungarian premier is at the moment the political victor of the refugee crisis which has shaken the Continent for weeks,' noted the German news magazine, whilst Kis, the first Free Democrat chairman after 1989 and today a professor at the Central European University, also stressed that the refugee crisis had strengthened Orbán's position. He added:

> Before the crisis he was a pariah in Europe. Now he is the leading figure in the coalition of those countries refusing to accept refugees. With the building of the fence he is, moreover, no longer reliant on the goodwill of others, especially as there are [in Hungary] practically no refugees.[7]

The international response was initially ambivalent. The representatives of the European People's Party held back, as usual, from any criticism of the Fidesz government or Orbán personally. However, neither the Social Democratic president of the European Parliament Martin Schulz nor the head of the liberal faction, former Belgian premier Guy Verhofstadt, minced their words in their judgement of Orbán.

The Hungarian leader, for whom the refugee crisis had proved a godsend, responded to all the public criticism with a forceful and unscrupulous offensive in interviews and speeches. In particular, he made common cause with the internal party critics of Angela Merkel, who had on 4 September 2015 opened Germany's doors to Syrian war refugees and sought support for this policy with her frequently quoted and overly self-confident sound bite '*Wir schaffen das!*'—'We can do it!' Abroad, Orbán first shared his populist narrative as truth-telling courage at a much-publicised meeting of the German Christian Social Union (CSU) held in a Bavarian monastery on 23 September 2015. The leader of the CSU and minister president of Bavaria, Horst Seehofer, who was vying with Merkel for influence within the Union, opportunistically seized the chance of inviting the German chancellor's most vocal foreign critic. The guest did not disappoint. Orbán delivered a speech, peppered with sarcasm, accusing the German government of 'moral imperialism' in the refugee crisis. 'Irrespective of how Germany decides, it will be only for itself,' said Orbán on the dispute about the proposed allotment of refugee quotas in the EU, adding that 'the Hungarians do not want that!'

This speech presented Orbán's deeds in a much better light then they deserved. At the closed meeting of the CSU, he once again gave a masterful and shameless performance of his famous dance of the peacock (see Chapter 12). On the one hand, he reaffirmed his admiration for Merkel and stressed that he did not want to interfere in German domestic politics. On the other, Orbán expressed pity for the refugees, who had been deceived by people smugglers and by politicians who had given the impression that they were welcome and that there was room for everybody. Though he did not mention Merkel by name, he in fact charged her with indirect responsibility for the deaths of refugees. With an easy cynicism, Orbán momentously and self-righteously declared that 'Hungary has cheated nobody.'

Seehofer also criticised Merkel at this event. Her decision to allow the refugees marooned in Hungary to enter Germany had created 'chaotic conditions' in Europe. Seehofer defended the dialogue with Orbán: 'It is a question of restoring European rules. And for this Viktor Orbán deserves support, not criticism.' In contrast, Thomas Oppermann, the head of the Social Democratic Party parliamentary group, censured the invitation to Orbán to address the CSU meeting. In dealing with the challenge of the refugee crisis in Europe, he maintained, Orbán was not part of the solution but part of the problem. 'Mr Orbán has trampled over human rights and Mr Seehofer rolls out the red carpet for him. That is not right.'[8]

Nevertheless, the impassioned public dispute ever since the refugee crisis on Orbán's role and the splits it has revealed within the European Union has provided ample proof that his calculated jingoism has paid off internationally. László Lengyel believes:

> Orbán has the feeling that the Hungarian liberals and the politicians of international liberal capitalism are just as much cynical hypocrites as

their Christian Democrat colleagues, who preach morality in order to maintain their position of power and to cloak their own crude interests ... When in the summer of 2015 he resolutely entered the European international arena he made it plain that liberal democracy was politically weak and non-functional; compared to its hypocritical and dishonest model there was, however, the exemplary, strong, functional and transparent model of illiberal democracy. Orbán's words are clear: the wolf should be a wolf and not pretend it is a sheep. But the sheep should also not wish to masquerade as a wolf.[9]

Orbán remains without doubt a radical fighter who thrives on confrontation. Brexit has confirmed his conviction that a weakened EU and the grand coalition led by Angela Merkel are on the verge of collapse and failure. According to Lengyel, after the unanimous rejection of Merkel's refugee policy by the four post-communist new EU member states—the Czech Republic, Hungary, Poland and Slovakia—after the abortive quota scheme and the shaky agreement with Turkey on refugees,[10] Orbán saw 2015 as the triumph of the Hungarian model in Eastern Europe. Against his liberal critics in Germany or the USA, Orbán can rely on the argument that even states such as the Czech Republic and Slovakia, governed (at least nominally) by social-democratic politicians, celebrate him as a trailblazer and role model; an argument that has gained weight since the October 2015 election victory of Jarosław Kaczyński's right-wing populist Law and Justice Party in Poland, the most significant central European state. It is reasonable to conclude that the majority of Romanians and Croatians think similarly. However, the difference is that, as Lengyel so aptly formulates it, the nationalists in those countries are still all in the chorus line—it is Orbán who is starring as the soloist. This is also confirmed by the Bulgarian political scientist Ivan Krastev: 'The Bulgarians have identified themselves completely with Orbán's reading of the refugee crisis; they feel they are represented by him.'[11]

It can of course be argued that it has been the failure of European leaders to deal with the twin crises of the euro and the refugees that has enabled both Orbán's success and the rise of populist and nationalist parties across Europe. Observers have dismissed the idea that Orbán, the bombastic and ferociously nationalistic leader of a landlocked country with a population of less than 10 million, could shape European politics and seriously challenge Merkel's dominant position as 'grotesque' and 'absurd'. Nevertheless, the effects of Orbán's rabble-rousing in Central and Eastern Europe should not be underestimated. It is primarily due to his influence that the four Visegrád states (the Czech Republic, Hungary, Poland and Slovakia) have emerged as a nationalistic group, blocking European integration, thereby also assisting Russia's expansive strategy. In the West, Orbán can boast of numerous admirers not only in Bavaria but also in neighbouring Austria. In September 2016 the leader of the far-right Austrian Freedom Party (FPÖ), Heinz-Christian Strache, publicly advocated Austria's joining the Visegrád alliance. Public opinion polls from spring 2017 confirm that one in three Austrians would vote for the FPÖ. Even critics of Hungary's brutal treatment of asylum seekers and the elimination of checks and balances admit that Orbán saw earlier than most of his EU colleagues that borders had to be controlled before relocation plans for refugees could be agreed upon. His public casting of doubt on the distribution of refugees has been borne out by the failure of the grand EU project to move 160,000 refugees even to willing countries.

Orbán's numerous declarations, speeches and interviews since the beginning of the refugee crisis offer an insight into his character and ambition, not to speak of his endeavours to emerge as a leadership personality on the European stage with the aim of starting what Jan-Werner Müller of Princeton University calls 'a pan-European culture war'. We need not have any illusions about his true role as a convinced wrecker of the supranational humane values and principles that underpin the EU. As he stirs up opinion against Angela Merkel behind the scenes, Orbán has become the 'most dangerous man in the EU'. Thus argued Gerald Knaus, the founding chairman of the European Stability Initiative (ESI) think tank, at the same international meeting in Vienna where Madeleine Albright, the former US secretary of state, condemned Orbán's behaviour over the refugee crisis as 'abhorrent' and 'shameful'.[12] The East European correspondent of the *Süddeutsche Zeitung*, Cathrin Kahlweit, described him as 'one of the most hated and most quoted politicians in Europe.'[13] The Hungarian János Kis notes that what represents success for Orbán means failure for the rest of Europe.[14]

In a speech held on 5 September 2015 in front of his party faithful before his appearance at the CSU in Germany, Orbán made no secret of his satisfaction at the misery of the refugees. 'The crisis offers the chance for the national Christian ideology to regain supremacy not only in Hungary but in the whole of Europe. This situation poses a big risk and a great opportunity: we are experiencing the end of all the liberal babble. An era is coming to an end.'[15] He gleefully announced at this closed meeting that the refugee issue had created 'the first good identity crisis' he had ever seen, because it was bound to destroy the 'hypocritical' liberals.

Three months later, the independent opinion research institute Median confirmed the shift towards Orbán, at least in Hungary, where his popularity rose in one year from 32 to 48 per cent. 87 per cent of respondents (including, in several interviews, even the well-known liberal author and sharp critic of the prime minister, György Konrád) approved the government policy on the refugee question, while the business magazine *HVG* declared Orbán the 'victor of the refugee crisis'.

It was thus hardly surprising that almost at the same time the Swiss weekly *Weltwoche*, now a mouthpiece of the right-wing conservative Swiss People's Party, published a gushing title story devoted to Orbán, praising him as 'the only European politician who correctly assesses the situation.' Beneath a veneer of seeming modesty the Hungarian politician replied with deeply rooted conceit: 'The monopoly of interpretation in Europe is dominated by the left. If you debate values, you need strong backing. Not many politicians have such strong electoral support as I do. It was not the dream of my youth to one day become the *enfant terrible* of Europe.' But he is 'ready to take on the task for the bourgeois, Christian Democratic camp, a burden no one else can cope with …' In his answers, riddled with sarcasm, there was a venomous reference to Merkel:

> To put it bluntly: what today dominates in European public life is only European liberal blah blah about nice but second-rank issues. Germany is the key. If tomorrow the Germans were to say, 'We are full up, it's over', then the flood would immediately ebb away. It is so simple, just a single sentence from Angela Merkel.[16]

For his Hungarian audience, Orbán has over and over again employed the method of deeming morally suspect more or less everything that does not correspond with his own ideas. A review of his statements on the domestic and international stages offers an inescapable conclusion: it is no exaggeration to say that there is not a single politician in Budapest or Brussels who has been able to hold a candle to Orbán with regard to his political cynicism, his gifts as an orator and his talent for intrigue. Experienced and astute, he has always avoided openly attacking Merkel by name. Even after his cleverly engineered symbolic visit in April 2016 to the gravely ill Helmut Kohl, he mentioned the old chancellor's (hated) successor in a friendly way when leaving his house in Oggersheim.

In a series of hardline speeches given in Budapest, beginning in the spring of 2015, as well as in interviews afterwards, Orbán launched absurd and overweening attacks against the various refugee distribution schemes of the European Commission. He presented himself and his government time and again as the 'last defenders of a Europe based on the nation, family and Christianity' in the face of an onslaught of millions of migrants bringing crime and terrorism. 'The most bizarre coalition in world history has arisen, one concluded among people smugglers, human rights activists and Europe's top politicians in order to deliver here many millions of migrants. Brussels must be stopped. We do not want and we will not import criminality, terrorism, homophobia and anti-Semitism.' Swept away by his own rhetoric, Orbán claimed that in Brussels it was forbidden to say that a mass migration was threatening, that 10 million were waiting to come to Europe; it was forbidden to say that immigration would bring in its tow criminality and terror, that European culture, customs and Christian traditions were under threat, that this was no accident but a planned and manipulated action to liquidate the nation states.

In one of his bizarre outbursts against those EU leaders who fail see that 'Europe is staggering towards its own moonstruck ruin', Orbán even offered asylum to future Dutch and French refugees fleeing from the terrible consequences of mass migration. His regular Friday broadcasts on the state-controlled radio and, above all, his impassioned nationalistic 15 March speeches on the steps of the National Museum (marking the failed revolution against Habsburg rule in 1848) employed almost identical extremist rhetoric to mobilise society for a seeming perpetual and total war 'to stop Brussels, to defend our borders and to prevent the resettlement of masses'. At an open-air meeting on the national holiday in 2017, he went even further, appealing to populists all over Europe to 'defend national independence and sovereignty against the holy alliance of Brussels bureaucrats, the liberal world media and insatiable international capitalists!'[17]

Despite such speeches, filled with alternative facts and fake news, Orbán has always been careful, in all his criticisms and warnings against the EU's complacent and faltering leaders, to avoid naming Angela Merkel. Yet politics is fought not only in the closed chambers of European institutions, but also in the language we use, the stories we tell and the images we conjure. We must therefore also cite the words of the cynics and xeno-phobic populists who do parade their prejudices and organise vile propaganda campaigns against their perceived opponents or the enemies of their supreme leader. In contrast to Orbán's own con-spicuous restraint in talking about the German chancellor, the Fidesz media empire has been authorised to attack Merkel head on. It was no accident but rather an important symbolic signal when columnist Zsolt Bayer, one of Orbán's oldest friends going back to the founding of Fidesz, lambasted the German leader in an open letter. 'We are flabbergasted and angry that you have joined the wreckers of Europe.'[18] Four months later, invoking his German blood, he went further, calling Merkel 'The lowest, mendacious, vile woman. Merkel has either gone mad or she is being blackmailed. She constitutes a public danger, she has to be removed from office as soon as possible.'[19] Another Fidesz scrib-bler declared: 'Merkel is Germany's and Europe's greatest dis-grace and danger.'

Mária Schmidt, the director of the controversial House of Terror Museum in Budapest and one of Orbán's closest advisers, launched in a mid-2016 long essay a frontal attack on Angela Merkel for sacrificing Christianity and German national inter-ests. Merkel is 'neither national nor Christian but global and an atheist, not Christian Democrat but liberal, not close to the people but elitist, not democratic but bureaucratic'. Schmidt's startling conclusion may well reflect Orbán's dream, though per-haps megalomania is a better word: 'Kohl and Stoiber (the for-mer minister president of Bavaria) see in the place of Merkel, who is giving up the legacy of Adenauer and Kohl, Viktor Orbán as their political heir and anticipate from him the continuation of this tradition.'[20]

In numerous speeches both in Hungary and at EU conferences and meetings, Orbán has furiously turned against both the various refugee schemes and, increasingly, against foreign-financed non-governmental organisations. However, in striking contrast to the vitriolic attacks launched by the Fidesz media, he continues to refrain from criticising Merkel by name. For example, at a congress of Europe's centre-right leaders in Malta at the end of March 2017, Orbán unleashed a blistering attack on EU policies in response to the 2015 refugee crisis, which he claimed had aided terrorists and threatened the continent's 'Christian identity', identifying migration as 'the Trojan horse of terrorism'.[21] But, yet again, he did not explicitly confront Chancellor Merkel, who was also present. In the same vein, she vigorously defended her refugee policy without even referring to Orbán.

Emboldened by the election of Donald Trump as US president, whose candidacy Orbán was the only head of government to publicly support in the summer of 2016, the Hungarian premier can now operate with boundless self-confidence in his perpetual war against liberal Western values.

19

THE END OF THE REGIME
CANNOT BE FORESEEN

The worrying thing about Orbán's 'illiberal democracy'—an increasingly authoritarian regime still concealed behind the figleaf of a parliamentary opposition—is that it is entirely unprecedented in Hungarian history, and its end cannot be foreseen. George Orwell in his modern classic *Nineteen Eighty-Four* analysed the 'huge system of organised lying upon which dictators depend.' But, he cautioned, 'it is quite easy to imagine a state in which the ruling caste deceive their followers without deceiving themselves'.[1] The way in which the media empire of the Fidesz government, through massive control of state television, radio and most newspapers, achieves the disappearance of objective truth and, with easy cynicism, falsifies the records about past supporters and adversaries of the group around Orbán is simply on a different plane from anything else we have seen since their takeover seven years ago.

Western observers often wonder why the octogenarian former benefactor of Fidesz, the billionaire and philanthropist George Soros, has since the end of 2015 become the Orbán regime's public enemy number one. For those not familiar with the Hungarian language, it is hard to imagine how far the vilification of the Hungarian-born US investor has gone, and how the media empires directly and indirectly controlled by Fidesz have disseminated vile and fabricated propaganda making a bogeyman out of a Holocaust survivor who, through his Open Society Foundation, has spent some $12 billion to promote liberal democracy, social justice and human rights in the post-communist countries as well as throughout the whole world.

On 30 October 2015, in his weekly Friday radio broadcast, Orbán personally gave the signal for the attacks on Soros, because of his views on refugees and his assistance to various human rights and refugee organisations worldwide. Specifically, Orbán named in the same breath people-smugglers and the activists who 'support everything that weakens the nation state. The best example of this type of Western thinking is George Soros, who maintains and finances the European human rights activism which encourages the refugees to start [out]'. Orbán has time and again repeated this smear, and has subsequently sharpened his attacks. When, in March 2017, the European Court of Human Rights found the Hungarian government to have violated various provisions of the European Convention on Human Rights in its detention and expulsion of two migrants from Bangladesh, Orbán said on public radio: 'It is a collusion of human traffickers, Brussels bureaucrats and the organisations that work in Hungary financed by foreign money ... Let's call a spade a spade. George Soros finances them'.[2]

Thus Soros, who has done more for the consolidation of democracy in post-communist Hungary and the other East European states than perhaps any other private individual, is portrayed at the age of 86 as a kind of 'demon of the refugee crisis', as the person responsible for the flood of refugees and as the mastermind behind a campaign against Hungary. To add insult to injury, this message is being spread by the very people who received substantial financial and moral aid from Soros both during the communist era and after the regime change. It is often recalled how, way back, an official Fidesz statement even defended Soros and his foundation from 'malicious attacks', since he had 'actively contributed to the creation of a freer and more open intellectual atmosphere through his support of the younger generation and university colleagues'.[3] Even at that time, in the early 1990s, the philanthropist was already under public and scurrilous attack from anti-Semitic and nationalistic politicians on the fringes of both the opposition and the then ruling party (the centre-right MDF).

As Soros was also involved in the financing of Vienna-based think tank the Institute for Human Sciences and has attended various conferences in Austria, I have met him several times in Vienna and even conducted a long English-language TV interview with him in 1995 for a special ORF (Austrian public broadcaster) programme. Though we have a similar background,[4] I hasten to add that I have never sought any subsidy from his foundations, nor do I share all his comments on the Euro crisis or on the role of the IMF. His speculations (for example against the pound sterling in 1992) on behalf of his Quantum hedge fund, currently worth about $25 billion, are certainly not above criticism.

At the same time, it must be emphasised that Soros' foundations have provided invaluable financial and moral support to all the reform states in Eastern Europe as well as in the succession states of the former Soviet Union. Hundreds of hospitals, welfare organisations, health research institutes, environmental activists, charities, non-governmental organisations and volunteer groups helping refugees or persecuted minorities such as Roma communities have received substantial grants. Naturally, the activities of the Soros foundations in more than 100 countries have also encouraged policies promoting democracy, human rights and freedom of speech. It was therefore not surprising that President Putin was the first to order a crackdown on foreign-financed institutions that had already, in the summer of 2015, been put on a 'patriotic stop list'. By the end of that year, Soros' Open Society Foundation and the OSI Assistance Foundation were declared to be 'undesirable' in Russia.

Not only Viktor Orbán, but also other East European politicians in domestic trouble have obviously drawn inspiration from Putin's shutting down of civil society groups financed by George Soros. From the nationalist Macedonian leader Nikola Gruevski (in the midst of corruption scandals after a decade in power) to the Romanian Social Democratic party chief Liviu Dragnea, faced with similar accusations, politicians fighting for survival in the post-communist countries blame Soros and his foundation for political upheavals threatening deeply rooted networks of corruption and political misdemeanour. The steamroller of Fidesz propaganda did not hesitate to use the complaints of discredited politicians embroiled in domestic crisis in neighbouring countries as proof that 'the Soros empire' seeks to overthrow governments and to impose his will on global institutions.

Orbán told the Fidesz website *888.hu* in December 2016 that 'the coming year will be about displacing Soros and the forces he symbolises. In every country efforts will be made to push Soros out. The sources of funding are being revealed, as are the secret service links, and which NGOs represent which interests'. His outspoken deputy at the helm of Fidesz, Szilard Nemeth, speaking at a news conference a few weeks later, made no bones of the plans to project fear and guilt: 'These organisations must be pushed back by all available means, and I think they must be swept out, and now I believe the international conditions are right for this with the election of the new president in the US.'[5]

The campaign against Soros and his Open Society Foundation launched by Prime Minister Orbán reached new heights on

4 April 2017, when the government used its majority to fast-track a law through parliament destined to close the Central European University (CEU), founded in 1991 with an endowment from George Soros. It is by far Hungary's most prestigious institute of higher education, with 1,440 students from 107 countries (including 400 Hungarians) and a distinguished faculty from forty countries. With 13,000 graduates since its founding, the CEU ranks among the top fifty institutions in the world. It is not a 'Soros university', as alleged in the vilification campaigns against him, because its administrative affairs are run by an international board that also appoints a fully independent rector, who is responsible for the academic staff and the education programmes. Fortunately, Michael Ignatieff, who was named rector on 1 October 2016, is an internationally respected scholar and former leader of the Liberal Party in Canada. Despite the protests of academics around the world, including twenty-four Nobel laureates and a series of protest demonstrations, the largest of which drew 80,000 to the streets of the capital, President János Áder, reelected a month earlier by the Fidesz parliamentary majority for a second five-year term, signed the controversial amendment into law without great ado. This means that the CEU must cease activities in Hungary if it fails to establish a base in the United States by February 2018.

Soon afterwards, in a clear imitation of Russian methods, the Hungarian government—instead of trying to find a compromise—has further broadened the search for convenient scapegoats by rushing through parliament a law affecting NGOs that receive foreign financial support of over 7.2 million forints (approximately €24,000), forcing them to register themselves as if they were foreign lobbies or agents. The main targets among the several dozens of NGOs are the Society for Freedom Rights (TASZ), the Hungarian Helsinki Committee (MHB) and the Hungarian branch of Transparency International, the respected watchdog reporting annually on worldwide corruption.

Rejecting the international criticism and ignoring the series of demonstrations at home, Orbán has intensified his efforts to create what *The Guardian* called 'a state of perpetual paranoia' and to demonise George Soros as 'the essential enemy' seeking through his foundations and his wealth to put pressure on Hungary. Orbán's blistering attacks are a telling reminder that the struggle over the CEU was not just about a unique university, but about the core values of liberal democracy. In a lengthy interview with a Fidesz paper in April 2017, he made clear that he was picking a fight with Soros and transferring aggression from domestic political opposition to foreign enemies and immigrants, as part of a 'dress rehearsal' for the 2018 election campaign. A verbatim quote can show how Orbán has become prone to inventing enemies:

There can be no special privileges, and no one may stand above the law—not even George Soros' people. I do not believe that the civic intelligentsia would be happy to be allied with people whom the impending legislation will clearly show to be operating with foreign funding, serving foreign interests, and following instructions from abroad. All this is about the fact that—through his organisations in Hungary, and hidden from the public gaze—George Soros is spending endless amounts of money to support illegal immigration. To pursue his interests he pays a number of lobbying organisations operating in the guise of civil society. He maintains a regular network, with its own promoters, its own media, hundreds of people, and its own university. He wants to keep the pressure on Hungary: the country that expects even the likes of George Soros to observe its laws. I believe that George Soros must not be underestimated: he is a powerful billionaire of enormous determination who, when it comes to his interests, respects neither God nor man. We want to protect Hungary, and so we must also commit ourselves to this struggle.'[6]

Because the target of such venomous personal attacks is an extremely rich US investor and philanthropist who happens also to be an elderly Hungarian Jew blamed for conspiring to let as many Muslims as possible into his native country and thus to destroy 'Christian identity and national pride', the Dutch vice-president of the EU Commission Franz Timmermans publicly accused Orbán of resorting to anti-Semitic rhetoric in this affair. The left-liberal weekly *Magyar Narancs* compared the prime minister's 'storyline' with the ill-famed 'Protocols of the Elders of Zion' about a Jewish world conspiracy, concocted by the Tsarist secret police in 1903. However, in his frequent references to migration as 'a Trojan horse of terrorism', Orbán himself never fails to mention that the migrants themselves bring with them 'a significant anti-Semitic potential.'

But, as *Magyar Narancs* put it, the word Jew has not been mentioned at all in the Soros context, as there is no need—everybody understands the reference. The British historian and political scientist Timothy Garton Ash was so incensed with Orbán's describing Soros as a 'predator' and the refugees from the Middle East as 'ants' that he attacked his 'poisonous language as fascistic' and called for the expulsion of his party from the EU centre-right faction (the European People's Party) if the Hungarian leader did not change course. Jan-Werner Müller of Princeton formulated his criticism of the Christian Democrats and centre-right parties in a similar vein in the *Financial Times*: 'How can Christian Democrats criticise the anti-democratic excesses of Recep Tayip Erdogan in Turkey, say, or Russia's Vladimir Putin, if they tolerate egregious violations of the rule of law by one of their own? One who slowly but surely undermines the union from within.'[7]

In addition to attacking the Central European University (CEU) and the nongovernmental organisations—'foreign agents financed by foreign money'—Fidesz and the far-right Jobbik party pushed through a law in March 2017 that forces all asylum seekers into detention camps, kept in converted shipping containers. Amnesty

International, the UN refugee agency and other civil rights groups condemned the measures as 'illegal and deeply inhuman' and 'a flagrant violation of international law'. Orbán rejected the accusations, continuing to claim in his speeches that migration is a security issue, representing 'a Trojan horse for terrorism.'

At the same time, the Orbán government has started a large-scale campaign against the EU, with newspaper advertisements and billboards calling on the Hungarians: 'Let's Stop Brussels'. Every household has received a leaflet with a personal letter from the prime minister introducing six leading questions to prove that 'Brussels' plans are endangering our national independence and the safety of our country.' The message is clear: the EU is planning to impose higher utility prices, 'illegal immigrants' and taxes on Hungary. This campaign, combined with the actions planned against the CEU and the NGOs and the law restricting asylum seekers' and migrants' freedom, was sharply condemned even by centre-right speakers at the special session of the EU parliament convened to discuss the Hungarian case. After a heated debate with Prime Minister Viktor Orbán at this plenary session, the European Commission announced on 26 April 2017 the beginning of infringement proceedings against Hungary over the law on the CEU, and criticised its false claims against the EU. In spite of the unprecedented personal outbursts against him, Orbán did not lose his temper. At both the session and a subsequent press conference, he vigorously defended his provocative actions. In tune with his usual tactics, he launched counter-attacks in defence of Hungarian national sovereignty, including several venomous remarks about Soros, the 'financial speculator who ruined the lives of millions of Europeans and seeks to send 1 million migrants yearly to Europe.'

Three days later, the presidency of the European People's Party issued an unprecedented warning to Orbán and to Fidesz: 'We will not accept that any basic freedoms are restricted or rule of law is disregarded. This includes academic freedom and the autonomy of universities. The EPP wants the CEU to remain open, deadlines suspended and the dialogue with the US to begin. The EPP believes that NGOs ... must be respected. The blatant anti-EU rhetoric of the "Let's Stop Brussels" consultation is unacceptable. The constant attacks on Europe, which Fidesz has launched for years, have reached a level we cannot tolerate.'[8] This statement was undoubtedly the sharpest ever official and public condemnation of Orbán's party by its right-of-centre partners. In contrast, and in spite of his alleged reassurances, Orbán's response has been ambiguous. He has continued to perform his 'peacock dance', confusing critics in Brussels while reaffirming his unchanged political line in Budapest. The same weekend as the EPP meeting, a new advertisement shown on state-controlled TV in Budapest condemned the Brussels bureaucrats, who, supported by the 'speculator Soros', were trying to force the country to accept illegal immigrants. In Fidesz parlance, the European Union is always described as 'Brussels', and external critics of the Hungarian regime are generally associated with the 'Soros network'.

Within two weeks however, on 15 May 2017, a strong majority in the European Parliament in Strasbourg voted for a resolution that may, for the first time, result in sanctions against a member country, suspending its voting rights under Article 7 of the EU Treaty. It calls on the Hungarian government to repeal laws tightening rules against asylum-seekers and NGOs, and to reach an agreement with the US authorities, making it possible for the Central European University to remain in Budapest as a free institution. It instructs the European Commission to strictly monitor the use of EU funds by the Hungarian government. This resolution was the hitherto strongest signal of EU disaffection, though it is unlikely that the Hungarian case will ever reach the European Council of member states' prime ministers and presidents. The procedure that might lead to a suspension of voting rights can only be initiated by a two-thirds majority of the European Parliament and a four-fifths majority of the Council. In any case, the current Polish government would veto such an outcome just as Orbán would in any similar case against Poland, as indeed he had already announced when the first sharp attacks from the EU were being directed against the right-nationalistic Polish regime.

Thus even this strongest critical resolution will have no immediate practical effect on Hungary and regime spokesmen tried immediately to minimise its importance. Nevertheless, neither the symbolic value nor the political impact of what happened in the European Parliament should be underestimated. The ill-conceived decision to launch a massive openly anti-EU campaign has alienated even former staunch Fidesz supporters, to such an extent that every third EPP member in the European Parliament voted for the resolution. It was adopted with 393 votes in favour 221 opposed, and 64 abstentions. The left, liberal, green and radical left MEPs, who wrote the resolution, were joined by sixty-seven members of the EPP, while forty abstained.

This means that more EPP members voted for the anti-Orbán resolution or abstained than voted against, although the leader of the group, the German politician Mandref Weber (CSU), still supported Orbán. His position within the European Union has weakened considerably due to his belligerent tone and also as a result of the Brexit referendum and the triumph of the pro-European Emmanuel Macron movement. The charges of the regime spokesmen—that those MEPs who voted for the resolution were in the pay of George Soros and 'his personal lobbying against Hungary'—belong to the repertoire of the far-right populists in Budapest. Orbán and his henchmen will always seek confrontation with Soros, the number one enemy of the Hungarian nation. Since Soros gave a major public speech at the Brussels Economic Forum on 1 June 2017, paying tribute to the young protesters defending the CEU in Budapest and referring to Hungary as 'a mafia state', Orbán and his apparatus have been on a war footing with his erstwhile benefactor. Attempting to convince the Hungarians that the nation is threatened by enemies within and without, the regime points repeatedly to the supposedly shadowy Soros networks as financing and organising both the civil society protests and the infringement procedures in Brussels against the Czech Republic, Hungary and Poland for breaching their legal obligations by failing to house a single asylum-seeker (relocated from Italy, Greece etc.). In reality, the proceedings are the result of more and more EU member state governments and the international media calling for financial retribution as a form of punishment for countries that refuse to cooperate when it comes to the refugee crisis.

In a paradoxical way, the EU decision about relocation and resettlement can be useful for both right- and left-wing populist governments in Budapest and Warsaw, Prague and Bratislava. Portraying all asylum seekers as illegal immigrants posing a grave threat to the Christian European identity of the Czech, Hungarian, Slovak and Polish nations, these governments present themselves with impeccable nationalist credentials in defending their countries against Brussels bureaucrats supported (or even steered) by Soros, who is trying to force them to take in illegal immigrants. Orbán has gloated that 'We want a Hungarian Hungary ... rejecting the blackmailing by Brussels and the obligatory resettlement quotas. Brussels has openly taken the side of the terrorists.' Adding the obligatory Soros reference, he added, 'It is absurd that a financial speculator decides the way ahead in Brussels. The European leaders are kowtowing to György Soros, who can say what Europe should do.'

Both liberal intellectuals in Budapest and foreign correspondents have tended to underestimate or even to ridicule the effects of the anti-Soros campaign conducted by the government media.

However, a poll conducted in June 2017 by the independent Republikon Institute in Budapest revealed that 28 per cent of the population think that Soros has 'considerable influence' on Hungarian politics, while 12 per cent think that he has 'some influence'. Thus 40 per cent of the adult population (and 70 per cent of Fidesz supporters) have more or less swallowed the government's propaganda.

The international reputation of the Orbán government might remain at a nadir for the forseeable future, but even EU sanctions would be unlikely to change political realities in Hungary. Nevertheless, the recent series of massive demonstrations, with tens of thousands taking to the streets to protest against the anti-CEU and anti-NGO law, clearly rattled the regime, which was unprepared for their size and spontaneity. The biggest surprise for the observers was the youthfulness of the crowds marching through the capital to Kossuth Square, in front of the parliament building. A previously apathetic generation has been aroused by the ugly and ill-prepared attack on an internationally admired symbol of academic freedom and independence and the values of liberal democracy.

The CEU affair has been Orbán's third major miscalculation within a year. The failure of the October 2016 referendum against welcoming migrants, supported by an enormously expensive advertising campaign, was followed in February 2017 by the humiliating defeat of the grandiose project of winning the right for Budapest to stage the 2024 Summer Olympics. This was a victory for the newly founded youth group Momentum, which collected 266,000 signatures in the capital to stage a referendum against the costly adventure. The powerful protests against the closure of the CEU, organised through Facebook and Twitter by different, mainly young groups, suggested a break with the lack of political interest exhibited by the youth vote in recent years. Young people have always been a catalyst for change. It is far from clear, however, whether their enthusiasm will be short-lived, or points to future turbulence. Both the fact of the protests and the posters carried by demonstrators also pointed to another object of their anger: the blatant and unabashed corruption at the top of Hungary's power structure. The journalists working for critical websites have stressed that the spontaneous actions of a handful of young protesters have mobilised crowds of a size that the opposition parties in parliament couldn't even dream of rallying. The ferment witnessed in the spring of 2017 within the ranks of Budapest's intellectuals and students does not necessarily mean that the tide has turned across the entire country, but something is definitely changing in the atmosphere, from sullen silence to more and more frequently organised and vocal protests. Brazen warning shots from Orbán and other Fidesz leaders have failed to muzzle the representatives of civil society in urban centres.

Critical observers and opposition figures have questioned the motives behind the dangerously self-defeating offensives led by Orbán on so many different fronts. The political scientist András Bozóki has listed four different explanations for Orbán's rationally inexplicable move against an internationally respected, high-quality educational institution, which has contributed to an attractive image of Budapest and the country:

> a) Orbán is seeking to find an additional enemy visage, to regain voters who have deserted to Jobbik; b) he is driven by resentments, even by hatred, against the liberals; c) he has been emboldened by the Trump era and is looking for new international opportunities; or d) he is complying with a request by Putin, who has been irritated by the impact of the CEU graduates from Russia and post-Soviet Asian republics after their return to their countries.[9]

After talking to a number of political insiders in Budapest during the CEU crisis, I personally assume that Orbán's high-risk campaign on several fronts has essentially been sparked off or encouraged by the intoxicating effect of Trump's triumph. He might also have been influenced by the initial elation of the Russian leadership and the rise of right populist parties across the EU. There is also no doubt that, as is so often reflected in his speeches, the animosity against the liberals in general and George Soros in particular is deeply imbedded in Orbán's thinking and feelings. Fanning the flame of xenophobia against refugees and migrants as well as stoking hostility against a political and socially liberal European agenda are used as tried and tested methods to whip up deeply-rooted nationalistic feelings in Hungary, and to project Fidesz as the only reliable shield for protecting national identity.

So much for Orbán's enemies—who, then, are his friends? In his annual state of the nation report for 2016,[10] the prime minister identified Berlin, Moscow and Ankara as 'our three points of reference', adding: 'We shouldn't let ourselves be dragged into an anti-German, an anti-Russian or an anti-Turkish international action'. We have already dealt with Orbán's tenuous personal relationship with German Chancellor Angela Merkel and his habit of currying favour with her chronic adversary within the ruling CDU-CSU party, the Bavarian leader Horst Seehofer. But regardless of the personal factors, Germany is Hungary's most important trading partner and foreign investor. The economic weekly *Handelsblatt* once carried the headline 'German investors love Orbánistan'; Audi, Daimler and Bosch have all erected large plants and research centres in Hungary, with car manufacturer Daimler currently constructing another factory at a cost of €1 billion. German companies employ 174,000 individuals in Hungary and have an annual turnover of €200 billion.

In his infamous speech on the 'illiberal state and illiberal democracy' in the summer of 2014, Orbán described Turkey, alongside Russia and China, as a 'success story', not least for the strong personalities of their leadership. At the height of the refugee crisis, Orbán was full of praise for Turkey: 'President Erdogan has for a long time been one of my personal friends. Our relationship with Turkey is close and commendable.'[11] Turkey's slide into a personal dictatorship and the brutal suppression of opposition have not changed Orbán's sympathy for Erdogan. He was the only EU head of government to immediately congratulate the Turkish president after his narrow victory in April 2017's controversial constitutional referendum abolishing the post of prime minister and the current parliamentary system, and thereby establishing an executive presidency.

As for Russia, we must bear in mind the memories of its crumbling rule over Eastern Europe as Orbán sprang onto the international stage in June 1989. The famous Polish fighter against Soviet communism, Adam Michnik, and the outstanding British chronicler of the Eastern Bloc's collapse, Timothy Garton Ash, were both 'watching with admiration as the then little-known 26-year old Orbán electrified the crowd on Heroes' Square in Budapest with a call for Russian troops to leave Hungarian soil. Now he is one of Vladimir Putin's best friends inside the EU'.[12] They, as well as such liberal figures as the French-German politician Daniel Cohn-Bendit and the liberal former Belgian prime minister Guy Verhofstadt, are among Orbán's sharpest critics.

It is a well-known phenomenon that strongman leaders often get on very well with one another. Was the lure of the Russian strongman responsible for the most puzzling and controversial turnaround in Hungarian foreign policy in general, and in Orbán's personal attitude to Russia in particular? The impact of such leaders is not confined within state borders, but spills over into international politics. There is barely a dictator in the world for whom Viktor Orbán does not have praise. To the chagrin of its democratic partners in the EU, the Fidesz government cultivates very close relations not only with Putin and Erdogan, but also with the authoritarian rulers of the Philippines and Azerbaijan.

The debasement of political communication into catchphrases and bizarre rhetoric is reflected in the blossoming of the personal friendship between Orbán and the president of Azerbaijan, Ilcham Aliyev. The birth of the effusive relationship between two states so geographically far apart, which historically had never cultivated close contacts, dates back to a highly disputed decision taken by the Hungarian prime minister alone. One night at the beginning of 2004, an officer from Azerbaijan murdered his neighbour, an Armenian officer, with an axe, during a NATO training course in Budapest. For this abominable deed motivated by national hatred, he was sentenced to thirty years' imprisonment at a Budapest court in 2006. However, on Orbán's personal instructions, and despite the opposition of Hungary's then foreign and justice ministers, he was prematurely released at the end of August 2012. The pardoned officer was welcomed back to his home country with much jubilation. Armenia immediately broke off diplomatic relations with Hungary in protest.

Since this incident, the grateful Aliyev has visited Hungary three times, while Orbán has been to Azerbaijan twice. Each has lauded the other to the hilt. Orbán has called one of the most corrupt dictatorships in the world (123rd of 176 countries on the Transparency International corruption list) 'a model state' and 'one of the most admired countries ... stable, predictable and successful!' During a visit on 6 March 2016, Orbán and his wife Anikó Lévai, under the glare of floodlights, laid a wreath on the grave of Aliyev's father, a former KGB general who was the then Soviet republic's party chief and a member of the CPSU Politburo for almost twenty years. This prompted sarcastic comments, and not only in Budapest. At any rate, relations are so good that Orbán personally awarded Mrs Aliyev a high Hungarian decoration in recognition of her charitable work in Baku. In March 2017, Anikó Lévai attended the Hungarian cultural festival in Baku and personally congratulated Mehriban Aliyeva on her appointment as vice-president—by her husband.

Another geographically distant friend is Kazakhstan. When Orbán visited the country to promote the 'opening to the East' policy, the official Hungarian news agency MTI reported his speech: 'It is a strange feeling that you have to travel to Astana to feel at home, whilst in Brussels you are certainly on an equal footing but nevertheless among strangers'. He also warmly praised Kazakhstan 'as an anchor of stability'. As is so often the case, hard facts contradict the political rhetoric of the Orbán regime here. These two new special friends—Azerbaijan and Kazakhstan—are not even among Hungary's top sixty trading partners. Trade with the two Central Asian countries actually has been declining over the last decade.

The most significant shift has occurred in Hungary's relationship with Russia. Resenting the pressure from the Obama administration and the denunciations by human rights groups, Orbán has deliberately intensified first his government's, contacts and then cooperation, with Vladimir Putin. As early as November 2009, when he was still only chairman of Fidesz in opposition, he accepted the invitation to attend the party congress of United Russia, the main government party, in St Petersburg. There, according to Hungarian press reports, he had a fifteen-minute conversation with President Putin. By this time it was already obvious that Fidesz would win an easy victory in the coming elections of spring 2010. Nevertheless, Putin remained cautious, and only three days later he met former Socialist premier Ferenc Gyurcsány in a Moscow restaurant for an informal chat, with only their wives and an interpreter present.

The most important development in Orbán-era relations with Russia has undoubtedly been the €12.5 billion deal signed on 14 January 2014 to expand the Soviet-built nuclear power station at Paks, 70 miles south of Budapest on the Danube, using technology and a thirty-year credit from Russia. Under the agreement Rosatom, the Russian state nuclear power holding, will build two new reactors. There was no international public tender. Hungarian and EU experts questioned the timing and feasibility of the project, and the secrecy provisions—also for thirty years—fostered further doubts. Opposition politicians and independent media have sharply criticised the absence of any relevant information about the financial, technical, environmental or safety conditions of what is by far the largest and most sensitive investment project in Hungary. Furthermore, from the outset there have been rumours and allegations of corruption regarding the choice of the Rosatom corporation. The fact that this highly controversial project was announced shortly before the EU and the US moved to impose sanctions on Moscow over the annexation of Crimea and its military intervention in Ukraine confirmed suspicions about the political consequences of the deal, at the very time when Brussels was urging EU member states to reduce their dependence on Russian energy.[13]

This watershed decision about Hungary's future energy supplies was taken at a time when Orbán frequently clashed with the USA, primarily because the State Department was regularly publishing extremely critical reports on the authoritarian tendencies in Hungary. Public tensions were also triggered by the visa ban placed on high-ranking officials (including the president) of the National Tax and Customs Agency in October 2014 because of suspicions of corruption. Further infuriated by the EU's efforts to force him to soft-pedal, even if only temporarily, some of the measures taken to promote 'illiberal democracy', Orbán has begun to stress the good understanding he has reached with the Russian president. A particular furore was sparked by Putin's visit to Budapest shortly after that of Angela Merkel in February 2015. By the beginning of 2016, George Soros had gone beyond analysing his differences with Orbán over the handling of the refugee crisis, and warned that the Hungarian prime minister was 'challenging Merkel for the leadership of Europe ... And it is a very real challenge. It attacks the values and principles on which the European Union was founded. Orbán attacks them from the inside, Putin from the outside'.[14]

With the international reputation of both leaders tarnished, relations between Putin and Orbán have become more and more intense. Strongman leadership is almost always accompanied by extreme sensitivity to criticism, particularly when it comes from abroad. Within three years between 2015 and 2017, Putin and Orbán have met three times, with the Russian president paying two visits (2015 and 2017) to Budapest, the second only a day before the EU summit meeting on Malta. One has to recall the first twenty years of Orbán's career, from his famously provocative speech on Heroes' Square in 1989 to his public quarrel with the Russian ambassador in Budapest over the Russian intervention in Georgia in 2008, to grasp the significance of this rapprochement in the seven years since Fidesz took power. In view of the evidence in politics and media reports, it is no exaggeration to conclude that the Hungarian leader has turned upside down both his personal attitude and his government's policy towards Russia.

Under the headline 'Wedding of the Pariahs', and with front-page photos of the foreign ministers Sergei Lavrov and Péter Szijjártó embracing each other in Moscow on the eve of Putin's visit to Budapest on 2 February 2017, the liberal weeklies *Magyar Narancs* and *HVG* published a series of articles about the ever closer ties between Russia and Hungary. Time and again, Orbán has publicly criticised the EU sanctions imposed on Russia, and the same line has been repeated by his foreign minister at international conferences and even on a visit to see his fiercely anti-Russian Polish counterpart in Warsaw. Independent Hungarian observers have pointed out the close resemblance between the Orbán regime's moves against the CEU and the NGOs and Putin's crackdown on similar institutions. Lajos Bokros, professor of economics at the CEU and head of the Movement for a Modern Hungary party, stated in an interview that Russian interests and, more specifically, Putin's dislike of this independent university's 'production' of free thinkers from the various post-Soviet republics had been responsible for the legal action aimed at the closure of the CEU. Though this claim has not yet been confirmed by other sources, the growing Russian influence is certainly reflected in its energy supply levels to Hungary (30 per cent of natural gas and 17.9 per cent of nuclear energy), in the opaque structure of the gas trading company MET Hungary Zrt (involving offshore firms of Russian background and one of Orbán's favourite oligarchs, Istvan Garancsi) and in the deals between Gazprom (majority-owned by Moscow) and the Hungarian state company MVM Partner Zrt., involving Russian gas deliveries at secret prices.

The fact that responses to the questionnaires issued in the spring 2017 anti-EU leaflet campaign ended up on the website of Yandex, a Russian digital firm said also to be connected with Moscow's secret services, caused a public uproar in parliament— but without any consequences, as usual, because the prime minister avoided a direct answer to a question from an opposition MP. When the news site *444.hu* checked MTV (state television)'s weekly news programme, it revealed that one of the programme's most important sources of information about events in Syria was the Russian Sputnik News network, which ranks jointly with Russia Today as the chief producers of fake news and disinformation. This did not trouble Foreign Minister Szijjártó, who explicitly praised Russia Today in an interview with the Moscow daily *Kommersant*. The independent media and opposition spokesmen have also drawn attention to the uncontrolled activities of the Russian secret services in Hungary, and to the fact that a Hungarian diplomat in Moscow sold 4,000 entry visas to Russians without the consulate having any information about these individuals. In general, Hungary is regarded as one of the countries in the EU and in NATO that gives most weight to Russia's interests; this, the economic weekly *HVG* concludes, is rewarded by Putin through his series of visits to the country.[15]

Concern about the growing Russian influence was expressed in a frank interview by the first foreign minister (1990–4) after the regime change, under the Antall government. Géza Jeszenszky was also the former Hungarian ambassador to the USA and later Norway. He said:

> Orbán's present policy brings us into dependence (on Russia) ... Hungarian foreign policy has no alternative to the Atlantic orientation. What has the opening to the East brought? Nothing ... As a result of the increasing friendship with Russia and of the onslaught on the freedom of the press, I see democracy endangered. But no power is irreplaceable power.[16]

Speculation about the reasons for the new pro-Russian orientation peaked in the spring of 2017, when Lajos Simicska, Orbán's once close friend and now implacable enemy (see Chapter 14), revealed new details of his conversation with the prime minister the day after Fidesz's electoral triumph in 2014. Orbán, he said, had sketched out a complete programme for control of the media, including his idea of buying the RTL TV broadcaster in order to liquidate it after purchase. He even asked Simicska for an estimate of how much such a project would cost. Simicska said that he did not know, but probably at least €300 million. 'No problem, Rosatom will buy it for me,' Orbán reportedly replied. One week later, in a further personal encounter, Simicska told the prime minister that, in view of the ever strengthening links with Russia, he refused to take part in this action. 'I have my principles. Had I gone ahead, my father would have turned over in his grave. I haven't signed a contract to become a mafia boss and a traitor to my country,' Simicska claims to have said, adding that this was the point of the rupture between him and Orbán.

The prime minister has continued with his tactic of not responding to Simicska's explosive revelations, just as he did at the time of the initial rift two years earlier. His spokesman voiced this approach:

> We do not want to deal with the absurd allegations of the billionaire boss of Jobbik ... It is amusing that the new boss of Jobbik is throwing about such allegations, the same Jobbik which still has and defends in its ranks the key figure of the Russian spy scandal, Béla Kovács.[17]

The fact that the prime minister has not accused Simicska of spreading untruths means that practically anything can be stated about him. Thus, in parliament the Jobbik leader Gábor Vona and his colleagues have repeatedly accused the prime minister and his family of enriching themselves. In the spring of 2017, giant posters put up by Jobbik showed the faces of Orbán and his alleged strawman Lörinc Mészáros, proclaiming in huge letters: 'They steal—you work'. By 2017 Mészáros, the mayor of Felcsút and Orbán's closest friend, had become the fifth richest Hungarian, after a fivefold increase of his assets in one year to €80 million. It was also noted that, between 2013 and 2015, the construction firms of Orbán's father and his two brothers yielded a net profit of almost €7 million.[18]

A few weeks later, the whispering campaign about the shady business deals of Orbán's cronies culminated in an astonishing claim. The former prime minister Ferenc Gyurcsány announced at a public meeting of his Democratic Coalition party that he had proof showing that the Russians possessed documents with which they could blackmail Orbán, and that this was the reason for his startling collaboration with Moscow. He challenged the prime minister to sue him. Neither Orbán nor Gyurcsány appeared at a subsequent meeting of the parliamentary subcommittee on national security, but the secret and intelligence services stated in a joint communiqué that there was no evidence in their files incriminating the prime minister. At the time of writing, Gyurcsány has failed to offer a shred of evidence to support his allegations. After a series of reports about controversial business deals concluded by Mészáros, Jobbik leader Vona accused the prime minister in parliament on 12 June 2017 of converting Hungary into a global frontrunner of corruption: 'You don't even deny that Lőrinc Mészáros is your strawman. He gradually swallows all the EU resources ... This is a mafia government, and you personally are the head of the mafia.'[19]

So far in his long political career, Orbán has been the beneficiary of spectacular luck with regard to the left-liberal opposition. His erstwhile potentially most dangerous challenger Gyurcsány (prime minister from 2004–9) is today considered simply unacceptable by an overwhelming majority of Hungarians. His position imploded as far back as 2006, under the weight of the 'lie speech' scandal, with the consequences fuelling Orbán's rise four years later. Gyurcsány's incessant political activity has succeeded in consolidating his estimated hardcore base of 300,000 to 500,000 voters after his 2011 break with the Socialist Party, but he has remained a convenient scapegoat for all that is wrong with the opposition.

In contrast to his predecessor, Orbán has played his hand with great skill from the very beginning, outmanoeuvring his opponents and maintaining his grip on power. He has managed to split and corrupt the discredited Socialists with a series of hapless leaders. It remains to be seen whether their new chief László Botka, successful mayor of the city of Pécs, will be able to regain popular backing. The liberal opposition, fragmented and permanently infighting, desperately needs to regain credibility. The inescapable consequence of public apathy is a remarkable indifference to the endemic corruption of the Orbán regime, as shown by all opinion polls. The smaller opposition groups have so far failed to show that they stand for more than noisy protests and simplistic slogans ('The rich should pay'). The most exciting question for the future is whether the young activists of the Momentum movement will be able to become a successful party with proper organisational structure.

As to the demands of the EU and the EPP addressed to the Fidesz government, Orbán has repeatedly shown that his promises are not worth the paper they are printed upon. If independent critics are right that only fundamental international changes could sweep away the Orbán regime, and that elections will fail to shatter the power structure, than one can only think in terms of a durable Fidesz leadership faced with a desperately weak parliamentary opposition. Viktor Orbán makes no secret of his will to power. In an interview with the German business magazine *Wirtschaftswoche*, he reaffirmed that 'I will remain in politics for the coming 15 to 20 years. Maybe in the front row, maybe in the third. Exactly where will be decided by the voters'.[20]

Despite the conflict with the EU and the stench of corruption and graft at all levels of the administration, I have never, since the regime change in 1989, seen so bleak a future for a progressive and liberal change in Hungary, or for Enlightenment values: tolerance, respect for the importance of fair debate, checked and balanced government, objectivity and impartiality in the media, recognition of international independence. The campaign against George Soros and his foundation has revealed a depth of cynicism and calculation shocking even by Fidesz standards. Yet, once again, Orbán has managed to diffuse international condemnation on grounds of perceived anti-Semitism by forging a political marriage of convenience with Israeli Prime Minister Benjamin Netanyahu, an equally cynical, ruthless and shrewd operator. Each side uses the other as a smokescreen to cover up ugly realities and offer pretexts to blunt liberal critics.[21] Meanwhile, in order to stay in power, Orbán and his acolytes continue to abuse those who disagree with them as unpatriotic scaremongers and traitors to their country. The government-controlled media outlets play on historical prejudices and ignorance, and the regime continues to blame the European Union for its own failings and mistakes.

Even for an opposition under more credible leadership, it is going to be a long, hard road ahead to break Orbán's grip on power. His decisive leadership is backed by a willingness (sometimes explicitly affirmed) to use force, if necessary, against 'the enemies of the state'. Nobody knows how far Viktor Orbán, who has so often surprised both his compatriots and the world, will go to avoid giving up power, with all its consequences for him, his family and his cronies.

NOTES

1. THE PERSONAL TOUCH

1. Lüthy, Herbert, *Der Monat*, Berlin, 1967.
2. Jahanbegloo, Ramin, *Conversations with Isaiah Berlin*, London, 1992, pp. 34, 149.
3. Except for the controversial case of Béla Biszku (1921–2016), minister of the interior in 1957–61, subsequently deputy premier and party secretary, who was sentenced to two years in prison for complicity in war crimes (suspended for three years) at the age of ninety-four, shortly before his death.

2. THE LONG CLIMB FROM BOTTOM TO TOP

1. Sárközy, Tamás, *Kétharmados Tulkormányzás*, Budapest, 2014; Sárközy, Tamás, *Magyarország Kormányzása*, Budapest, 2012.
2. Weber, Max, *Wirtschaft und Gesellschaft*, Tübingen, 1972.
3. For details of Habony's career, see Chapter 15.
4. For all citations about Viktor Orbán see: Debreczeni, József, *Viktor Orbán*, Budapest, 2003 & *Arcmás*, Budapest, 2009; Kéri, László, *Viktor Orbán*, Budapest, 1994; Pünkösti, Árpád, *Szeplötelen fogantatás*, Budapest, 2005; Kende, Peter, *A Viktor*, Budapest, 2002; Petöcz, György, *Csak a narancs volt*, Budapest, 2001; Richter, Anna, *Ellenzéki Kerekasztal*, Budapest, 1990; Lengyel, László, *Uj Magyar Bestiárium*, Budapest, 2015; Janke, Igor, *Hajrá Magyarok*, Budapest, 2012; Bozóki, András, István Javorniczky and István Stumpf, *Magyar Politikusok Arcképcsarnoka*, Budapest, 1998.

5. István Bibó (1911–79) was a legal scholar and political scientist. He took part in the resistance movement in 1944, wrote basic texts about Hungarian contemporary history and in November 1956 became a minister in the revolutionary government. After the Soviet intervention he was imprisoned for six years. The Bibó College is located in the prominent quarter of Buda in a two-storey villa with a large garden, which was built at the beginning of the twentieth century by József Madzsar, a Socialist doctor, and his wife Alice Jászi, a famous dancer and pedagogue; before the collapse of the Dual Monarchy it served as a meeting place for liberals and left-wing intellectuals.

6. Paris, Rainer, 'Herrschen und Führen', *Merkur* (November 2011).

3. THE RISE AND FALL OF A SHOOTING STAR

1. Pataki, Ferenc, *Hosszú menetelés, A Fidesz-Jelenség*, Budapest, 2013.
2. *Népszabadság* (1 September 1990).
3. Also an author, civil rights campaigner against the communist regime, and representative of the CSCE (Conference on Security and Co-operation in Europe) for the freedom of the media, 2004–10.
4. *Mozgó Világ* (October 1993).

4. THE ROAD TO THE FIRST VICTORY

1. Debreczeni, József, *Arcmás*, Budapest, 2009, pp. 197–108
2. Cf. Janke, Igor, *Hajrá Magyarok!*, Budapest, 2013, pp. 17–18. The story was first recounted by László Kéri in his book *Viktor Orbán* (Budapest 1994). Boris Johnson's 2014 biography of Churchill records that during the Second World War the British prime minister watched Alexander Korda's film *Lady Hamilton* no fewer than 17 times.
3. In this affair the treasurers of the Socialists, the Free Democrats and Fidesz all obtained money not only for party finances but also considerable sums for themselves.
4. Under this agreement, ratified in 1999, church schools in Hungary received the same support as public and self-governing schools; furthermore, part of the former Church property that had been nationalised would be returned to Church ownership. Finally, the Church would receive 0.5 (later raised to 0.7) per cent of income tax, and private indi-

viduals could deduct up to 1 per cent of their taxable income for Church charity. Liberal and left-wing circles have criticised the magnitude of these concessions.

5. THE YOUNG COMET

1. Debreczeni, József, *Arcmás*, Budapest, 2009, p. 420.
2. Janke, Igor, *Hajrá Magyarok!*, Budapest, 2013, pp. 198–207.
3. Debreczeni, op. cit., p. 199.

6. THE GRAVEDIGGER OF THE LEFT

1. Inotai, András, *Gesellschaft und Politik*, Vienna, 2015.
2. *Népszabadság* (21 September 1996).
3. *Die Welt* (28 August 2004).
4. Antal Apró (1913–94), a construction worker and pre-war communist, held high office throughout the four decades of communist rule in Hungary: as a member of the Politburo, head of the trade unions and president of the parliament. His wife and son also filled important positions. His daughter Piroska Apró, an economist, held many posts, including deputy minister for foreign trade, chef de cabinet for Gyula Horn when prime minister, chair of the board of the Magyar Hitelbank etc. Her husband Petar Dobrev worked in the Bulgarian foreign trade organisation, and their daughter Klára Dobrev was, inter alia, deputy secretary of state in the national development agency. The marriage between Klára Dobrev and Ferenc Gyurcsány has produced three children. Gyurcsány's two sons from his second marriage also at times lived in the villa in Buda, which Antal Apró's widow and daughter purchased after his death and later rebuilt.

7. A MEGA SCANDAL: GYURCSÁNY'S 'LIE SPEECH'

1. For the events that unfolded after the revelations of the 'lie speech', see: Debreczeni, József, *A 2006-os ösz*, Budapest, 2012; Janke, Igor, *Hajrá Magyarok!*, Budapest, 2013; Mayer, Gregor and Bernhard Odehnal, *Aufmarsch. Die rechte Gefahr in Osteuropa*, St. Pölten/Salzburg, 2010; Adrowitzer, Roland and Ernst Gelegs, *Schöne Grüsse aus dem Orbán-Land*, Graz, 2013; Lendvai, Paul, *Hungary*, London, 2012.

2. In Hungarian the name Jobbik is a pun on 'better' and 'on the right'.
3. Adrowitzer and Gelegs, op. cit., p. 34.
4. Mayer and Odehnal, op. cit., p. 49.

8. ORBÁN'S VICTORY IN THE COLD CIVIL WAR

1. Despite these attacks Mária Schmidt, an historian, was able bask once again in Orbán's favour after the Fidesz electoral victories from 2010. She was named a member of the government commission for the commemoration of the sixtieth anniversary of the October Uprising of 1956, and plays a key role in the campaigns against Angela Merkel and George Soros. A similar case is that of Zsolt Bayer, a talented journalist but one internationally notorious for his crude anti-Semitic and anti-Roma remarks. He was a founding member of Fidesz and chief press officer of the party from 1990 to 1993. Orbán has long forgiven him for writing leading articles in the Socialist daily newspaper *Népszabadság* in 1993–4 and other left-of-centre newspapers.
2. Cf. Széky, János, *Bárányvakság—Hogyan lett ilyen Magyararország?*, Budapest, 2015.
3. Széky, op. cit., p. 130.
4. Sárközy, Tamás, *Magyarország kormányzása*, Budapest, 2012, p. 364.

9. THE EARTHQUAKE

1. In the first round 265 seats were distributed as per the popular vote for the parties; in the second round 121 seats were allocated to the parties in the constituencies. For the impact of the electoral law passed in 2011, see Chapter 13.
2. By exploiting to the full its two-thirds majority, in just two months Fidesz had passed fifty-eight resolutions, including twelve new laws and forty-four legislative amendments; it had also elected two Fidesz politicians as state president and speaker of parliament. Moreover, a further forty-two resolutions were announced for the autumn session. *HVG* (31 July 2010).
3. *Népszava* (17 May 2014).
4. In *Bárányvakság* (Budapest 2015) János Széky points out that the possibility of one party achieving a two-thirds parliamentary majority was always inherent in the political system created in 1989.

5. Of the 37 per cent of the electorate that voted in the referendum on 5 December 2004, only 19 per cent voted for dual citizenship—short of the 25 per cent needed to carry the reform.

6. Cf. Sárközy, Támas, *Magyarország kormányzása 1978–2012*, Budapest, 2014, vol. 2, p. 124.

10. THE NEW CONQUEST

1. *Magyar Polip. A Posztkommunista Maffiaállam* appeared in three volumes in 2013, 2014 and 2015; its editor Bálint Magyar, who in 2015 also published a summary of the work, is a sociologist and a former liberal Free Democrat politician, who was minister of education for almost seven years.

2. See Magyar, op. cit., p. 240. Sárközy cites, albeit anonymously, a Western politician on Orbán's activities: 'This is a weird mixture of the mentality of a great statesman and that of a horse thief from the Balkans.' The quotation is repeated on p. 52 of vol. 2 (2014), again anonymously, but this time attributed to an English journalist. In a personal response, Sárközy expressly confirmed the quotation, adding that the quoted journalist had later become a politician.

3. János Kornai, professor emeritus at Harvard, is the most respected economist in Hungary. Lajos Bokros is a former finance minister and professor at the Central European University in Budapest. For the following quotations, see Magyar op. cit..

4. The speech was first published in its entirety in Fidesz's magazine *Nagyító* on 17 February 2010.

5. For the problematic and the thought processes that lay behind it, see 'Zugügyvéd-állam', Sándor Radnótis' excellent article in the literary weekly *Élet és Irodalom* (10 February 2012).

6. László Sólyom, the first chair of the constitutional court (1989–98), publicly criticised Prime Minister Ferenc Gyurcsány several times during the autumn 2006 crisis, but would also sharply censure the Orbán regime after the pruning of the competences of the constitutional court; see his writing in *Népszabadság* (13 March 2013).

7. See Chapter 8 for the tensions between Orbán and Áder after the election defeat in 2006.

8. For further details, see Kerekes, Zsuzsa 'A maffiaállam "Parlamentje"' in *Magyar Polip* vol. 3; Sólyom op. cit.; *HVG* magazine (26 March 2016).

11. THE END OF THE SEPARATION OF POWERS

1. The twelve questions did not deal with any of the controversial aspects of the proposed Fundamental Law of Hungary such as the character of the Horthy era after the Germans marched into Hungary on 19 March 1944, the Hungarian nation as a 'Christian community' or discrimination on the basis of sexual orientation and sexual identity.

2. Cf. the critique of the constitutional lawyer Gábor Halmai in *Élet és Irodalom* (22 October 2015).Some commentators believe the questionnaire, the results of which cannot be verified, also enabled the identification of the respondents by means of a special code. After his public criticism of this, the data protection ombudsman was replaced and his duties were integrated into the Prime Minister's Office. Cf. Magyar, Bálint, *A magyar Maffiaállam anatómiája*, Budapest, 2015, p. 118.

3. See Kovács, Mária M. 'Holocaust-Gedenkjahr und Horthy-Rehabilitierung in Ungarn', *Europäische Rundschau*, (2014/1), pp. 33–44.

4. See Ungváry, Krisztián, 'Hitler, Horthy und der ungarische Holocaust', *Europäische Rundschau*, (2014/1) pp. 11–21; for the roots of Hungarian anti-Semitism and the anti-Jewish and anti-Roma campaigns of the radical right, see also Chapters 4 and 12 of Lendvai, Paul, *Hungary*, London, 2012.

5. Szapáry comes from the Hungarian high nobility. After 1956 he completed his studies abroad and upon his return to Hungary became a long-serving vice-president of the Hungarian National Bank. The criticism is not directed against the person of Szapáry himself but rather against Orbán's tendency to arbitrary manipulation of the law. Szapáry eventually left his ambassadorial post aged almost seventy-seven.

6. Müller, Jan-Werner, *Wo Europa endet—Ungarn, Brussel und das Schicksal der liberalen Demokratie*, Berlin, 2013; since the publication of this book, Fidesz has won the 2014 elections—but this prediction holds equally true of the next elections in 2018.

7. Cf. *Osteuropa* (4/2013).

8. Cf. Magyar, op. cit., pp. 128–135.

9. For the figures quoted, see also *HVG* magazine (9 April 2016).

10. Cf. *Osteuropa* (4/2013); for Vörös' analysis, see Magyar, op. cit., pp. 69–96.

12. THE NATIONAL LIBERATION STRUGGLE

1. See inter alia Lendvai, Paul, *The Hungarians: A Thousand Years Of Victory In Defeat*, London and Princeton, 2003; and *Hungary: Between Democracy and Authoritarianism*, London, 2012.

2. See Johnston, William M., *The Austrian Mind*, Berkeley 1983.

3. Cf. Bibó, István, *Die Misere der osteuropäischen Kleinstaaterei*, Frankfurt, 2005.

4. For Reding's statements, see her interview http://derstandard. at/1369362296023/Reding-an-Orbán-Die-Verfassung-ist-kein-Spielzeug (last accessed 4 July 2017) and her article in *Die Welt* (26 September 2015); cf. Adrowitzer, Roland and Ernst Gelegs, *Schöne Grüsse aus dem Orbán-Land*, Graz, 2013, pp. 156–7.

5. The economist András Inotai estimates that EU transfer payments between 2013 and 2015 accounted for at least 3 per cent of Hungarian GDP: 'Das ungarische "Wirtschaftswunder" ist nicht nachhaltig', *Europäische Rundschau*, (2015/3), pp. 59–66; see also Inotai 'Ungarnheft— Hungary's Path Toward an Illiberal System', *Südosteuropa*, (2/2015).

6. Cf. Vásárhelyi, Mária in *Magyar Polip—A posztkommunista Mafiaállam*, vol. 1, pp. 308–392; Magyar, Bálint, *A magyar Maffiaállam anatómiája*, Budapest, 2015, pp. 212–17; for concrete examples of news manipulation and how pressure is put on the media, see also Adrowitzer and Gelegs, op. cit., pp. 65–81.

7. For extracts from this speech, see https://www.youtube.com/watch?v= 0s5gzvb87ZY (last accessed 11 July 2017). Orbán gave the speech at an event held by two foundations close to Fidesz. The improvised reference to the dance of the peacock is absent from both the official text and his website.

8. Cf. Vásárhelyi, op. cit.

9. The Humiliation of Canossa takes its name from the journey made in the winter of 1076–77 by the German king Henry IV from Speyer to the castle of Canossa in Italy, to beg for the revocation of the excommunication Pope Gregory VII had imposed on him.

10. Cf. Inotai, András, 'Krise, Krisenbewaltigung und Schaffung neuer Krisen in Ungarn', *Gesellschaft & Politik*, (December 2015).

11. The Austrian Embassy in Budapest estimates that Austrians own about 200,000 hectares in Hungary, approximately 4 per cent of the country's agricultural land.

12. See Androwitzer and Gelegs, op. cit., pp. 65–81; see also the descriptions of the many smear campaigns against me in my books *Blacklisted* (London 1998) and *Leben eines Grenzgängers* (Vienna 2013).

13. András Schiff, knighted by Queen Elizabeth II in 2015, was the target of a hate campaign in the Fidesz media following the publication of a critical reader's letter in *The Washington Post* at the beginning of 2011. He decided never to perform again in Hungary.

14. These quotations are taken from interviews given in the *Frankfurter Allgemeine Zeitung* (4 March 2012) and the *Bild Zeitung* (19 January 2012).

15. For a summary, see Androwitzer and Gelegs, op. cit., pp. 159–73.

16. See *Die Welt* (26 September 2015).

17. Cf. Müller, Jan-Werner, *Was ist Populismus?*, Berlin, 2016; see also Müller, *Wo Europa endet—Ungarn, Brussel und das Schicksal der liberalen Demokratie*, Berlin, 2014.

13. A QUESTIONABLE ELECTION VICTORY

1. See Scheppele, Kim Lane, 'Eine Potemkin'sche Demokratie in Europa', *Europäische Rundschau*, (2014/2). The expression 'Potemkin democracy' derives from the story of the Russian prince Potemkin (1739–91), who had fake villages erected to simulate prosperity for Empress Catherine II; it means a democracy of illusion, deception—only a facade with nothing behind it.

2. In a pact sealed on 14 January, less than three months before the election, the Left Alliance comprised the Socialists, the Democratic Coalition founded by Ferenc Gyurcsány in 2011, the green-liberal Dialogue for Hungary, the Together party led by former Prime Minister Gordon Bajnai, and the new Liberal Party led by Gábor Fodor (following the dissolution of the Free Democrats in 2013).

3. This stance of the already deeply divided LMP was incomprehensible

to many. As with the tactical manoeuvrings of Attila Mesterházy, the leading Socialist candidate (since resigned), it naturally gave rise to unproven but persistent rumours that Orbán had sown division among his opponents, and not only through his words and speeches.

4. Scheppele, op. cit.

5. According to Zsolt Semjén, Orbán's vice-premier and minister without portfolio, as of April 2016 825,000 Hungarians from over the border(s) had received citizenship. It seems probable that by the end of the current legislative period (2014–18) this number will have increased to 1 million; see *Propellor* (1 April 2016).

6. Scheppele describes these votes 'from across the border' as 'not clean'. These voters did not need to prove their identity, register a concrete address or even appear personally to cast a ballot.

7. Of the ten ministers, eight had been members of the previous government. The greatest change was the departure of Lászlóné Németh, minister of national development, and an ally of the now disgraced Lajos Simicska. Incidentally, she has been Fidesz's only woman minister since 2010.

14. THE PRICE OF 'ORBÁNISATION'

1. Ildikó Vida rejected all these accusations but resigned in July 2015. She had been a member of the Fidesz inner circle since her days at the Bibó College, albeit as a confidante of Lajos Simicska.

2. See, for example, *Frankfurter Allgemeine Zeitung* (2 January 2015).

3. The former minister Tibor Navracsics, who was being sent to Brussels, had won the seat the previous year by a margin of twenty percentage points; Zoltán Kész overturned this huge lead and captured the seat with a margin of nine percentage points.

4. On 28 November 2014, Hungary's Supreme Court did not condemn the historian Lászlo Karsai for calling Jobbik a 'neo-Nazi party'.

5. The Quaestor affair, in which close associates of Orbán are apparently implicated, continues to exercise the media and courts.

6. See Sárközy, Támas, *Magyarország kormányzása 1978–2012*, Budapest, 2014, vol. 1, p. 240.

7. *Der Standard* (15 December 2015).

8. The speech was held on 26 July 2014 at Băile Tuşnad and given, as every year, to ethnic Hungarian students; see Chapter 18 for details and the consequences of this speech.
9. See Sárközy op. cit., vol. 1 p. xxx.
10. See the interview with Gyurgyák in *Heti Válasz* (10 January 2013).
11. See the interview with Gyurgyák in *Heti Válasz* (11 February 2016).
12. The conversation took place in March 2015 and *444.hu* published extracts in October 2015; see http://444.hu/2015/10/12/Orbán-korulirta-az-utodjat.
13. Ibid.
14. See *444.hu*, 13 December 2015.
15. Nevertheless, on the list of the fifty most influential people in Hungary published by Péter Szakonyi (*A száz leggazdagabb 2015*, Napi.hu), Kövér fell from thirteenth to twenty-second place between 2014 and 2015.
16. One of the crudest words in Hungarian is *geci*, the slang word for male ejaculate. *Orbán egy geci* was the frequently cited vulgarity used by Simicska in his live interview on his own TV station HírTV. It translates roughly as 'Orbán is a douchebag.'
17. *Magyar Narancs* (6 February 2015).
18. Wikileaks, reported in the left-wing daily newspaper *Népszava* (9 September 2011).
19. See *Der Standard* (9 February 2015); *Süddeutsche Zeitung* (7 February 2015).

15. POWER, GREED AND CORRUPTION

1. Jay, Antony (ed.), *Oxford Dictionary of Political Quotations*, 3rd edn, Oxford, 2006, pp. 1, 311.
2. Janke, Igor, *Hajrá Magyarok*, Budapest, 2012, pp. 14–16.
3. Janke, op. cit., pp. 284–7.
4. See *Magyar Idők* (21 December 2015).
5. See *HVG* (12 May 2016).
6. See *The Economist* (2 May 2016), *HVG* (5 May 2016), *Élet és Irodalom* (6 May 2016), *Magyar Narancs* (19 May 2016), *Népszabadság* (6 & 9 June 2016); see also *Süddeutsche Zeitung* and *Der Standard* (29 April 2016).
7. Initially Orbán and the present speaker of parliament Kővér were listed

as staff members. Stumpf was head of the Prime Minister's Office in the first Orbán government (1998–2002), and then directed the foundation until 2010, when he was elected a member of the constitutional court.

8. See Petöcz, György, 'Századvég: System or Nightmare', *Élet és Irodalom* (8 January 2016).

9. See Petöcz, op. cit.

10. Finkelstein and his Israeli partner George E. Birnbaum have been working for Fidesz since 2008. Both are known as masterly organisers of negative and smear campaigns; see *Magyar Narancs* (15 February 2013).

11. See *Magyar Narancs* (26 May 2016).

12. For further details on Habony, see *Népszabadság* (9 October 2010) and *Magyar Narancs* (28 February 2013, 21 May 2015, 23 June 2016).

13. See 'Butaságunk története', *Élet és Irodalom* (3 June 2016); see also *Magyar Narancs* (26 May 2016), *Népszabadság* (10 May 2016), *Népszava* (25 May 2016), *HVG* (16 April 2016) and *Magyar Nemzet* (9 April 2016).

14. See *HVG* (15 December 2016).

15. See *Frankfurter Allgemeine Zeitung* (15 October 2016).

16. THE GREAT AND GOOD OF THE COURT

1. Lengyel, László, *A halott ország*, Budapest, 2016.

2. As he admitted, Szigetvarí arbitrarily included in this figure the estimated fortunes of five Orbán intimates and, despite the rift between the two men, a third of Simicska's fortune; cf. *Népszabadság* (18 May 2016) and *The Daily Telegraph* (20 June 2016). For similar statements and smaller estimates see *Magyar Narancs* (14 April 2016) and for more on strawmen the Internet news site *444.hu*.

3. See Chapter 5, footnote 1.

4. Cf. *Népszabadság* (8 December 2015).

5. 'A 100 leggazdagabb', *Napi.hu*; see also *Süddeutsche Zeitung* (28 January 2016), *Die Welt* (13 January 2015), *Népszava* (4 November 2015 & 12 April 2016), *HírTV* (11 February 2015), *Magyar Narancs* (14 April 2016) and *444.hu* (16 January 2016).

6. *444.hu* (16 January 2016) and *Népszabadság* (3 May 2016); according to

József Ángyán, a former secretary of state in the Fidesz government who resigned in protest against agricultural policy, the Mészáros family and their companies lease more than 3,000 hectares of land in the Fejér region; according to *Magyar Nemzet* (4 July 2016) the Mészáros family owns as much as 6,500 hectares of land in the region. On the Orbán family and the reports on its business contacts see *HVG* (10 November 2016 & 22 December 2016) and *Magyar Narancs* (2 June 2016 & 5 January 2017).

7. See Chapter 2.

8. See *Népszabadság* (30 January 2016); see also *Die Welt* (13 January 2015) and *Süddeutsche Zeitung* (27 January 2016).

9. See *Magyar Narancs* (23 July 2015 & 21 April 2016), *Népszabadság* (5 & 6 November 2015) and *Napi.hu*, op. cit.

10. The pleasure of the prime minister was certainly tempered by the report that, following charges of fraud made by an opposition Hungarian MEP, the European Anti-Fraud Office has investigated whether deliberately false figures for the numbers of anticipated passengers (2,500 to 7,000) were provided. In the first three weeks of operations only 1,220 tickets were sold. A covered sports hall costing €20 million is also being built in Felcsút (*Népszabadság*, 8 July 2016).

11. *Népszabadság* (4 April 2016).

12. Ibid.

13. Cf. Hankiss, Elemér, *Társadalmi csapdák*, Budapest, 1979.

14. Cf. Lendvai, Paul, 'The "Golden Age" of the Millennium: Modernization with Drawbacks', in Lendvai, Paul, *The Hungarians*, Princeton, 2003, pp. 310–28.

15. *HVG* (23 June 2016). Among these suspicious investments the media count, for example, the sale of 4,700 special bonds (as of end of 2016), which foreign investors from non-EU states are able to purchase for €300,000 each for five years in order to acquire, with immediate effect from July 2016, a permanent residence permit in Hungary. With this, they are able to move freely within the Schengen area. The bonds are offered by six offshore companies. These firms receive €60,000 in fees as commission per bond and are scrutinised by no external body. The whole project was launched in 2013 by a special (Fidesz-dominated)

committee headed by Antal Rogán, who today, as Orbán's chef de cabinet with the rank of minister of state, is placed seventh on the list of most influential Hungarians, and who in the summer of 2016 was linked by the media to various real estate scandals (cf. *Magyar Nemzet*, 31 March 2016). The offshore companies are alleged to have earned almost €400 million with one third originating from public funds (*Magyar Nemzet*, 14 January 2017).

16. *HVG*, 23 June 2016.
17. The deputy director-general of HírTV, Péter Tarr, related to the trade journal *Médiapiac* how the broadcaster functioned in the time of the friendship between Simicska and Orbán. 'Those responsible for [government] communications informed the management what the party message for that week was to be, what should be advertised in the programmes, who should be invited to appear, who should speak on what matter, where and how and what they should emphasise. The truth is we served the regime' (*Népszabadság*, 15 February 2016).
18. This was an unprecedented leak of 11.5 million files from a financial outfit in Panama, revealing money laundering, tax evasion and so on, including by government and government-linked figures from across the world. It was reported by a group of newspapers, including *The Guardian*, with the first details published on 2 April 2016.
19. See *Népszabadság* (16 April 2016).

17. HUNGARY'S 'FÜHRER DEMOCRACY'

1. *Mozgó Világ* (January 2016).
2. Carl Schmitt (1888–1985) was an extreme right-wing German jurist and political theorist who wrote widely on the effective exercise of political power.
3. Lengyel, László, *A halott orszag*, Budapest, 2016.
4. *Mozgó Világ* op. cit. Kálmán Tisza held the office of prime minister for fifteen years between 1875 and 1890, the longest premiership in Hungarian history.
5. Professor István Magas, director of the Institute for Global Economy at the Corvinus University in Budapest, in *Népszava* (2 July 2016). The Vienna Institute for International Economic Studies has calculated that,

measured by purchasing-power parity in Hungary, a superior annual growth rate of 5.4 per cent would be required to overtake Austria by 2040.

6. Cf. 'Eltorzult Magyar alkat, zsákutcás Magyar történelem 1948', in *Bibó István összegyüjtött munkái*, Bern, 1981, p. 267.

7. Cf. *Mozgó Világ* (March 2016). Csillag was the minister for economic affairs in the Socialist–Free Democrat government between 2002 and 2004 and president of the Export-Import Bank from 2005 to 2010.

8. 168 Óra (3 March 2016). See also *Portfolio.hu* (6 November 2015), *Népszabadság* (5 December 2016), 168 Óra (7 April 2016) and *Élét és Irodalom* (12 February 2016).

9. See *Vasárnapi Hírek* (6 March 2016), 168 Óra (7 April 2016) and *Élet és Irodalom* (12 February 2016).

10. *HVG* (24 November 2015).

11. See Tellér, Gyula, 'Született-e "Orbán rendszer" 2010 es 2014 között?', *Nagyvilág*, (March 2014).

12. Woller, Hans, *Mussolini, der erste Faschist*, Munich, 2016.

18. 'THE MOST DANGEROUS MAN IN THE EU'

1. For Hungary see Gábor Halmai in *Élet és Irodalom* 22 October 2015; for Austria see Statistik Österreich.

2. Le Bon, Gustave, *Psychologie des foules*, Paris, 1895.

3. Pew Research Center, Washington DC, 11 June 2016. The poll was conducted in the spring of 2016 in Hungary, Poland, the Netherlands, Germany, Italy, Sweden, Greece, the UK, France and Spain.

4. See interview with the Hungarian news agency MTI (11 January 2015).

5. See interviews with Soros in *Wirtschaftswoche* (12 November 2015) and the *New York Review of Books* (11 February 2016); on the subject of Orbán and Fidesz as recipients of Soros scholarships and financial support, see also Chapter 3. Between 1979 and 2015 Soros donated approximately $11 billion to various aid projects, all in post-communist countries, including money for the establishment and running of the Central European University in Budapest.

6. *Index.hu* (29 December 2015).

7. *Der Spiegel* (9 December 2015); for the János Kis quotation see the interview in *Vasárnapi Hírek* (22 February 2016).

8. *Frankfurter Allgemeine Zeitung* (23 September 2015).

9. Lengyel, László, 'Orbáns Weltbild', *Europäische Rundschau* (2016/1).

10. Under the agreement of 16 April 2016 between Turkey and the EU, Turkey stops the flow of refugees to Greek islands (and thus into the Schengen zone) in exchange for €6 billion in funding for refugee camps in Turkey; Greece sends refugees back to Turkey, in exchange for Syrian refugees being distributed among and hosted by EU states. Turkey was also promised abolition of visa requirements for Turks to enter the EU and an acceleration of its own EU accession talks.

11. *Frankfurter Allgemeine Zeitung* (25 May 2015).

12. *Die Presse* (20 April 2016).

13. *Süddeutsche Zeitung* (11 September 2015).

14. *Vasárnapi Hirek*, op. cit.

15. *Index.hu* (16 September 2015).

16. *Weltwoche* (12 November 2015).

17. www.kormany.hu (28 February 2015, 20 February 2017 & 15 March 2017).

18. *Magyar Hírlap* (11 October 2015).

19. *Magyar Hírlap* (9 April 2016).

20. Schmidt, Mária, 'Das verwaiste Vermächtnis', *Budapester Zeitung* (28 May 2016).

21. *Financial Times* (30 March 2017).

19. THE END OF THE REGIME CANNOT BE FORESEEN

1. Quoted from Bernard Crick, *George Orwell: A Life*, London, 1982, p. 348.

2. Citations from *MTI-Magyar Távirati Iroda* (Hungarian Telegraphic Agency)

3. *MTI*, 22 February 1992. The left-liberal weekly *Magyar Narancs* published on 13 April 2017 a detailed account of the grants Orbán and more than a dozen leading Fidesz politicians received from the Soros Foundation for study abroad. Ironically, one of the top beneficiaries in 1992–9 was a certain Zoltán Kovács, who has become internationally known as the government spokesman, and particularly for the abusive campaign against both the CEU and the Soros foundations.

4. We are both Holocaust survivors of the same age from Budapest, refugees—he fled from Hungary in 1948, I did in 1957—and our fathers were both lawyers.

5. Marton Dunai, 'Soros-funded charities targeted by Trump-inspired crackdown in Eastern Europe', *Reuters*, 23 March 2017. See also the Fidesz paper *Magyar Idők* (3 June 2016, 18 November 2016, 6 April 2017); interview with Orbán (15 April 2017); *Der Spiegel online*, 'Half of Eastern Europe hates Soros', 26 February 2016.

6. Interview with *Magyar Idők* (15 April 2017); English translation from the government website.

7. For the quote from Timothy Garton Ash, see *The Guardian* (12 April 2017) and for Jan-Werner Müller, *Financial Times* (11 April 2017).

8. See press releases from the EU Commission and the EPP presidency (Brussels, 26 and 29 April 2017).

9. See his article in *Élet és Irodalom* (7 April 2017).

10. Citations from *MIT* (28 February 2016).

11. Interview with *Bild* (24 February 2016).

12. *The Guardian* (17 April 2017).

13. See the analysis by Zoltán Sz. Biró, the foremost Hungarian expert on Russia, in *Élet és Irodalom* (31 March 2017); for the details and doubts on this matter see *Süddeutsche Zeitung* (30 December 2016), *Népszava* (2 February 2017), *Financial Times* (3 March 2017), *Magyar Narancs* (17 March 2017).

14. *New York Review of Books* (11 February 2016).

15. For the Szijjártó-Lavrov photo see *Népszava* (24 January 2017). For bilateral relations see *HVG* (26 January, 13 April 2017); *Magyar Narancs* (16 March 2017); *Frankfurter Allgemeine Zeitung* (3 February 2017).

16. *HVG* (13 April 2017).

17. Simicska told *24.hu* that he had originally granted Reuters a two-hour, sharply worded interview about the political situation in Hungary, but that the final version of the text had been so heavily 'censored' that he withdrew it. The most important part was the account of his talk with Orbán in 2014. The government spokesman's reference to the Jobbik MEP Kovács concerns the inquiries in Brussels and Vienna over an

alleged espionage affair. The accusation has been rejected both by him and by his party. Simicska expressed his hope in a statement that Jobbik would win the next elections. In their critical coverage of the government, the TV station and newspapers controlled by him give space and airtime to interviews with opposition spokesmen, including those of Jobbik, which still ranks as Hungary's second largest party in both parliament and all opinion polls.

18. See figures in *Napi.hu*'s '100 Richest Hungarians 2017' for the links between Mészáros' 120 firms and the Orbán family; *Magyar Narancs* (23 March 2017) for the net profit of the family enterprises.

19. See his interview on ATV (21 April 2017), *Magyar Nemzet* (23 April 2017), *Népszava* (10 May 2017), *Népszava* (12 June 2017).

20. *Wirtschaftswoche* (23 April 2016).

21. During a three-day visit to Budapest on 19–21 July 2017, Netanyahu met not only Orbán but also the prime ministers of Poland, Slovakia and the Czech Republic (the other members of the so-called Visegrad group, of which Hungary became president in that month). The meeting was used to criticise EU policies regarding migrants and the Middle East, and was widely regarded as a political success for Orbán.

INDEX

INDEX

FPÖ (Freiheitliche Partei Ös-
terreichs), 84, 138, 200
Hypo Alpen Adria, 161
Kreisky chancellorship
(1970–83), 61
immigration, 192
ORF (Österreichischer Rund-
funk), 6–8, 69, 122, 190–91,
209
property rights in Hungary,
121
and refugee crisis, 189–91, 193
refugees from Hungary, 189
Social Democratic Party, 117
TV stations, 121
Vienna Capital Partners, 161
Austria-Hungary (1867–1918),
44, 111, 114, 148, 173, 194,
234
Austrian Empire (1804–67), 112
authoritarian system, 92–4
Azerbaijan, 221–2
Aznar, José María, 144

Bãile Tuşnad, Romania, 68, 242
Baja, Ferenc, 67
Bajnai, Gordon, 79–80, 132, 240
Baka, András, 104
Balatonöszöd, 66
Balog, Zoltán, 50
de Balzac, Honoré, 11
Bangladesh, 208
Bárányvakság, 236
Barnás, Ferenc, 185
Bauer, Tamás, 92

Bavaria, Germany, 197–8, 200,
204, 220
Bayer, Zsolt, 204, 236
Belarus, 10
Belgium, 83, 172, 197, 221
Berlin, Isaiah, 2
Berlin International Film Festival,
122
Berlin Wall, fall of (1989), 40, 189
Berlusconi, Silvio, 158
Bertelsmann, 139, 161
Bibó István Special College,
17–18, 19, 23, 38, 44, 104, 141,
142–4, 234
Bibó, István, 113, 181, 234
Bicske, 172
Bild Zeitung, 240
Birnbaum, George E., 243
Biszku, Béla, 233
Blair, Anthony 'Tony', 61
Bokros, Lajos, 40–41, 92, 225–6,
237
Boldvai, László, 174, 175
Bosch, 220
Boston University, 48
Botka, László, 229
Bozóki, András, 92, 179, 219
Brandt, Willy, 3, 37
Brexit, 199, 216
Bronson, Charles, 39
Brussels Economic Forum, 216
Buda Cash, 138–9
Budapest
Andrássy Avenue, 6, 122
Bibó College, 17–18, 19, 23,
38, 44, 104, 141, 142–4, 234

252

INDEX

INDEX

INDEX

INDEX

INDEX

INDEX

INDEX

INDEX

INDEX

Szekeres, Imre, 67
Székesfehérvár, 14, 171
Széky, János, 77, 88, 236
Szemerey, Tamás, 153
Szigetvári, Viktor, 166, 243
Szijjártó, Péter, 225, 226
Szili, Katalin, 67

Tapolca, 137
Tarr, Béla, 122
Tarr, Péter, 245
Tavares, Rui, 117, 124
taxation
  advertising, 139, 146
  Bokros package (1995), 41
  on foreign companies, 109, 120, 121, 140, 182
  Gyurcsány government (2004–9), 62
  income tax, 180, 234
  on Internet, 135–6, 139, 186
  and Jobbik, 166
  on minimum wage, 55
  and Puch, 175
  on severance pay, 105
  and sports, 170
  VAT (value-added tax), 79, 135
Tellér, Gyula, 187
Tiborcz, István, 168
Timmermans, Franz, 213
Tisza, Kálmán, 180, 245
Tito, Josip Broz, 3
tobacconists, 109, 138
Tocsik scandal (1996), 41
Together Party, 240

Tölgyessy, Péter, 194
Total Recall, 157
Tóth, Krisztina, 185
Transparency International, 173, 222
Transylvania, 88
Treaty of Trianon (1920), 37, 77, 88–9, 112, 194
Trump, Donald, 205, 219
tuition fees, 76
Turin Horse, The, 123
Turkey, 112, 114, 141, 168, 173, 199, 213, 220–21, 247
TV2, 119, 158–60
Twitter, 137, 218
two-thirds majority, 9, 11, 84–5, 87–8, 114, 236
  and chief justice, 104
  and constitution, 93, 97, 98, 99, 107, 110
  in elections, 9, 11, 84–5, 88, 127, 128, 137, 140
  and Manifesto of National Cooperation (2010), 87
  and media law, 115
  and president, 94

Ukraine, 88, 185, 224
unemployment, 25
Ungváry, Rudolf, 92, 138
United Kingdom, 23, 61, 108, 149, 155, 156, 158, 173
  Brexit, 199, 216
  Hungary, migration from, 125, 130, 180
United Russia, 223

INDEX

United States, 48, 115, 122, 201
  Obama administration (2009–
    17), 223
  travel ban, 136, 141, 224
  Trump administration (2017–),
    205, 219
University of Frankfurt, 92
'unreal sphere', 172
Upper Hungary, 88

Vajna, Andrew, 119, 157–9, 163,
  165, 175
Varga, Mihály, 150, 178
Vásárhelyi, Mária, 118, 160
Vásárhelyi, Miklós, 8
VAT (value-added tax), 79, 135
Vatican, 42, 51
Venice Commission, 105, 116
Veres, János, 60
Verhofstadt, Guy, 117, 197, 221
Veszprém, 137
vezérdemokrácia (Führer democ-
  racy), 186
Vida, Ildikó, 136, 241
Videoton, 171
Vienna Awards (1938–40), 37
Vienna Institute for International
  Economic Studies, 245
Visegrád Group, 200

Vojvodina, 88
Vona, Gábor, 165–6, 228–9
Vörös, Imre, 110
VS.hu, 158

Wall Street Journal Europe, 144
Warsaw Pact, 4
Washington Post, 240
Weber, Mandref, 216
Weber, Max, 10
welfare system, 55, 79, 136
Welt, Die, 60
Weltwoche, 201
West Germany (1949–90), 3
Wirtschaftswoche, 230
women, 143
workers' militias, 4
World Bank, 41, 78
World Cup, 16, 62
World Economic Forum, 182
World Union of Hungarians, 89

xenophobia, 121, 124, 195, 204,
  220

Yandex, 226
Young Communist League, 14,
  16, 22, 58
Yugoslavia, 3, 37